Software
Inspection
Process

Software Inspection Process

Robert G. Ebenau • Susan H. Strauss

McGraw-Hill, Inc.

New York   San Francisco   Washington, D.C.   Auckland   Bogotá
Caracas   Lisbon   London   Madrid   Mexico City   Milan
Montreal   New Delhi   San Juan   Singapore
Sydney   Tokyo   Toronto

Library of Congress Cataloging-in-Publication Data

Ebenau, Robert G.
   Software inspection process / Robert G. Ebenau, Susan H. Strauss.
      p.   cm. — (McGraw-Hill systems design & implementation series)
   Includes index.
   ISBN 0-07-062166-7
   1. Computer software—Quality control. I. Ebenau, Robert G.
  II. Strauss, Susan H. III. Title. IV. Series.
  QA76.76.Q35S77   1993
  005.1'068'5—dc 20   93-2618
                                         CIP

ISBN 0-07-062166-7

The sponsoring editor for this book was Jeanne Glasser, the editing supervisor was Jim Halston, and the production supervisor was Pamela A. Pelton. It was set in Century Schoolbook by Carol Woolverton Studio, Lexington, Massachusetts, in cooperation with Warren Publishing Services, Biddeford, Maine.

Printed and bound by R. R. Donnelley & Sons Company.

Contents

Preface

Software engineering is a relatively young field, but one that is changing so rapidly that it's easy for software engineers to become obsolete in a very short period of time. New languages, new hardware, new procedures, new concepts pop up daily. Buzzwords of yesterday are constantly replaced with the buzzwords of today. Yet amid all this change, software inspections have survived for 20 years, and are at least as useful today as they were when Michael Fagan first introduced them at IBM in the early 1970s.

In the earliest days of computing, programs were often experimental and ad hoc. What a programmer could learn by trying them was frequently as important as what they did. Understandably, many of these programs were sloppily written. But as programs began to be used more pervasively for repeated and more critical applications, the need for stability and quality grew, giving rise to the concept that today is known as software engineering. The inspection process was an early and successful application of software engineering techniques.

One reason for this success is that, like software engineering in general, the inspection process has been able to evolve. In part, the evolution of software inspections has been directed by the authors' involvement with inspections at IBM and Bell Laboratories. A bit of history about the authors' experience with inspections will provide a clearer understanding of the background that influenced the form of the inspection process described in this book.

Inspections were developed by Michael Fagan while he was a software development manager at IBM in 1972. The process was used and refined within IBM, and in 1976 Fagan published the defining article on the inspection process, *Design and Code Inspections to Reduce Errors in Program Development,* in the IBM Systems Journal. Fagan had developed the inspection process for software development as it was practiced by IBM at that time. Robert Ebenau became involved with the inspection process while he was a senior instructor with the IBM

Systems Science Institute software engineering curriculum in the late 70s.

Because of the success of the IBM inspection program, Bob was asked to develop and teach a software inspection workshop for the Systems Science Institute. After successfully developing the course and teaching inspections for IBM, Bob subsequently became an independent consultant for inspection training and implementation.

At about this time, in 1981, Priscilla Fowler, a training manager at Bell Laboratories, had the foresight to recognize the potential for inspections at Bell Labs. Fowler had a fledgling software engineering curriculum under development, and needed a vehicle to convince the technical population of the value of software engineering, and software inspections in particular. Fortunately, her group was in Dan Clayton's training department and he supported her efforts.

Her initial attempts, working with Frank Ackerman, to advertise the inspection concept, to develop inspection training, and to run the first series of inspection seminars were somewhat disappointing, and they didn't reach enough people in any one project to make an impact.

Dan Clayton brought Bob Ebenau on board to help the troubled program, and Bob worked with Fowler and Ackerman to revise inspection training and aim it more specifically as an implementation program, not just training. Also, the entire project now became the client, not the individual developer. Management was included as an integral part of the implementation. In addition, they began adapting the inspection process to each particular project's needs, further enhancing the value of the process. The program succeeded and grew over the following years, and became an institutionalized part of Bell Laboratories software development under the leadership of Susan Strauss.

The inspection process described in this book is centered around the same inspection methods that Fagan espoused. But in adapting inspections to fit the needs of the many different projects at Bell Labs, a more flexible and widely applicable inspection process has resulted. The inspection procedures presented here are a hybrid of Mike Fagan's original process, the Bell Labs' adaptations, and further evolution that has resulted from our experiences.

The additions to the original process include:

- Focus on the project as the client. Inspections are not an individual skill, like mathematics, but a coordinated group effort concentrating on improving the quality of the project's products.

- An emphasis on universal inspection training. In the Bell Labs model, the technical training organization performs the role of evaluating a project's inspection training needs and adapting inspection training appropriately to the entire project.

- Procedures for inspection management. Seminars let managers know specifically what to do and how to do it to run an effective inspection program. Also, evaluation seminars inform managers of the status of the inspection process. Data collection and analysis provide supporting data for determining strengths and weaknesses of the inspection process.

- Existence of an inspection coordinator. The inclusion of an inspection coordinator guarantees project ownership of "their" inspections.

- Tailoring inspections to a project's needs. Seven tuning parameters enable projects to define inspections in terms of their own requirements, and recognize the need for a variety of customized inspection types.

- Inclusion of entry criteria. The need to satisfy these ensures the readiness of materials for inspection.

- Application of inspections to other areas. As a result of the ability to tailor inspections, the procedures have been readily applied to other than software projects: hardware, documents, course development, etc.

Bell Labs was the major influencing environment where this current representation of inspections was developed. The Labs environment consisted of a large number of diverse projects involved in the development of software, hardware, and embedded systems. Each project, which varied from having only a few people to having over one thousand persons, had its own development methods and procedures. This diversity of projects called for a way of flexibly defining inspections to meet their varying needs. The definition of inspections was parameterized, so that each type of inspection could be defined to match the project, yet retain all of the precepts of inspections.

In addition, each project prepared its own version of an inspection procedures manual. It turned out that the preparation of an inspection manual was a time-consuming task that was being repeated by each of the early projects. Therefore, we decided to build a central, general, inspection procedures manual that could be used as a template for the projects, so that they did not each have to replicate the material that was common, and could edit that material which was particular to the project. The central manual was then distributed electronically to the projects for their modification and use.

As inspection data began to be collected, it was analyzed to evaluate the inspections and to determine trends in the project's development process. With more and more data, and more projects requiring evaluation of their inspections, it soon became apparent that manual methods of data analysis were inadequate. Although projects were advised to create their own inspection data base and analysis tools, this was often too great a burden to be undertaken by the smaller projects, and many of the medium sized ones as well. Thus, a need was evidenced for a central data base system that could be used by the projects. This led to the development of LIDS, which was provided to the projects and modified for their unique naming conventions and defect types.

Today, these principles have helped Bell Laboratories establish an extensive range of inspections that contribute to product quality in a wide variety of applications. They are fully supported by a number of tools and documentation, including being part of the company's series of "Best Current Practices." And, they continue to evolve.

Over the years many people have helped to influence the direction of inspections and the concepts presented in this book. Our thanks to them all: to Mike Fagan, but for whom there would be no process to write about; to Priscilla Fowler, who had a vision, and to Dan Clayton who let her pursue it; to Frank Ackerman, an early pioneer in inspection training at Bell Labs; to Sig Rosenthal and Frank Lewski, later players in inspection training; to Dennis Christiansen, who not only profited from his use of inspection metrics, but who helped improve the process by feeding back to us what he learned about inspections; to Al Maione who was the first engineer at Bell Labs to apply inspections to hardware design; to Janey Cheu who brought inspections to international development; and to other Bell Labs colleagues who played a role in enhancing our knowledge and use of inspections.

We thank also John Musa and Ed Weller, who reviewed pieces of this book and encouraged us to complete it; and Jeanne Glasser, our very patient editor.

And a special thanks to Bill Brykczynski and David Wheeler for diligently compiling the inspections bibliography that appears at the back of this book, and for graciously allowing us to reprint it.

Without all of these people, and others we may regrettably have overlooked, this book could not have been written.

Software
Inspection
Process

In-Process Inspections

The English language is rife with sayings that reflect on the cost of procrastinating.

"Don't put off 'til tomorrow what you can do today."

"A stitch in time saves nine."

"You can pay me now, or pay me later."

These and other sayings recognize that delay too often results in additional work and expenditure. This is true whether the delay is in repairing a seam, a car engine, or a piece of software. In-process inspection stems directly from a recognition of the principle that time and delay are money, and offers a method for paying for quality early, and thus saving the greater expense of trying to achieve quality later in a completed product.

But sooner rather than later seems to be the opposite of what inspections are commonly understood to be; that is, an examination of a product after it is completed to make sure that it is right. In fact, Edwards Deming[1] says "Cease dependence on inspection to achieve quality. Eliminate the need for inspection on a mass basis by building quality into the product in the first place." Companies around the world have taken Deming's principles to heart, and have profited by it. But yet we say that in-process inspection is a path to quality improvement. Is there a conflict between our advice and that of Deming? We don't believe so. Consider these two points.

First, the term "in-process" implies a difference from the usual interpretation of inspection. In-process inspection refers to the use of the inspection method during the process of development, by examining intermediate representations of the product for defects at each stage of their preparation. Most importantly, the results of in-process in-spections are analyzed and fed back to control the production process to further reduce the occurrence of defects—while the process is on-going.

Second, Deming goes on to say "there are exceptions [to inspection], circumstances in which mistakes and duds are inevitable but intoler-able." Where are errors inevitable and intolerable? In the part of the process that is the product of the "intellectual artisan," the application of human intelligence to the manipulation of information, adding value to it, resulting in further enhanced and more complex information. The intellectual artisan works with and produces objects of the mind, illus-trated by Fig. 1.1. It is to these products, exemplified by software, hardware designs, documentation, and courses that in-process inspec-tions are meant to be applied.

In this book, we explain the benefits and limitations of in-process inspections, and show where inspections fit into an overall quality management program. (For simplicity, we frequently use the term "in-spection" as synonymous with "in-process inspection.") We describe the inspection process, through its stages from preparation to follow-up, in-cluding how to implement in-process inspections and how to keep them

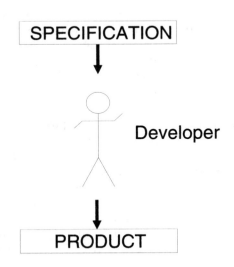

Desired:

Information (specification) ➡ **Information (product)**

Figure 1.1 The intellectual artisan.

running smoothly. We discuss management of in-process inspections, and its impact on the success of an inspection program. We describe techniques for the analysis of inspection data to evaluate the product, the development processes, and the inspection procedures. We also present an in-process inspection training program. In these chapters we have included in-process inspection rates, product dispositions, and defect densities that have been successfully used by a variety of projects. We also provide an example in-process inspection procedures manual that includes techniques for the inspections of a variety of software, hardware, documentation, and course products. In the Appendix, we have also included a model, called Lotus™ Inspection Data System (LIDS), for an in-process inspection data base system.

In this first chapter, we explain what in-process inspections are and are not, how inspections started, and how they grew, what their results were, and conclude with a few words about who we think will benefit from this book, and how best to use it.

1.1   What In-Process Inspections Are

In-process inspections are a means of verifying intellectual products by manually examining the developing product, a piece at a time, by small groups of peers to ensure that it is correct and conforms to product specifications and requirements. The purpose of in-process inspections is the detection (and subsequent correction) of defects. The underlying concept behind inspections is that a small group of peers, concentrating on one part of the product, can detect more defects than the same number of people working alone. This increased effectiveness results from the thoroughness of the inspection procedures and the synergy achieved by an inspection team.

To bring this about, inspectors must be well versed in the product and the project environment, knowledgeable about in-process inspections, prepared for the inspection meeting, and committed to improving product quality. For these reasons, in-process inspections are closely controlled by a formal process, that is defined on a per-project basis, and managed by project management. Part of this control is the collection and analysis of reported inspection data.

A further prerequisite for the success of in-process inspections is a clearly delineated development process that has established checkpoints at key development stages. Within such a development process criteria are established that determine when an interim work product is ready to enter the inspection procedure, and when it is ready to exit.

A relatively self-contained, well-defined interim work product is presented to an inspection team using a predefined and structured meeting format. Defects are sought and identified and documented, but not resolved. Solution of defects is left to the author of the work product; however, verification of the success of the solution is again controlled by the inspection process.

Data collected during inspection meetings is analyzed, and the results fed back into the inspection and development processes. This enables one to detect error patterns and possible overall weaknesses in the product or project procedures. The data also provides a concrete measure of product quality.

The structure and formality of the inspection process result in a high rate of defect detection. Moreover, inspection data analysis reveals that inspection results are repeatable, provided the inspection process is consistently applied.

1.2   What In-Process Inspections Are Not

In-process inspections are not a panacea for a haphazard product development process. They are not a forum for design decisions. They are not brainstorming sessions. Nor are they product reviews or walkthroughs, which are distinctly different processes with different objectives.

In-process inspection also is not the only method of quality control. In-process inspection is one of many quality control mechanisms, a mechanism that has proven extremely effective for the specific objective of product verification in many, but not necessarily all, development activities.

What differentiates in-process inspections from reviews, walkthroughs, and other methods of quality control are their singleness of purpose and the formality of the process. For a process to be an inspection it must follow a specified series of steps that define what can be inspected, when it can be inspected, who can inspect it, what preparation is needed for the inspection, how the inspection is to be conducted, what data is to be collected, and what the follow-up to the inspection is.

Less structured procedures can have many purposes and many formats. Reviews can be used to form decisions and resolve issues of design and development. They can even be used as a forum for information swapping or brainstorming. Walkthroughs are used for the resolution of design or implementation issues. Each of these methods can range from being formalized and following a predefined set of procedures, to the completely informal. What such methods most frequently lack is the close procedural control associated with in-process inspections, and because of this, they also lack repeatability of their results.

1.3   The Origins of In-Process Inspections

In-process inspections were first introduced and used in the early 1970s at International Business Machines (IBM). The in-process inspection concept was the brainchild of Michael E. Fagan,[2] who was seeking a means of improving programming quality and productivity. Large software products were plagued by poor reliability and the soaring costs of fixing bugs. A plethora of methods for improving software reliability were being proposed at the time: top-down program design, structured programming, structured walkthroughs, code reviews. The buzzwords were endless, as were the courses and books offered on each new method. The results were inconsistent.

Fagan recognized the need to eliminate errors as close to their source as possible. He also recognized the need for structure, control, and focus in the code verification method. His solution was software inspections. Fagan established inspections as gating and control procedures within the software development process.

Software inspections (he called them design and code inspections) as defined by Fagan form the basis for the inspection process described in this book. It was Fagan who first couched inspections within the larger concept of process management. He recognized that for a product verification method to succeed, the product development process must first be well defined and controlled, as illustrated in Fig. 1.2. Without this underlying structure to the development process, without product requirements, design specifications, and defined outputs, there is nothing to verify a product against. Therefore, Fagan established the need for program development checkpoints, with clearly stated exit criteria.

To ensure the measurability and repeatability of inspections, Fagan defined a set of inspection process steps, the same steps presented in Chapter 3 of this book: planning to establish the inspection, an overview to prepare the team, preparation of individual team members, the inspection meeting to detect defects, rework to resolve the defects, and follow-up to certify when the inspection was complete.

Fagan also identified key participants and ascribed roles to them. The participants he cited included the moderator, who acts as an inspection team coach and as the recorder; the program designer; the program coder; and the program tester. If a programmer filled more than one of these roles, another programmer with the requisite coding or testing skill would be selected to round the team to four and provide separate representation for each functional role.

The effectiveness of these procedures was repeatedly verified in use. For instance, as shown by Fig. 1.3, the results of similar software development projects at IBM were compared by Fagan—one using formal

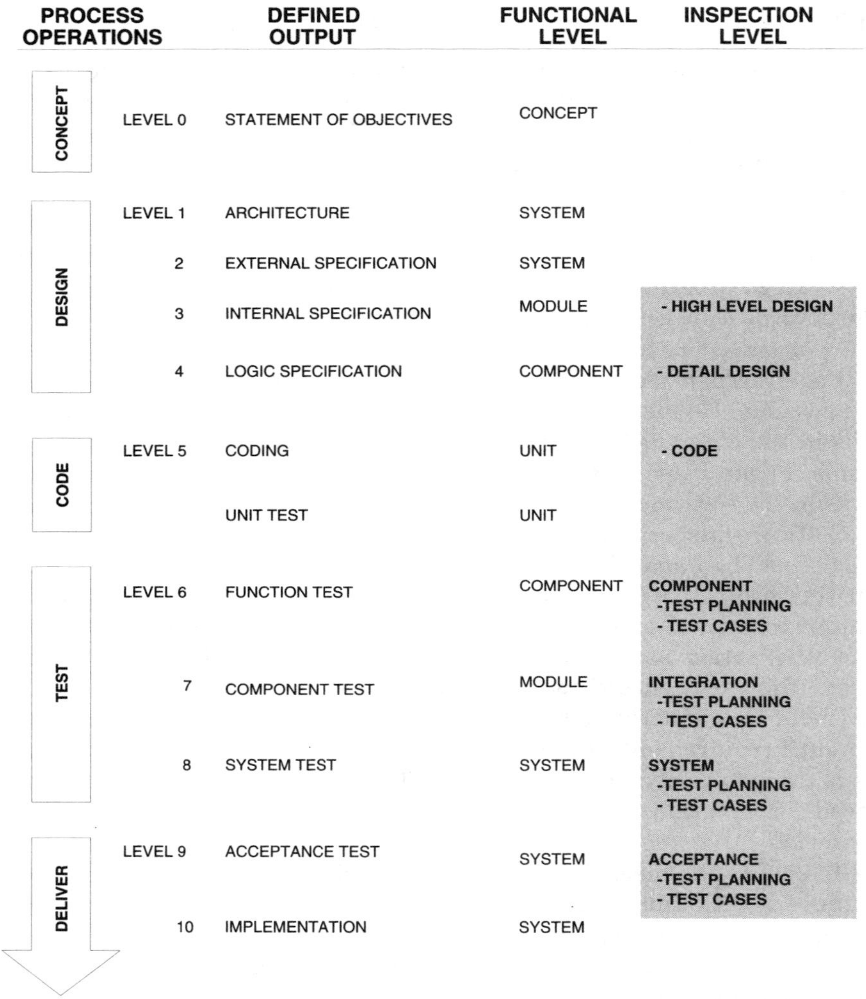

PROCESS OPERATIONS	DEFINED OUTPUT		FUNCTIONAL LEVEL	INSPECTION LEVEL
CONCEPT	LEVEL 0	STATEMENT OF OBJECTIVES	CONCEPT	
DESIGN	LEVEL 1	ARCHITECTURE	SYSTEM	
	2	EXTERNAL SPECIFICATION	SYSTEM	
	3	INTERNAL SPECIFICATION	MODULE	- HIGH LEVEL DESIGN
	4	LOGIC SPECIFICATION	COMPONENT	- DETAIL DESIGN
CODE	LEVEL 5	CODING	UNIT	- CODE
		UNIT TEST	UNIT	
TEST	LEVEL 6	FUNCTION TEST	COMPONENT	COMPONENT -TEST PLANNING - TEST CASES
	7	COMPONENT TEST	MODULE	INTEGRATION -TEST PLANNING - TEST CASES
	8	SYSTEM TEST	SYSTEM	SYSTEM -TEST PLANNING - TEST CASES
DELIVER	LEVEL 9	ACCEPTANCE TEST	SYSTEM	ACCEPTANCE -TEST PLANNING - TEST CASES
	10	IMPLEMENTATION	SYSTEM	

Figure 1.2 The programming process.

inspections and the other using an informal walkthrough process. During development (design and coding), the inspected product showed a *net* savings (including inspection and rework time) of 23 percent. After testing for 7 months, an analysis of the results showed that 38 percent fewer defects were found for the inspected product. These and similar results were so compelling that the inspections process is now widely used throughout the IBM company.

Fagan also recognized the importance of documenting inspections

---

Selected project of sufficient size:

- 3 person design team
- 13 programmers
- Moderate complexity (operating system component)
- Control selected using walkthroughs

Results:

- 23% net productivity increase
- 38% fewer errors—as compared with walkthroughs

Inspections are now extensively used throughout IBM

Figure 1.3 IBM experience.

and analyzing inspection results. Inspection information was used to identify error-prone modules that warranted more rigorous testing, or in the worst case, redevelopment. An analysis of the frequency of certain defect types pointed to particular trouble spots, especially when defects occurred consistently in certain types of code.

The inspection process Fagan conceived was specifically oriented to program development. Therefore, he applied inspections to two categories of materials: the program itself, including design and coding; and the program test plans. In each of these categories, in-process inspection is used to verify the correctness of the materials and thus increase the quality and integrity of the overall product.

1.4   And How They Grew

The inspection process presented in this book is adopted without apology from the process conceived and implemented with such success by Michael Fagan, a process which has proved effective over years of use. But the process has been introduced into new environments, applied in different ways. It has been nurtured—and it has grown.

The major difference between in-process inspections as presented in this book and Fagan's original definition is a difference in perspective. Fagan was providing a method for improving the quality of software products. The inspection process we present provides a means for improving the quality of a variety of products: software, of course, but also hardware, documentation, and courseware. In fact, any intellectual product.

Fagan envisioned inspection as a process management tool. We recognize this use of inspections, but expand on the concept by embedding inspections within a larger quality management framework. By providing this framework, we are able to further clarify the role of in-process inspections in achieving overall process quality—and control. The roles of inspectors have been slightly modified in our view of inspections. The recorder role is recognized as separate from the functions of the moderator. And where Fagan recommended training only for the moderator, we emphasize the need for training for all inspection participants and their management.

But the most significant modification in our approach to in-process inspections is the emphasis placed on customizing the process to a particular project environment. When inspections were first introduced in Bell Laboratories in the late 1970s, they were treated as a generic process and taught through a class open to one and all. The results were disappointing. It quickly became apparent that teaching an employee here and there was not the answer. Staff members who were enthusiastic about the procedure had an uphill battle trying to convince peers and managers to try it out. To make inspections work, it was clear that the process had to be sold to the entire project.

So a new approach was taken, aimed at first selling the idea of in-process inspections to project managers, then, with their support, selling staff and training them in inspection techniques. This approach led to immediate positive results, but still did not attain the level of return expected. The key lay in the nature of the Bell Laboratories structure.

Each project at Bell Laboratories is generally under the direction of a separate department, or a small group of cooperating departments. Each department tends to have different skills, tools, and procedures, in short, drastically different environments. Even among cooperating departments, the environments often differ. This is especially true when the tasks performed are widely variant, as when hardware and software organizations work on a joint project. Clearly, one set of inspection procedures would not suffice for the entire population.

It was decided to devise a method for tailoring the inspection process to meet the needs of each development environment within the scope of projectwide inspection training. Thus the concept of inspection types evolved, allowing the inspection process to be tailored not only for a particular department, but also within that department to accommodate as many variations as necessary to achieve the maximum benefit. And a new concept of inspection training, consultative training, was instituted to assist projects in defining their inspection types and procedures.

A by-product of these activities was the recognition of the need for inspections to be closely controlled. The management role in the inspection process was formally defined, and an inspection coordinator position was defined to aid in the project's conversion to inspections and to provide continued support and improvement of the inspection process.

And so the concept of an adjustable inspections process evolved. And although this concept was derived from the particular needs of Bell Laboratories, it has resulted in a matured inspection process with widespread applicability.

1.5   Who Should Use In-Process Inspections

It would be facetious and wrong to claim that every development project should use inspections. Inspections can play a significant role in a quality management system when used consistently and correctly. But they are of little value if applied haphazardly or without controls or for the wrong tasks. For example, inspections are of no use if what you really need to do is evaluate alternative algorithms or approaches. Nor are they of any use if there is not follow-up to an inspection meeting. They are of only limited use if data is not collected and analyzed, or if they are used by only some of the developers within a project.

Moreover, even if applied correctly and consistently, inspections are not effective in all project environments. They will not work well on unstructured projects, such as research, or on projects that have no interim checkpoints. They will not work on a project that is not closely managed.

So the answer to who should use in-process inspections is anyone who

- Is committed to the inspection process and well trained in its use

- Works on a well-structured, closely managed project that has identified checkpoints

- Is guided by a quality management process that has identified defect detection goals

1.6   Why You Should Use In-Process Inspections

What should you expect to gain for your efforts? Nothing less than increased quality, increased productivity, and increased customer satisfaction. If that seems a tall order, let's consider for a moment what the real cost of poor quality is. Basically, it's the cost of doing things over, possibly several times, until we get it right. In addition, it's the cost of lost time, lost productivity, lost customers, lost business. These are real costs, and they're the costs that eat up businesses, because there is no return on them.

On the flip side is the cost of quality. Surely it costs something to perform yet another set of procedures within the development cycle.

TABLE 1.1 JPL Experience*

Averages per Inspection	
Major defects found (product performance)	4
Minor defects found (product representation)	12
Pages of material	38
Number of participants	5
Total staff time	28 hours
Approximate savings	$25,000

*JPL estimates they have saved over $7.5 million for 300 inspections.

However, experience with inspections shows that time added to the development cycle to accommodate the inspection process is more than gained back in the testing and manufacturing cycles, and in the cost of redevelopment that doesn't need to be done.

Citing one result, the Jet Propulsion Laboratory (JPL),[3] a supplier of software to National Aeronautics and Space Administration (NASA), adopted in-process inspections on a broad basis, using more than 10 types of inspections in their development processes. Their experience, summarized in Table 1.1, has been the realization of a net savings of $7.5 million from performing 300 inspections.

The key is that in-process inspections provide a means of keeping defects out of the deployed product, of avoiding the cost associated with trying to build quality into a defective product. Although it is possible to retrofit quality, it is only possible to do so at great expense. So the conclusion is that you should use in-process inspections because they make good business sense, because they can contribute to your bottom line.

1.7 And What They'll Do for You

The key reason for using in-process inspections is to obtain a significant improvement in quality, as measured by defects that are found in the product when it is used. In addition, you should expect that the productivity and manageability of the development process will be improved. Three examples illustrate these benefits.

1.7.1 Quality

Typical of many companies, AT&T decided to trial in-process inspections for a portion of the Integrated Corporate Information System (ICIS) project.[4] ICIS had very large maintenance costs for prior releases. This time, using inspections at four phases in their development cycle, summarized in Fig. 1.4, the resulting product had one-

```
┌─────────────────────────────────────────────────────────────┐
│ Project:                                                    │
│   ▪ Data base accounting                                    │
│   ▪ 14 persons                                              │
│   ▪ 3 month duration                                        │
│   ▪ 20 modules; 7,000 LOC (lines of code)                   │
│                                                             │
│ Inspection Results:                                         │
│   Analysis                        23 defects                │
│   High-level design               83                        │
│   Detail design                   85                        │
│   Code                            77                        │
│   ────────────────────────────────────────                 │
│   Totals:                         268 defects               │
│                                   37 inspections            │
│                                                             │
│ Evaluation:                                                 │
│   ▪ Product delivered on-time, within budget                │
│   ▪ Only 4 defects found in production                      │
│   ▪ Stability Index* of 0.2% vs. 15% expected               │
│   ▪ Development personnel very favorable                     │
│                                                             │
│   *Stability Index = % LOC Maintained/Total LOC             │
└─────────────────────────────────────────────────────────────┘
```

Figure 1.4   AT&T ICIS project software inspection results.

tenth the production defects that they had been experiencing. Most significantly, maintenance was also reduced by an order of magnitude, with an incalculable improvement in staff morale and customer relations. This was achieved while delivering the product on schedule, and within budget.

1.7.2 Productivity

Bell Northern Research has been using in-process inspections since 1984 for key projects, and in 1986 established the technique as standard for nearly all software development.[5] Their results for the inspection of 2.5 million lines of code over eight software releases indicated that inspections

- Detected 37 defects per thousand lines of code
- Found one defect for each staff-hour invested
- Discovered defects two to four times faster than by testing
- Found 80 percent of all defects
- Avoided 33 hours of subsequent maintenance effort per defect

Mike Fagan pointed out that inspections shorten the development schedule in his 1976 paper, as illustrated in Fig. 1.5. By detecting defects early, and consequently clarifying the following stages of work, inspections allow subsequent phases to progress more quickly and reduce costly testing.

1.7.3 Manageability

The Network Software Center of AT&T determined that in-process inspections were a reliable source of early project management data.[6] Analysis of inspection data from previous releases (Fig. 1.6) identified a significant relationship between inspection results and end-product quality: *Software features and subsystems with defects "different" from the inspection process mean had the highest failures.*

This allowed appropriate corrective action to be initiated before re-

WITHOUT INSPECTIONS

```
        ┌──────────────────────┐
        │       DESIGN         │
        └──────────────────────┘
                    ┌──────────────────────────┐
                    │           CODE           │
                    └──────────────────────────┘
                              ┌──────────────────────────────┐
                              │            TEST              │ ──► SHIP
                              └──────────────────────────────┘
                              ↑ FIRST QUANTITATIVE INDICATION
                                OF QUALITY - FROM TEST RESULTS

        ├──────────── SCHEDULE ────────────┤
```

WITH INSPECTIONS

```
        ┌──────────────────────┐
        │       DESIGN         │
        └──────────────────────┘
                    ┌──────────────────────┐
                    │         CODE         │
                    └──────────────────────┘
     I₀       I₁       I₂
                                    ┌────────────────────────┐
                                    │          TEST          │ ──►
                                    └────────────────────────┘
        FIRST QUANTITATIVE          ↑ STILL GET TEST RESULTS
        INDICATION OF QUALITY

        ◄═══════════════════════════════════════
                              DEFECT REPAIR COSTS

        1.5       1       1.5      10 | 60                  100
```

- Point of management control over quality is moved up much earlier in schedule
- Defect rework is 1/10 as expensive at this level

Figure 1.5 IBM determined effect of inspections on schedule.

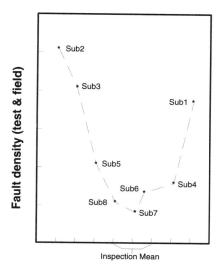

Mean log defects/inspection

Subsystems with inspection defects that were
statistically different from the inspection mean
had the highest subsequent fault densities

Figure 1.6 AT&T data for the early identification
of fault-prone units.

lease of the product. For the current release, 3 of 7 subsystems and 5 of
18 features were identified as exceptions, and management reevaluated the features and subsystems and instituted more effective testing.

Results like these are not an exception, but rather are consistent
from one company to another, using various development methodologies, and regardless if the product is hardware or software. What
should you expect from inspections? Nothing short of improved

- Product quality
- Development productivity
- Process manageability

1.8 Who Should Use This Book—And in What Ways

Anyone who uses in-process inspections, manages inspections, teaches
inspections, consults on inspections, or who is just curious as to what
in-process inspections are all about should find something of interest in

this book. And those who think inspections aren't worthwhile should find lots to consider, as well as object to.

The following terms try to summarize the intent of the remaining nine chapters to provide a guide for your further reading:

- Chapters 2 to 5 define in-process inspections and describe how to use, implement, and manage them within a project framework. These chapters combine educational material, of the "what are inspections made of" variety, with practical advice, such as how to conduct an inspection.

  —*Chapter 2:* Understanding the use of inspections in development

  —*Chapter 3:* Performing inspection procedures

  —*Chapter 4:* Defining an inspection process

  —*Chapter 5:* Managing inspections within development

- Chapter 6 discusses the analysis of inspection data, with application for the assessment of the inspection process and the feedback of information for guiding development.

- Chapter 7 describes a program to educate the staff and management about in-process inspections, along with techniques for inspection support.

- Chapter 8 contains a sample software inspection procedures manual, as a template that may be useful for preparing your own customized documentation.

- Chapter 9 provides information about applying the inspection process to other types of development: documentation, hardware, and training.

- Chapter 10 compares in-process inspections to the more general review technique, highlighting the differences and similarities to guide the appropriate application of each.

- The Appendix describes an inspection data base management system, LIDS, that can be used to ease the preparation of one tailored for your project and system requirements.

Taken together these pieces provide a blueprint for creating your own inspection process, a textbook that can be used to supplement your inspection training program, a reference for inspection procedures, or an in-process inspection management handbook. Individual pieces can be used for establishing in-process inspection procedures. Checklists and inspection forms can be used as is, or tailored for your process. In fact, each of the chapters of this book are designed to provide guidelines and models that can be followed and/or improved on.

1.9 Conclusion

Our recommendation is that you read the first five chapters of this book for a consistent understanding of in-process inspections and the steps needed to successfully apply them. Then refer to the other chapters as needed. Use the pieces that work best within your environment, modify the pieces that are near-misses, and come up with your own replacements for the pieces that are completely foreign. If we've done our job well, there should be very few of the last category.

1.10 References

1. Deming, W. Edwards, *Out of the Crisis,* Massachusetts Institute of Technology Center for Advanced Engineering Study, Cambridge, November 1989.
2. Fagan, M. E., Design and code inspections to reduce errors in program development, *IBM Systems Journal,* Vol. 15, No. 3, 1976.
3. Bush, Marilyn, Formal Inspections—Do They Really Help?, NSIA Sixth Annual National Joint Conference on Software Quality and Productivity, Williamsburg, Va., April 19, 1990.
4. McCormick, K., Results of using inspections for the AT&T ICIS Project, Second Annual Symposium on EDP Quality Assurance, March 1983.
5. Russell, Glen W., Experience with Inspection in Ultralarge-Scale Development, *IEEE Software,* Vol. 17, No. 1, January 1991.
6. Graden, M. and Horsley, P., The Effects of Software Inspections on a Major Telecommunications Project, *AT&T Technical Journal,* May–June 1986.

2

Process Management

The most critical problems faced by industry today are low productivity and poor quality. Faced with global competition, huge import figures, and a shrinking share of the market, clearly the success of our industrial capability lies in regaining our ability to produce products of the highest recognized quality at the lowest possible cost. Our proven innovative abilities are no longer enough to guarantee success in the marketplace. We must develop the ability to implement our ideas so they are both highly saleable and economical.

The most effective way to improve both quality and productivity is to improve the processes and procedures that are used to develop our products. Deming claims that 85 percent of our quality problems are directly attributable to the processes we use to get things done. If this is the case, we need a quality management approach that focuses on the procedures and processes we use, with the aim of continually improving and fine-tuning them—an approach that provides a new set of processes that enable us to consistently provide products and services that meet customer's quality, schedule, and cost requirements. Or, in the words of American Telephone and Telegraph (AT&T) Network Systems President Bill Marx,[1] "the best way to get [results] is to improve the process that produces them. And then improve it again."

2.1 Process

Generally speaking, the purpose of an organization is to provide goods or services to some customer group. Organizations do this by using the resources at their disposal to create a product. This product may be something as tangible as a car or a shirt, or something less tangible, like accounting. Whatever the product, some process is involved, some series of steps that turns inputs into the desired output.

Like the product, the process can assume many forms. It can be a physical process, such as converting logs to lumber, a paper handling process, such as providing insurance, or a service, such as arranging accommodations. Or it can be some combination of these, such as developing an idea into a system of electronic and software components. Whatever the process, it involves a series of activities, and may include several groups of people, and the commitment of facilities and equipment.

If we consider a process to be the series of productive actions resulting in a product, and management to be the act, manner, or practice of control, then *process management* can be defined as the series of actions that control product evolution, especially with regard to the resultant quality of the product.

2.1.1   Process stages

A process can be broken down into three basic stages: planning, development, and deployment. Each of these stages involves several activities, which must be controlled, monitored, and adjusted throughout the process. And each stage produces one or more outputs. Table 2.1 shows activities and outputs associated with each process stage.

Each process stage is, in turn, a process itself. Ideally, each stage is formally defined and assigned to separate areas of an organization, each reporting to an overall project manager. For large organizations, this ideal is often at least partially achieved. For smaller organizations, the stages and responsibilities are less likely to be distinct, and activities such as market analysis may be rudimentary or even nonexistent. However, for any organization to provide a product, some product development process must exist. That process requires the

TABLE 2.1   Process Stages

Stage	Activities	Outputs
Planning	Data collection Market analysis Goal setting	Objectives Concepts Project plans
Development	Definition Design Implementation	Internal, intermediate work products
Deployment	Testing Production Maintenance	Customer product

commitment of personnel and resources, and involves many steps, which must be completed in a given order. Except in the most trivial processes, each step should include checks and balances to verify its completion and correctness, and to ensure the overall success of the process. The process must be planned, organized, monitored, and controlled. Or simply put, it must be managed.

2.2 Process Quality

In order to define a quality management approach, we must first get a handle on what quality is. Quality has been defined in many ways. One often-quoted description is, "I can't tell you what quality is, but I know it when I see it." Juran[2] defines it broadly as "fitness for use." Each of these descriptions tells us something about quality, but neither is useful in deriving a measure of the quality of a product.

More helpful for product development is the Department of Defense's software development standard 2167A,[3] which defines a set of quality attributes. These include

- Correctness
- Consistency
- Understandability
- Traceability
- Performance
- Testability

Although there is still some degree of subjectivity to these attributes, they help reduce the definition of quality to terms that are meaningful to developers and clients, and that are controllable within the development process.

One key to quality management is to recognize that quality issues are as inseparable from the development process as schedule and cost considerations. That in fact quality and productivity are directly related, and that the cost of ignoring quality is the expense related to doing things wrong—an expense no development process can afford.

2.2.1 Defects and product development

The true cost of a product includes the costs of product development, quality control, and defect repair. Even with the best development and quality control processes in place, it is not likely that a product will be defect-free through all its development stages. Much of product development work is of a highly cerebral nature, relying on specifications, development guidelines, and prior experience. In transforming a set of specifications into a product, the producer often encounters a number of problems which are not a function of his or her own errors, problems endemic to the nature of highly intellectual work. These may include incomplete or incorrect specifications, misunderstandings between the product specifier and the customer, and differing interpretations of what the specifications call for. Changing requirements, tight or inadequate schedules, and restricted resources all add to the possibility of inadvertently incorporating defects.

When these and other problems are entered into the development process, defects occur. An implementation may be incorrect; the product may not conform to specifications or comply with standards. This phenomenon is depicted in Fig. 2.1.

Yet the inevitability of defects is not the true source of concern for quality management, but rather at what point in the product cycle these defects are detected and corrected. If we recognize that development is an error-prone process, and gear our quality program to finding

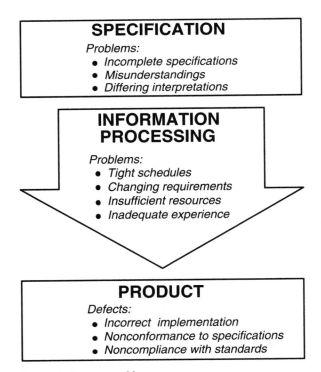

Figure 2.1 Process problems.

and correcting defects early in the process, we reduce the cost of defect correction and increase productivity—while we improve quality.

The value of early defect detection and correction cannot be overemphasized. Statistics gathered on software projects from several major corporations establish that the cost of defect correction increases dramatically the further from their source defects are detected. Figure 2.2 illustrates this.[4]

In later stages of development the cost of defect repair may increase by as much as a factor of 10 from one stage of development to the next. Defect detection and repair at the requirements phase was approximately $200 per defect, while the direct cost of defect repair in the deployed product was greater than $20,000.

For large products, defect removal and repair typically account for 50 percent or more of all costs. As products become even larger and more involved, the cost of defect repair can actually exceed all other production costs. For example, one large communications switching program, that required 9 months to develop, took another 14 months to test and debug.

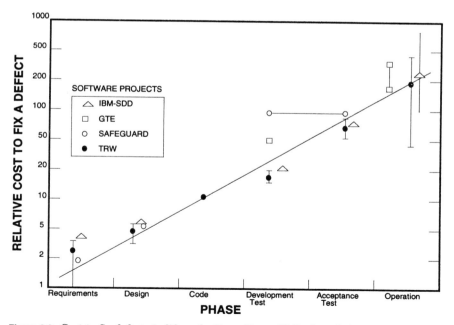

Figure 2.2 Cost to fix defects in life-cycle. From Barry W. Boehm, *Software Engineering Economics,* © 1981, p. 40. Reprinted by permission of Prentice-Hall, Englewood Cliffs, N.J.

2.3 Development Models

There are many development process models. Commonly these models break the development process into a series of activities, such as conception, definition, design, construction, testing, and operation. The specific steps involved in any given product development cycle depend on the nature of the product being developed, the environment in which it is developed, and the underlying principle on which the development model is based. What many development models have in common though, is that they delay verification until after the product has been developed, then begin by testing the last stages of development first.

2.3.1 The waterfall model

This characteristic of development models is demonstrated in the composite view of the waterfall model shown in Fig. 2.3. Here product creation is divided into four tasks, proceeding from a general, conceptual description of the product, to a functional definition of the requirements, a structural formulation of the design, and finally procedural construction of the product itself. In each stage the product idea becomes more refined, and each stage depends on the quality and accuracy of the previous stage.

The upper portion of the model consists of a series of testing stages.

- First, the individual pieces of the final product
- Then, the pieces integrated together
- Then, the product as part of the system it serves
- Finally, the operation of the product in the environment in which it was designed to perform

This testing pattern, which is an attribute of the waterfall model, results in early occurring errors of conception and definition being found last, which leads to the following problems.

1. As development progresses, products become more complex, increasing the likelihood of incorporating defects.
2. As work progresses from one step to another, undetected defects proliferate and become embedded in the emerging product.
3. As defects are detected farther from their source, a dramatic increase in the cost of detection and removal, shown in Fig. 2.2, is experienced.

The lesson is clear. To increase the reliability of work done at each step, to decrease the complexity of detecting defects, and to reduce the cost of defect detection and removal, find defects as early in the development cycle as possible.

2.3.2 The rapid prototyping model

An alternative development model which has gained popularity recently is the *rapid prototyping* model shown in Fig. 2.4.

In this model an initial version of the product is defined, often without the full capability of the proposed final product. This version is quickly developed and tried out with the user. The result of the exercise is evaluated, leading to an enhanced design. The new design is then used to redevelop the product, and the process is repeated.

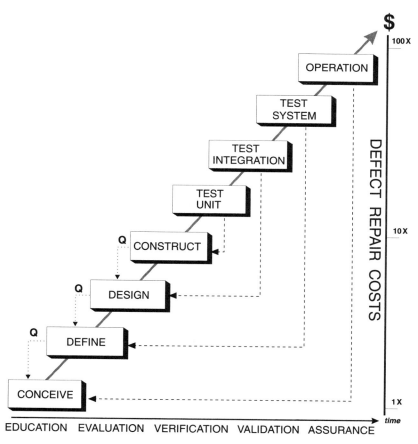

Figure 2.3 Quality management in the development cycle.

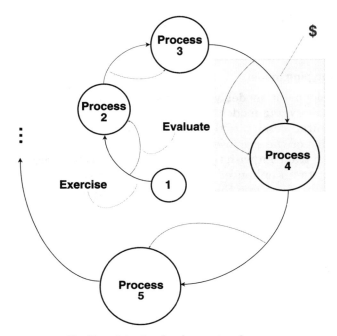

Figure 2.4 Rapid prototyping development cycle.

Although the rapid prototyping model avoids much of the inverse order of testing that results from the waterfall model, it also has its problems. Because an inherent characteristic of the model is that each stage is based on specifications that may not be complete, it is difficult to know when the final product has been fully specified, and therefore when the process should be terminated. There is also a tendency to keep refining the process past the point of efficiency and cost-effectiveness. In addition, as the cycle progresses, the cost of testing becomes increasingly more significant.

These deficiencies can be somewhat alleviated by including a verification procedure within the model. Verifying the specifications and development procedures for each stage, as well as the exercise plan itself, can improve the predictability of the rapid prototyping method. In fact, a significant reduction in development time and cost can be achieved if internal verification can reduce the need for one or more cycles.

However, regardless of the model of the life-cycle that is used, the best assurance of quality and cost effectiveness is to employ the quality objective that is most appropriate for the development stage. The education, evaluation, verification, validation, assurance (EEVVA) model is offered to help guide this choice.

2.4   The EEVVA Model

The EEVVA model emphasizes a quality objective for each development stage, and matches each objective with a method for achieving it, shown in Table 2.2.

The quality objectives in EEVVA follow directly from the product development stages. During the early stages of product concept and definition, the model emphasizes communicating the emerging product concepts to project members. In the specification and design stages, the emphasis switches to evaluation of functional requirements and assessment of alternative design choices. During product construction, the model prescribes procedures for verifying the implementation of the specification. Once the implementation is completed, EEVVA calls for testing to validate product performance. Finally, the model recognizes the need to provide the user with assurance that the product works the way it is expected to, and provides the development organization with assurance that they complied with all required development procedures, standards, and practices.

The procedures associated with each stage in the EEVVA model represent one alternative among many. However, each procedure shown is typical of the type of activity best suited to each quality objective. Moreover, these choices have been found to be highly effective across a large range of development projects. In particular, inspections offer definite advantages over less formal product verification procedures; the major advantage being their effectiveness of defect detection.

TABLE 2.2   The EEVVA Quality Management Model

Quality Objective	Procedure
Education Communication of information	Tutorial
Evaluation Assessment of alternatives	Review
Verification Conformance to specifications	Inspection
Validation Proof of performance	Test
Assurance Compliance with procedures	Audit

2.4.1 Education

The education objective of the EEVVA model provides project members with information that will enable them to do their jobs more successfully. Typically, tutorials are used to

1. Inform project members of the project concept, plans, and product designs
2. Establish development procedures
3. Familiarize project members with the customer and the customer's needs
4. Provide any other pertinent project information

Much of this information is imparted early in the project life cycle. But the educational component of EEVVA is not limited to the start of a project; it continues as needed throughout all stages of a project.

2.4.2 Evaluation

The purpose of project evaluation is to allow project personnel to assess alternative approaches to product function, design, and creation. This activity takes place at a point in the development process when the product is not yet completely defined. The review procedure allows participants to air ideas and concepts, to consider questions of usage and optimization, and to identify and consider alternatives. In general, a review also seeks to resolve issues whenever possible. (See Chapter 10 for a more complete discussion of reviews.)

2.4.3 Verification

The verification objective has as its express goal the detection and elimination of defects. The verification procedure of inspection is applied to a well-defined, completed segment of work, which is judged against a given set of entry criteria and specifications to establish that the work product complies with its specifications, is correctly implemented, and complies with applicable standards of development and use. The inspection procedure is expected to identify defects through examination of the work, not to offer solutions. However, solutions to identified problems are expected to be accomplished within the whole process of verification that incorporates the examination. Verification takes place in-process, as segments of the product are completed.

2.4.4 Validation

Validation is the more traditional type of product testing. Validation takes place when portions of the work product can be exercised, and when the entire product is completed. It tests not only the individual components of the product, but also the interaction of the components, and the product responses within its intended environment.

2.4.5 Assurance

The assurance objective provides the final check of compliance to the originating concept and with project procedures. The product is checked to be sure it has all the features that the were requested, and that they work the way the customer expects them to in application. An audit, as an assurance procedure, also checks that the product does not have additional features that the customer did not request and does not want. In addition, the audit checks that product support features such as documentation, training, and customer service facilities are in place.

2.5 Defect Detection

Recognizing the inevitability of defects and the compelling need to detect and correct them as early in the development process as possible leads us to the question of how best to detect defects early, cheaply, and efficiently. In many cases, there are few automated tools available early in the development process, and most of these are highly specialized. When automated processes are available, use them! But for most products, manual examination is likely to be the only currently available method. Manual examination should be used to verify those parts of the product that cannot be verified automatically.

As we see from the EEVVA model, product verification is an integral part of managing product quality during development. In order to apply verification effectively, we must first look at the development process flow.

2.5.1 The work unit

Product creation results from the execution of a series of steps, each of which produces an interim output, or work product. Work products then become input to later development steps. Each development step that produces a work product is a potential point of verification. The activities that occur at a verification point comprise an element called a work unit. The *work unit* is a reasonably self-contained division of the production process. It may produce a single feature, a particular circuit, or even a document.

The work unit combines the tasks of construction, verification, and baselining. The input to each work unit is a set of specifications and previously baselined work products. The output of a work unit is one or more verified and baselined work products, as depicted in Fig. 2.5.

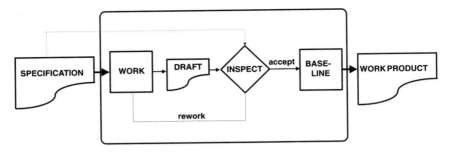

Figure 2.5 The work unit.

Work products are tangible evidence of the progress of the work unit. The accumulation and integration of all assigned work units and their work products is the development process and the resulting end product.

2.5.2 Why consider work units?

The work unit provides a mechanism for achieving the effect of "doing it right the first time," by providing a means of defining "the first time" and "right" within the development context of the work unit. In terms of the work unit, as illustrated by Fig. 2.6, the first time is an end-to-end measurement, from the point input arrives at the work unit to the point a work product is delivered. Draft results within the work unit

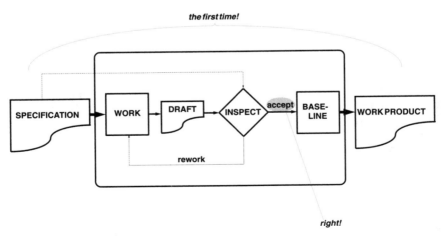

Figure 2.6 The work unit—the "first time."

are incomplete work products, requiring some number of iterations until the draft is accepted and baselined.

The work unit's internal quality control mechanism determines when the work product is right and can be released. Since all detected defects in the draft work product are reworked and reexamined until the product is accepted by the peer inspection team for use by others, the completed work product is thus considered "right the first time!" That is not to claim that all work products that have undergone verification will be perfect. The degree of "rightness" depends on how well the quality control process detects defects and how effectively the work procedures correct them.

As illustrated by Fig. 2.7, the work unit provides a framework for defining development and quality responsibilities and for measuring product quality and progress.

The developers, and the quality control procedures that they follow, are within the scope of the work unit. Management activities are outside the work unit, since their contribution is to enable the development and quality processes, not to apply them. Likewise, quality assurance tasks, those that measure and evaluate work products at the interstices between work units, reside outside the work unit.

The development staff perform the operations of work, verification, and baselining. Management, which is outside of the boundaries of the work unit, does not perform any of the internal tasks, such as the work or its verification, but, importantly, "provision" the work unit. Provisioning includes the critical tasks of scheduling the work unit, providing the necessary resources of staff, tools, and workplace. In addition, management monitors and controls the activities of the work unit.

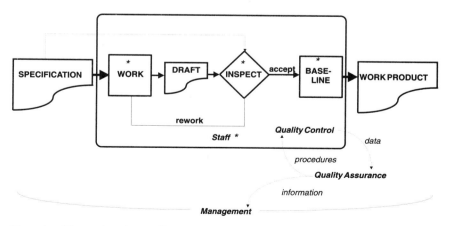

Figure 2.7 The work unit—quality responsibilities.

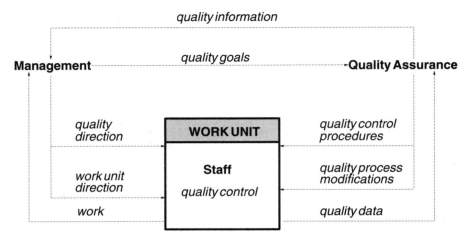

Figure 2.8 Relationship of quality responsibilities.

But management requires information to control the activities of the work unit. This information is provided from quality assurance. Quality assurance provides information from measurements of the work product outside of the work unit, and derives its data for these measurements from the quality control activities that are performed inside the work unit by the staff. There is a path of product information from quality assurance to management, and of product data from the quality control activities in the work unit to quality assurance. In addition, quality assurance provides quality control procedures that will be performed by the staff within the work unit. These relationships are further highlighted in Fig. 2.8.

2.6   Verification of Work Products

Given the work unit view of the development process, the key to successful product verification is to make each work product as defect free as possible. We contend that the best way to do this is to use a formal verification procedure rather than an informal one. The difference as we define it is not in how rigorously the procedure is performed. Both formal and informal procedures may be performed in a rigorous or a slipshod fashion. Rather, a formal procedure is distinguished by knowledge and control of the quality control process by the project. An informal quality control procedure is controlled by and provides knowledge only to the individual developer, and is transparent to the project. A look at the properties of formal and informal examination procedures in Table 2.3 illustrates these differences.

What is most notable about the two types of verification procedure is

TABLE 2.3   Comparison of Key Properties

Property	Formal inspection	Informal examination
1. Purpose	Verification	Alternatives Education Defect detection
2. Organization	Small group with defined roles	Variable, from small to very large
3. Leadership	Impartial moderator	Producer
4. Procedures	Standardized and documented	Variable
5. Training	For all participants	None
6. Follow-up	All rework monitored	None
7. Data recording	Described, encoded, and stored	Listed
8. Data analysis	Product Development process Inspection process	Data not available

the degree of focus and control provided by the formal procedure. Informal procedures are much more variable, both in what they are intended to accomplish and in assuring that they have accomplished it. Informal procedures can work as a means of obtaining feedback and information for the developer to assist in creating the work product. However, when it is time to verify the work product, formal procedures offer much better odds for success for the project.

2.6.1   Inspections as a means of verification

Although inspections are just one type of formal verification procedure, we emphasize them because of their proven track record. Our earliest data, from Mike Fagan's 1976 *IBM Systems Engineering Journal*[5] article, shows that he found formal verification of work products using inspections resulted in 38 percent fewer defects in the final product than attained when walkthroughs were used. This is money in the bank. To see why such dramatic improvements are possible, let's examine how inspections are used.

To apply inspections, the product specifications and the quality attributes to be measured must be clearly stated and understood. All design conflicts must be resolved before implementation begins. These are the goals of the first two stages of the EEVVA model. Inspections then verify quality by assessing the conformance of each work product to the stated specifications and quality attributes. (For example, a functional specification of an elevator would be its capacity, while a quality attribute would be safety.) Each detected instance of noncon-formance becomes a measure of the product's departure from quality, its departure from the ideal final product. While we may never quite reach that ideal product, with each defect that is detected and corrected, we inch a little closer to it.

Inspections are especially effective in detecting defects, because that is precisely the focus of an inspection meeting. When you collect a group of knowledgeable people in a room, with the express purpose of finding how a work product diverges from the ideal specified, it is not surprising that they come up with results. Since they are not only under no obligation to figure out how to fix the problems they find, but are in fact told not to even think about fixes, there is nothing to distract them from concentrating on detecting defects.

Moreover, an output from each inspection meeting is a classified list of identified defects. The data from each inspection meeting is combined into a data base that tracks the results of inspections over the entire project. Figure 2.9 shows the flow of inspection data within a project. Following analysis, the inspection data is fed forward into the test plan to help identify areas that are defect-prone, or types of defects

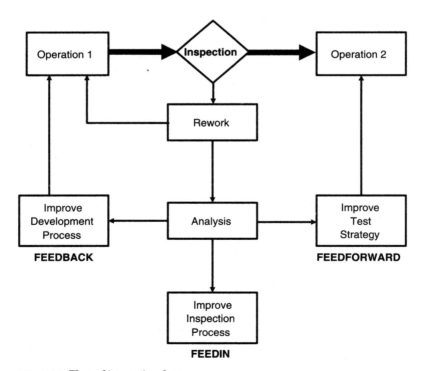

Figure 2.9 Flow of inspection data.

that recur throughout the project. The data is also fed back into the development process to improve development procedures. Finally, the data is fed into the inspection process itself, to help tune the verification procedures for greater efficiency.

Part of the success of inspections is this ability to help monitor and control the inspection process as well.

All examinations benefit the developer and the product, since all examinations tap into a broader base of project expertise, help find defects earlier in the development cycle, and encourage communication among project members. Additionally, inspections provide

- A quantitative definition of how to measure product quality
- Formal procedures for the control, accuracy, and repeatability of inspection results
- Required entry and exit criteria to reinforce project milestones and provide a measure of progress
- Assigned accountability for work product quality to the inspection team, while in no way lessening the author's accountability for the work product itself
- Impartiality of the inspection meeting moderator to ensure that the process will be objectively and consistently applied
- The use of past and current inspection data to reduce the occurrence of defects and provide for continuous process improvement

2.6.2 Where to apply inspections

When inspections are used for product verification and quality control within the EEVVA model, there are logical places in the product development process where they apply. Figure 2.10 identifies these inspection checkpoints.

The figure shows the quality procedures associated with each step and product in this example of a development process. The checkpoints shown correlate with the evaluation, verification, and validation objectives of the EEVVA model.

Since it is characteristic of the development process that each step builds on preceding steps, the outputs of earlier steps become entry criteria for subsequent steps. In particular, inspections use not only the outputs of the planning, design, and requirements steps as entry criteria, but also work products from earlier implementations.

2.6.3 Cost of inspections

The obvious question is, "What are all these benefits going to cost me?" For the answer let's look at what happened at a major financial corpo-

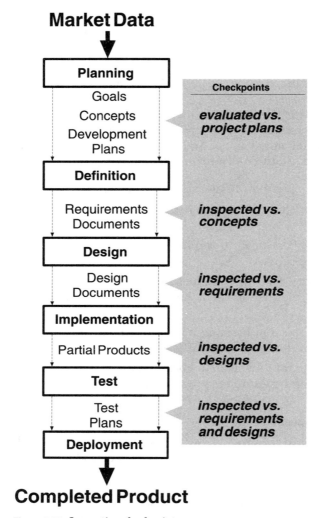

Figure 2.10 Inspection checkpoints.

ration. When their first attempt at a new communications system failed miserably at a cost of almost $2 million, the corporation employed a new vendor, and specified inspections as a means of quality control. This time the project was successful. After 3 years in operation, the communications system could boast a defect rate of only three defects per 15,000 lines of code, or 0.2 percent.

And what had it cost them? Inspections accounted for 18 percent of their total project budget. However, the project was completed on schedule, at a total net cost of 10 percent less than originally estimated. The bottom line was that with the aid of inspections, the corporation got a high-quality system, at a 10 percent discount.

Harold Geneen[6] said it best, "Quality is not only right, it is free! And it is not only free, it is the most profitable product we have!" The real question is not how much a quality management system will cost, but how much the lack of one will cost.

2.7 Conclusion

To the achievement of any goal, there is a process. That process can be simple or complex, haphazard or well defined, uncontrolled or managed. In some cases, how well the goal is achieved may be independent of which of these adjectives describes the process. But for most organizations, where an organizational goal is likely to be product excellence, the process is best not left to chance. Defining and managing the process will ensure more consistent, more successful quality results.

Part of managing a process for quality involves providing a quality management program as an integral part of the development process. EEVVA and the work unit provide a framework for such a quality management program, and in-process inspections a successful procedure for product verification. In this chapter we have described how inspections fit into quality management as a means of quality control. In the next chapter, we take an in-depth look at the inspection process, what it is, and how it functions.

2.8 References

1. Address telecast to AT&T employees, Basking Ridge, N.J., April 25, 1990.
2. Juran, J.M., *Quality Control Handbook,* McGraw-Hill, 1974.
3. Military Standard, Defense System Software Development, DOD-STD-2167A, Department of Defense, Washington, D.C., February 29, 1988.
4. Boehm, Barry, *Software Engineering Economics,* Prentice-Hall, Englewood Cliffs, N.J., 1981, p. 40; reprinted with permission of Prentice-Hall publishers.
5. Fagan, M.E., "Design and code inspections to reduce errors in program development," *IBM Systems Journal,* Vol. 15, No. 3, 1976.
6. Crosby, Phil, *Quality is Free: the art of making quality certain,* McGraw-Hill, 1979; statement quoted from Harold Geneen, CEO of the ITT Corporation.

3

Performing Inspections

Until now, we have viewed in-process inspections externally, concentrating on how an inspections program fits into the larger scope of process management. In this chapter, we turn our attention to the internal view of inspections, concentrating on the "performance structure" of people and procedures that enable inspections to function correctly and effectively. In this chapter we discuss in-process inspection according to its definition, consisting of the six stages shown in Table 3.1.

3.1 Inspection Stages

The inspection process goal is to eliminate defects from a given, well-defined work product. To achieve this goal, objectives are set for each stage in the process flow illustrated in Fig. 3.1.

3.1.1 Planning

During the planning stage, the objective is organization. The author collects the necessary materials and selects a moderator. The moderator consults with the author to determine the other inspection participants, and reviews the material against the inspection entry criteria to verify its readiness for inspection. The moderator then determines the inspection preparation and meeting times, schedules the inspection, and sends the materials, along with an inspection meeting notice, to each inspector.

3.1.2 Overview meeting

When an overview meeting is held, as applicable, the objective is education. A presentation is made by the author to educate the other in-

TABLE 3.1   In-Process Inspection Stages

Stage	Description	Objectives
1. Planning	Establish schedules. Choose inspectors. Obtain and distribute materials.	Ensure that schedules, participants, and materials are available.
2. Overview	Presentation by author of work to be inspected	Provide educational background to understand materials
3. Preparation	Individually study inspection material	Prepare participants to identify defects
4. Meeting	Formal examination of distributed materials	Find and record defects as a team
5. Rework	Revise product	Resolve problems
6. Follow-up	Verify satisfactory resolution of identified defects	Certify author's revisions and complete inspection reporting

spectors about the materials to be inspected. The presentation explains the material's functions and relationships, and provides a description of the techniques and the representations that are used. The overview is attended by all inspectors. The moderator arranges and conducts the overview session, although the author does the presentation.

3.1.3   Preparation

Preparation is an individual exercise performed by all the inspectors to allow them to become thoroughly familiar with the materials so that they can better find defects. Without adequate preparation, the inspection meeting is missing its most important element—knowledgeable inspectors. Using the information provided at the overview, if there was one, and guided by the preparation checklists, each inspector is responsible for his or her own adequate preparation. The inspectors note any suspected defects that they have found for discussion at the inspection meeting. They record their preparation time for collection at the meeting.

3.1.4   Inspection meeting

The objective of the inspection meeting is verification of the work product. It is attended by the author of the material to be inspected, the moderator, and other inspectors—the entire inspection team. Since the

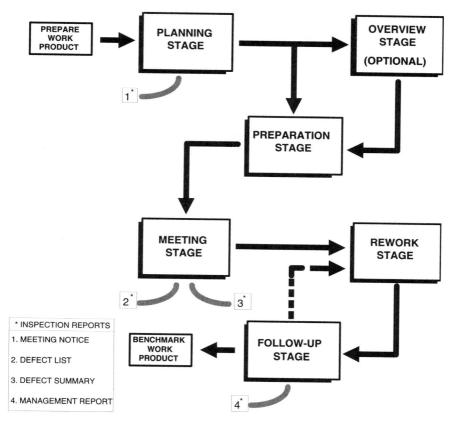

Figure 3.1 Inspection process flow.

purpose of the meeting is defect detection and not education, no one else should be present. At the beginning of the meeting, the moderator reviews the agenda for the inspection meeting. The moderator, not the author, conducts the meeting. The reader, who is selected by the moderator in the planning phase, leads the other inspectors through the materials by paraphrasing them. As all the materials are "read," each inspector looks for defects and discusses the notes and findings that he or she has made during preparation. As defects are recognized and accepted by the moderator, they are recorded and classified on the inspection defect list by the recorder. At the conclusion of the inspection meeting the moderator establishes the inspectors' agreement with the inspection defect list and decides on a disposition for the inspected materials.

3.1.5 Rework

During rework, the objective is to resolve all defects. The author revises the materials according to a copy of the inspection defect list, supplied by the moderator.

3.1.6 Follow-up

The objective of the follow-up stage is to verify rework. After the defects have been resolved to meet the exit criteria, the moderator follows-up to verify the author's defect resolution. Follow-up is performed according to the product disposition that was determined at the inspection meeting. When the work product has met the inspection exit criteria and is certified complete, the moderator submits a completed inspection management report to the inspection coordinator.

3.2 The Inspection Team

The inspection process is performed by small teams of peers, usually project members. It is repeated many times on many work products during the development of any given product. Inarguably, this often results in longer development times than are typical without inspections. Assuming the inspections are performed completely and correctly, they lead to shortened total production and test times, and to increased product quality and reliability. In fact, when development and test times are considered together, there should be a net decrease in the overall development schedule and an increase in net productivity, leading to significant cost savings! But this all depends on how well the inspection teams do their job.

3.2.1 Procedural roles

The inspection consists of a team of people working together to detect and remove defects in the work product of a development activity. To carry out the inspection, there are always five specific procedural roles that are assigned. These are called procedural roles because they are specified by and enable the performance of the inspection process procedures. These five roles each have clear responsibilities and are:

- *Author:* The role of author is assumed by the individual who is responsible for effecting changes to the document (usually, but not necessarily, the same person who wrote it). The author's role at the inspection meeting is to address specific questions which the reader is not able to answer, and to detect defects based on his or her special

understanding of the product. The author must not serve as moderator, reader, or recorder.

- *Moderator:* The moderator ensures that the inspection procedures
  are followed, and that the other inspectors perform their responsibilities for each step of the inspection process.

- *Reader:* The reader, not the author, leads the team through the work
  in a complete and logical fashion at the inspection meeting. The
  reader shall be prepared to describe the various parts and functions
  of the work, paraphrasing the material, in detail, at a moderate pace
  suitable for thorough examination. (*Paraphrasing* means that the
  reader attempts to explain and interpret the material a small section
  at a time, rather than necessarily reading it literally.)

- *Recorder:* The role of the recorder is to record and classify all of the
  defects detected at the inspection meeting on the inspection defect
  list, and to assist the moderator in preparing the other inspection
  meeting reports.

- *Inspector:* All of the inspection team members are inspectors, including the author, regardless of their other procedural roles. It is the
  responsibility of the inspectors to detect defects, not offer solutions,
  as the material is presented by the reader at the inspection meeting.

3.2.2 Overall guidelines for roles

It is obviously desirable to have the inspection process run as smoothly
and efficiently as possible, to minimize any increase in development
time. This can be achieved through careful management of the inspections and the use of well-formed and prepared inspection teams. To ensure the quality, effectiveness, and efficiency of inspection teams, they
should not just be allowed to happen. Inspection teams need to combine
several factors.

1. The minimum inspection team size is three: a moderator/recorder,
   a reader, and an author. All team members are considered to be
   inspectors.

2. When an inspection team is composed of only three people, the moderator is also the recorder. At other times, the moderator may elect
   to have a separate recorder. Keep in mind that all of the team members are also inspectors.

3. The author is always present, but cannot hold any other procedural
   role except inspector.

4. Keep the inspection team small, with a suggested maximum of
   seven persons, including the author. Have only enough team mem-

bers to ensure having the necessary expertise to adequately verify the work product for the intended purpose of the inspection. Any more persons will tend to reduce the efficiency and effectiveness of the process.

5. The inspection is a peer process—*no* managers should be present at the inspection. Where the inspected work product is for management's use, such as plans, or has been produced by a manager, then other managers and senior technical staff may comprise the inspection team. Inspections are a technical, not a management, meeting, and the unnecessary presence of managers strains the dynamics of the inspection meeting and disturbs peer level communication.

In addition, the team must combine knowledge of the specific work product with professional expertise in the more general product area. To function correctly, the team members must be familiar with inspection procedures, and know what is expected from their role assignments. To this end, all inspectors should be trained in conducting inspections, including the author. Readers and recorders should be chosen from experienced inspectors. Inexperienced inspectors should receive training prior to participating in an inspection, and the number of inexperienced inspectors should be limited if possible.

3.2.3   Selecting the moderator

A good summary of the moderator's role is an often-used quote by former President Harry Truman, "the buck stops here!" The moderator assumes responsibility for the inspection process and ensures that inspection team members perform their roles to the best of their abilities. He or she has ultimate responsibility for the success or failure of the inspection.

The moderator decides whether the author's material is ready for inspection, by verifying that the entry criteria are met. The moderator has the major responsibility for assembling the right inspection team, and for assigning their roles. The moderator must keep the inspection meeting on track and facilitate the reader's progress through the materials. The moderator must certify that the materials finally meet the inspection exit criteria. Clearly, to do all this the moderator must be thoroughly familiar with the project's inspection process.

The ideal moderator is, therefore, a senior staff member, generally possessing broad experience and responsibility. He or she has received training in the inspection process. The moderator should have participated in several prior inspections, and be experienced in several roles. Moderators who are knowledgeable, open-minded, sensitive, yet firm prove the most successful.

The selection of a moderator for an inspection should not be left to chance. Four methods, although not inclusive, for selecting a moderator are:

1. *The moderator is assigned with the author when the product development plan is prepared.* This method gives equal weight to product development and product verification. The assignments are usually made by the development manager, who has an overview of the skills, responsibilities, and available time of project personnel. Moderating inspections is viewed and handled as a project responsibility with little emphasis given to any "honorific" value associated with the role. Adequate time for inspection responsibilities is built into the moderator's overall work schedule.

2. *The inspection coordinator assigns the moderators.* This method gives slightly less weight to product verification, but still benefits from early notice and inclusion of the moderator within the fairly broad planning horizon of the project inspection plan. Although the inspection coordinator is less knowledgeable of the project plans than the development manager, he or she still brings a large measure of objectivity into the process of moderator selection. Again, there is no assumed status associated with the role.

3. *The author selects the moderator from an "approved moderators list."* This method assures that moderators are selected from those having met a set of minimum qualifications. But care must be taken that moderators receive notice of impending inspections early enough to ensure adequate personal inspection planning.

4. *The author selects the moderator.* The major advantage of this method is simplicity. There is no need for management or coordinator planning of the inspections. The major disadvantage is that the author, who has a limited perspective on the project as a whole, can only select a moderator for local reasons. In the worst case, the author may select a moderator who is unqualified. Further, the moderator may be notified late, causing inspection activities to be rushed, and other project or personal plans to suffer.

Any of these methods for moderator selection is acceptable; those that involve a greater degree of planning help to improve the inspection process and project quality.

3.2.4   Selecting inspectors

It is often useful for individuals with differing viewpoints or interests in the work product to participate in an inspection to sharpen the team's collective understanding of the work and improve defect detection. These views should be present, even when there are only three persons on the inspection team, to achieve a multifaceted perspective of the product. It is always easiest to question the correctness of the work, but more difficult to determine if it is complete, in conformance with requirements, and to standards. It is in addressing all of these considerations that an inspection makes its greatest contribution. Therefore, in general terms, these "functional" viewpoints are

- *Leader:* Must be the moderator, who uses the various talents and viewpoints of the team members to verify the product, and ensure that the inspection is impartially conducted and follows all of its required procedures.

- *Requester:* Represents the customer or someone responsible for the product requirements at an earlier phase of development, and ensures that the product conforms to specifications.

- *Peer:* Is especially familiar with the techniques used by the author, and ensures that the product is correct.

- *Receiver:* Views the use of the work product in the next phase of development, and ensures that the product is complete, clear, and consistent.

- *Validater:* Designs tests for the product, and ensures that it performs as required.

- *Standardizer:* Is especially familiar with standards to which the product must adhere.

An inspection team should be composed of a small group of people with an appropriate balance of these points of view. Actual requesters and receivers should participate in inspections whenever possible. When choosing the inspectors, keep in mind that the participants should be familiar with the subject matter of the inspected material; this helps prevent the meeting from degenerating into a training session.

3.2.5 Participation of inspectors

An inspection is a cooperative activity that brings together professional software developers with differing viewpoints and levels of experience. The purpose of the inspection is for the team to work together to improve the product being inspected by uncovering its flaws, i.e., the points at which the product does not meet the specifications. Participa-

---

*Functional versus procedural roles address the down-to-earth defect detection activities of the inspection team, not the procedures necessary to carry out the meeting.

TABLE 3.2 **Inspection Roles**

Stage	Moderator	Author	Reader	Recorder	Inspector
Planning	X	X			
Overview	X	X	—	—	—
Preparation	X	X	X	X	X
Inspection meeting	X	X	X	X	X
Rework		X			
Follow-up	X	X	(X)	(X)	(X)

tion in an inspection begins when the team members receive the inspection meeting notice and the materials to be inspected. Their participation ends when the moderator certifies that the work product meets the inspection exit criteria.

Table 3.2 shows how roles are assigned in each stage of the inspection. The dashes indicate that these team members do not hold any procedural roles, but are present. The parentheses indicate that involvement of these participants in the follow-up stage depends on the disposition of the work product at the inspection. Only when a work product must be reinspected would these team members participate. As the table shows, the author participates in each stage of the inspection.

In the sections that follow we will specify the tasks in each of the six successive stages of the inspection process, and the responsibilities involved in carrying out each stage. These guidelines are defined in the sequence normally encountered in conducting an inspection.

3.3   The Inspection Planning Stage

Inspections are not haphazard meetings called together by the author at the last minute, so he or she can get a work product signed off. Inspections are scheduled and prepared for.

Responsibility for planning the inspection lies jointly with the moderator and the author. When the author believes his or her work product is ready for inspection, the author brings the material to the moderator. The moderator evaluates the material against established inspection entry criteria to determine whether the work product is ready for inspection. If it is not yet ready, the moderator informs the author of what is required to bring the work product to inspection readiness. If the work product meets the entry criteria, the moderator and author consult on an appropriate inspection team and an overall inspection schedule. The moderator verifies the availability of the proposed inspectors, negotiates role assignments, determines the

1. PLANNING

- Purpose: Organization

- Tasks: Approve entry criteria
             Establish schedules
             Designate participants
             Determine overview
             Prepare inspection meeting
              notice
             Distribute materials

- Roles: Moderator
             Author

preparation requirements, and establishes the inspection meeting and overview schedules. The moderator then prepares the inspection meeting notice.

3.3.1 Moderators' planning tasks

Since in-process inspections should be a planned procedure within the development cycle, authors' requests to have their work products inspected are generally anticipated. For each inspection, the moderator

- Verifies that the work product meets the entry criteria. If the criteria are not met, works with the author to bring the material to the point where it can be effectively inspected. All materials must be fully understandable as they are presented to the moderator, or expected to be so with the aid of an overview meeting. Entry criteria specify both the materials that are to be inspected and what condition these materials should be in. The moderator uses entry criteria as a "pro forma" check to ensure that the work product is ready for inspection. The moderator's verification of the entry criteria ensures that good use is made of the inspectors' preparation and examination efforts.

- Determines the need for an overview meeting. The purpose of an overview is educational. Whenever you think that the inspectors have insufficient information about the work product or the techniques that are used to be successfully inspected, an overview meeting should be scheduled.

- Selects the other inspectors and appoints a reader and recorder. An inspection team should be a small group with an appropriate balance of relevant technical points of view. In some cases, participants may come from other departments to properly verify one or another aspect of the product that they are most familiar with, and dependent upon.

- If an overview meeting is to be held, schedules it for a few days before the inspection meeting, with enough time for subsequent individual preparation. Inspection materials may be distributed before, during, or after the overview, provided all inspectors receive them and have adequate time to prepare.

- Schedules the inspection meeting. Estimates the preparation and meeting times that are required to prepare for and examine the work product, using the appropriate rates determined by the project for this type of inspection. (Inspection rates are described in more detail in Chapter 4.) No inspection meeting should exceed 2 to 3 hours. Multiple meetings may be required at times. Then, the moderator schedules the meeting(s), reserves a meeting room, and sees that the materials are distributed to the other inspectors enough in advance of the meeting to allow for adequate preparation.

  The moderator obtains a quiet room, large enough to comfortably accommodate the inspection team, equipped with a central (preferably round) table. If the reader specifies a need for visual aids, or if the recorder requires a special recording device, the moderator arranges for the appropriate equipment to be present.

- Prepares the inspection meeting notice. The inspection meeting notice requires that the moderator indicate: the type of inspection (or overview), date, time, location, estimated meeting(s) duration, and the preparation time expected of each participant. For materials that are examined at multiple inspection meetings, or where modified materials are distributed throughout a base product, the preparation time is the time required to examine the new material, and any interfaces and dependencies with other material. Include some notation of where the inspected materials are located for each inspection meeting.

TABLE 3.3   The Planning Stage

Inputs	Process	Outputs
1. "Completed" work product	1. Moderator verifies that work product meets entry criteria	1. Entry criteria verified
2. Inspection entry criteria	2. Moderator selects inspectors	2. Inspection meeting notice
3. Inspection rates	3. Moderator determines need for overview	3. Scheduled meeting room(s)
	4. Moderator schedules inspection	4. Inspection materials

3.3.2   Authors' planning tasks

It is up to the author to make an initial determination that his or her work is ready to be inspected. On making this determination the author

- Reviews the materials to be inspected with the moderator to verify that they satisfy the inspection entry criteria, and provides the moderator with a copy. The moderator, not the author, schedules the inspection.

- Works with the moderator to bring the materials into compliance with the entry criteria if necessary.

- Gathers and distributes the materials to the inspection team members.

- Suggests inspection team members, as appropriate.

- Recommends whether an overview meeting is indicated.

Table 3.3 summarizes the planning stage.

3.4   The Inspection Overview Stage

An overview meeting is an optional tutorial presented by the author of the work product to be inspected. It is scheduled as part of the inspection process if the moderator and the author believe that such a discussion will substantially increase the inspectors' understanding of the work product. Some reasons for scheduling an overview are:

1. The work product is critical to the project, and sets the direction for subsequent work.

PLANNING
- OVERVIEW
PREPARATION
INSPECTION MEETING
REWORK
FOLLOW- UP

2. OVERVIEW

- Purpose: Tutorial (optional)

- Tasks: Presentation

- Roles: Moderator
              Author
              Inspectors
              Others

---

2. The work product is large, or complex, or interrelates extensively with other work products.

3. The work product represents a use of technology that is new or infrequently used by the other inspectors.

4. The work product is the result of a "one-person" project, and the other inspectors require background information in order to adequately understand the material.

5. There is a division of technical responsibility among the inspectors, with a sharing of the role of reader because of differences in inspector expertise.

The purpose of the overview is to educate the inspectors, and possibly other project personnel, about the work product, its functions, organization, technology, and techniques. The duration of the overview is usually about that of an inspection meeting, 2 or 3 hours, and the work product is stabilized (or baselined) as for the inspection meeting. Any obvious defects that are apparent at the overview should be revised prior to distribution of the materials to the inspectors for their preparation.

The overview can be used to show how this work product fits into the overall project picture and may indicate what other work products it affects or is affected by. Such a meeting is extremely useful for projects where individuals work independently, or, conversely, where many people contribute to interrelated products. It is also useful for setting the stage for a series of inspections that are held during the development cycle of a large or complex product.

3.4.1 Moderators' overview tasks

The moderator's role in the overview stage is to act as a facilitator. Specifically, he or she

- Arranges, announces, and conducts the overview meeting.
- Attempts to maximize the exchange of product information, and minimize defect detection efforts or other attempts to "improve" the product.
- Guides the discussion toward providing the information necessary for a successful inspection.
- Assigns and partitions inspectors' preparation, reading, and examination activities if required. This may be done for complex materials, and where the inspectors have diverse expertise.

3.4.2 Authors' overview tasks

The author's role in the overview meeting is to describe the work product to be inspected. Specifically, he or she

- Prepares as for a technical presentation.
- Presents whatever information is necessary for a complete understanding of his or her work by the other inspectors. This might be a general review of an overall design so that the function of a particular part may be understood, or it might be a tutorial on some special techniques that are used in the inspected materials.

3.4.3 Inspectors' overview tasks

The overview meeting is for the inspectors. Their task is to obtain an understanding of the work product for them to adequately prepare. At an overview meeting, the inspectors

- Question the work product, its assumptions and representation. Clarify its meaning and implications sufficient for further individual preparation.
- Do not review design or implementation alternatives.

Other members of the project, such as management, may attend the overview meeting as the dissemination of this information may be helpful to a broader audience than just the inspection team members.

TABLE 3.4   The Overview Stage

Inputs	Process	Outputs
1. Work product	1. Moderator conducts overview meeting	1. Increased understanding of work product
2. Related materials	2. Author presents work product to attendees	2. Responses to questions
3. Visual aids (as required)	3. Moderator determines need for partitioning, preparation, and reading responsibilities	3. Assigned responsibilities
4. Overview room		

However, keep in mind that the overview is meant to satisfy the objective of education for the inspectors, and this objective must be met.

Table 3.4 summarizes the overview stage.

3.5   The Inspection Preparation Stage

Each participant at an inspection meeting, no matter what other role he or she may be serving, is expected to act as an inspector, including the author. To enable participants to do so effectively, each participant is given a complete copy of the material to be inspected and its references, beforehand, so that he or she may study it. Each inspector should use the overview, if held, the preparation checklist, and the in-

---

PLANNING
OVERVIEW
- *PREPARATION*
INSPECTION MEETING
REWORK
FOLLOW- UP

3. PREPARATION

- Purpose: Understanding
            Identify potential defects

- Tasks: Study materials

- Roles: All inspectors

spection materials to attain an individual understanding of the work product.

Preparation time should be guided by the preparation rates that are used by the project for this type of inspection. Too little preparation time will leave the inspector with a spotty knowledge of the material, which reduces his or her effectiveness at the inspection meeting, while too much detracts from the cost-effectiveness of the inspection process.

Potential defects that are identified during preparation should be noted, but with the understanding that not all personal findings are defects! The actual identification of defects occurs during the inspection meeting, and is often the result of synergy among the participants, which is based on the participants being well versed in the product, but not having invested so much time that they develop an attachment to "their defects."

There is mixed opinion as to whether preparation should be focused on individual defect detection. Our opinion is that each inspector must first and foremost understand the work product, and then secondarily identify potential defects. Any analytic tools and techniques that help to achieve this purpose and are reasonable in their demands on preparation time can be used.

3.5.1 Inspectors' preparation tasks

For inspectors, the preparation stage begins as soon as soon as the inspection notice and work product are received. To prepare for an inspection, inspectors

- Study the material to be inspected for the approximate time noted on the inspection meeting notice.

- Use the appropriate inspection checklists to help find common defects at this time.

- If assigned the role of reader, consider how to present and paraphrase the work product.

- Record the time spent preparing for the inspection. Report this time to the moderator at the inspection meeting.

The total preparation time of all the inspectors is collected at the inspection meeting. This data is used to continually evaluate the effectiveness of the inspection process. Note any questions and potential defects that you have identified during preparation directly on the materials you received.

During preparation, you should thoroughly understand the material. Secondary emphasis may be placed on finding defects. Without a thor-

TABLE 3.5 The Preparation Stage

Inputs	Process	Outputs
1. Work product	1. All inspectors study the work product	1. Knowledge of work product
2. Inspection meeting notice	2. Reader determines how to present work product	2. Noted findings
3. Appropriate inspection checklists	3. Inspectors record their preparation time	3. Noted preparation time
4. Recommended preparation time		

ough understanding of the work product, you will not be able to contribute effectively to the meeting. Be cognizant of the existence of a "point of diminishing returns" for identifying defects during preparation, which, if exceeded, sacrifices some of the synergy that can be used to find defects most efficiently during the actual inspection meeting.

Table 3.5 summarizes the preparation stage.

3.6 The Inspection Meeting Stage

The inspection meeting is the crux of the inspection process. It is not a review or a walkthrough or a brain dump. Nor is it intended to impress or to educate. Its sole purpose is the identification of defects. It is a small, narrowly focused meeting for this alone.

The inspection meeting is attended by the author, the moderator, and the other selected inspectors only. To avoid any chance that the meeting might take on the trappings of a performance review, management is specifically excluded.

The meeting focuses on the work product, not on the person responsible for it. Therefore, the inspectors need to be peers who can recognize both defects and nonadherence to requirements and standards.

The moderator conducts the inspection meeting, using a predefined format. The moderator reviews the agenda for the meeting, introduces the participants, and identifies their roles. The moderator then turns the meeting over to the reader, who leads the inspectors through the materials, paraphrasing the work product a line, or a small clause, at a time. Inspectors look for errors in each section as it is "read." There are often discussions of purported defects. These discussions center around whether in fact something is a defect, and if so, what kind of defect it is. Discussions of other issues are not permitted. All development issues are assumed to have been resolved prior to inspection. It is the moderator's responsibility to keep the meeting focused on defect detection—

PLANNING
OVERVIEW
PREPARATION
- *INSPECTION MEETING*
REWORK
FOLLOW- UP

4. INSPECTION MEETING

- Purpose: Verify product

- Tasks: Introduce inspection meeting
             Establish preparation
             Reading and recording defects
             Review listed defects
             Determine product disposition

- Roles: Moderator
             Author
             Reader
             Recorder
             Inspectors

---

only! It is the responsibility of all the inspectors, especially the moderator, to keep the meeting fixed on this purpose.

As defects are recognized and agreed on, the recorder enters them on an inspection defect list which becomes the basis for the author's rework of the materials. The author should leave the meeting with a clear understanding of the specific defects that need correction before the inspection is complete. Classify all defects reported by the project-determined defect classification. A sample defect classification scheme consisting of defect type, class, and severity (with appropriate forms) is described in Chapter 4. (Inspectors should be familiar with the classification documented in the project's inspection procedures.) Describe defects as crisply as possible, but avoid the temptation to correct the defects during the meeting. Also, be aware that it is easy for the meeting to drift into a discussion of "good" programming practice, alternative techniques, special coding tricks, etc. If there is interest in conducting such a discussion, a separate review may be held.

The inspection process is a cooperative effort of co-workers which, when used well, improves the productivity of the work team and the quality of the product. It can be thought of as "getting a little help from your friends." In a good inspection meeting the total effect is more than the sum of the individual contributions—synergy. One inspector's remark triggers another inspector's thoughts, and ideas are developed until they lead to the uncovering of a defect that no individual inspector had recognized. Vague misgivings are examined until they yield the cause. And often it is the author, listening to the discussion, who pinpoints the actual defect. It is this process of seeing material through the eyes of other, respected peers, that can give each inspector insights that he or she would not have had in isolation.

Good inspection meetings in which this synergy is evidenced, are not accidental. They are skillfully conducted, focusing not on the author, but on the work product, and concentrating their efforts on identifying defects, not trying to fix them.

3.6.1 Inspection meeting agenda

The inspection meeting starts promptly, but not until all the participants are present. If shortly after the scheduled start of the meeting, the moderator, reader, or author is not present, the meeting must be rescheduled. If other inspectors are absent the moderator decides whether to begin the meeting or to reschedule it, depending on the criticality of their presence.

To cover all of the essential points, we recommend that an inspection meeting follow this agenda.

1. Introduce the inspection meeting.

2. Establish the preparedness of the inspectors.

3. Read the work product, and identify and record defects.

4. Review the defects.

5. Determine the work product disposition.

3.6.1.1 Introduction. For an inspection meeting to be successful, it is important that all participants feel comfortable with the process. At the start of the meeting, the moderator introduces the inspectors, describes their roles, and acknowledges the work of the author. The moderator states the purpose of the inspection and directs the inspectors to focus their efforts toward defect detection, not solution hunting. The moderator reminds the inspectors to direct their remarks to the reader and to comment only on the product, not the author.

3.6.1.2 Establish preparedness. It is pointless to have an inspection meeting unless the inspectors are prepared. The moderator verifies preparedness by asking each inspector to state their total preparation time. The total of all of the inspection team's preparation time is recorded by the moderator on the inspection management report for entry into the inspection data base. If the moderator is satisfied that the inspectors are well prepared for the inspection, the meeting proceeds. If the moderator does not believe that the inspectors are adequately prepared, he or she stops the meeting and reschedules it for a later time or date.

Of course, "well-prepared" is subjective. It is the moderator's judgment that there is or is not enough knowledge of the work product by the inspection team to support adequate defect detection. As a quantitative guideline, if the total of the inspection team's preparation is less than half the amount the moderator estimated would be needed, reschedule the meeting. Studies of the relationship between total preparation time and defect detection have demonstrated that whenever the total preparation time was less than half the recommended amount, defect detection was significantly reduced.

Rescheduling an inspection meeting is not meant pejoratively, but is done to increase the expected effectiveness of defect detection. The time that was originally scheduled for the meeting may be used effectively in preparing for the new meeting. In many cases, the inspection meeting might be deferred for an hour or so to allow additional preparation time for the inspectors, while still maintaining the original inspection schedule.

3.6.1.3 Read and record defects. Once it has been determined that the inspection meeting should proceed, the moderator turns the meeting over to the reader, who begins presenting the work product. The material is presented in logical segments, paraphrased by the reader, clearly reflecting his or her understanding of the work. The reader is responsible for choosing the most effective way to present the materials to the inspectors. (Note that the order in which the material appears in the work product may not be the best order for inspecting.)

As the material is presented, the team identifies defects, makes comments, or asks questions. All questions and comments are directed to the reader, who may defer to the author for clarification. As defects are identified, both those that were discovered during preparation and those that come to light as the team systematically examines the work, they are classified and noted by the recorder on the inspection defect list. Defects should be classified as they are recognized, as later attempts to classify them, out of context, are not as accurate. The moderator's job during this phase of the meeting is to make sure the participants focus on creating the inspection defect list.

Questions or comments as to defect classification are directed to the recorder, who may answer them or direct the question to the moderator for resolution. If it is still unclear after discussion whether an issue raised is, in fact, a defect, it should be included as a defect on the defect list, where it is a controlled item, subject to later resolution by the author. An appropriate resolution of the issue may be an explanation by the author as to why the item in question is correct.

3.6.1.4 Review defects. At the close of the inspection meeting, the recorder reviews the inspection defect list with the team to verify its completeness and accuracy. The inspection defect list records what items the author needs to resolve before the work product is considered complete and meeting its exit criteria. Therefore, it is important that all of the inspectors agree on its content.

3.6.1.5 Determine product disposition. When the defect list is completed and accepted, it is used by the inspection team to determine the disposition of the work product. The moderator is responsible for the product disposition, although he or she generally solicits the opinion of the inspection team in determining the disposition. The moderator is not, however, bound by the team's recommendation.

The product disposition is not the inspection team's opinion of the presumed quality of the work product. It is simply a determination of the procedure that will be used for the subsequent verification of the author's rework. There are three product dispositions.

1. *A:* Accept the work product as complete, without any further verification of rework. This does not require the work product be totally defect-free. But it does require that there be no defects that cause the product to deviate from its specifications, and that there are only a very few trivial defects (such as misspellings) that can be left to the author's discretion. Under these conditions, the work product is certified as meeting the inspection exit criteria, and any incidental defect resolution is left to the author.

2. *C:* Conditionally accept the work product, with verification of the rework by the moderator in review with the author. In this case there are some major defects, but they are few, relative to the work product, and their rework is not expected to create any substantial changes in the "design premise" of the work product. The rework is also within the moderator's expertise.

3. *R:* Reinspect the author's rework. This disposition requires that the rework be examined by the moderator, the author, and at least one other member of the inspection team in a reiteration of the inspection meeting. For this case, there are either a substantial number of major defects, or rework that will change the original design

premise of the work product. The rework, its interfaces, and any of its dependencies to the original product are verified before the moderator can certify that the inspection is complete and the work product meets its exit criteria. This may or may not comprise all of the original work product.

The difference between a disposition of C and one of R is frequently subjective, but there is a quantitative guideline that was used by IBM; if the number of major defects exceeds 5 percent of the total number of noncommentary lines inspected, assign a disposition of R. This works out to be 50 major defects per 1000 lines, which is a substantial defect density and calls for a reinspection of the rework.

If the rework is expected to substantially change the work product, or to be extensive, reinspection is called for. If one or more inspectors are vitally interested in the work product, or if the moderator feels that another inspector has expertise that is essential to verify the rework, the moderator should stipulate reinspection with those inspectors participation.

Remember, reinspection may involve the entire original inspection team or just one member in addition to the moderator and the author. Inspectors from the original inspection team are usually preferred in order to capitalize on their investment in preparation and their experience with the work product.

In the final analysis, the disposition of the product demonstrates the objectivity of the inspection; how it is able to control product quality without ever assessing it!

3.6.2 Moderators' meeting tasks

The moderator's fundamental job is to make the inspection process work for the good of the project—to be responsible for the effective conduct of the inspection meeting. He or she is the presiding officer at the meeting, making sure it is kept within due bounds, is not extreme in opinion, and is reasonable and calm. The moderator must ensure that during the inspection meeting the inspection team concentrates on finding defects and does not bog down in disagreement, discussing trivial issues, in solution-hunting, or in seeking alternate solutions. The moderator must be unbiased to the area under inspection and must be sensitive to each participant. During the inspection, the moderator is the key to ensuring that resources are efficiently utilized and maximum effort toward finding defects is achieved.

The moderator's responsibilities during the inspection meeting are

- Certainly, never be the author of the inspected work product.

- See that all the physical needs for the meeting are satisfied.

- Start the meeting on time and move it along so that it finishes on schedule.
- Follow the outlined inspection meeting agenda.
- Defer arguments over style or technique.
- Counteract any attempt at developing solutions or alternatives.
- Maintain an appropriate pace for the examination based on the project's estimated inspection rates, the inspectors' expertise, and the complexity of the material.
- Avoid examining too much material at the inspection meeting—the tendency will be for the team to finish them by going too quickly for thorough inspection.
- Retain the participation of the recorder as a contributing inspector by pausing the meeting for a short time for adequate notation of each defect.
- Keep the synergy of the meeting high by being aware of, and correcting any conditions, either physical or emotional, that are draining off any participant's attention. This includes everything from calling a stretch break to repairing the effects of inappropriate personal remarks.
- Bring to the inspection meeting any references that may be useful (e.g., standards references, programming language references, etc.). Also bring copies of the inspection defect list, inspection defect summary, and inspection management report. At the end of the meeting make a copy of the inspection defect list for the author.

At the completion of the meeting, the moderator

- Completes the inspection defect summary and the inspection management report forms.
- If the inspected work product receives a disposition of either A, accept or R, reinspect, submits the paperwork to the inspections coordinator and the inspection is complete.
- Alternatively, if the inspected material receives a disposition of C, conditional, the moderator's examination of the author's rework is required. When this examination is complete, submits the inspection defect list, inspection defect summary, and the inspection management report to the inspection coordinator.

3.6.3   Authors' meeting tasks

The author's role at an inspection meeting is a difficult one since the focus of the meeting is to uncover defects in work for which he or she is responsible. The author is present at the inspection meeting and should focus on understanding all of the comments, and helping, as possible, to find defects. The author is asked to make a "best effort" offering of the work product to the inspection team for their objective assistance in finding defects that may still remain despite the author's diligent efforts.

Specifically, the author should

- Not hold any other procedural roles at the inspection.

- Above all else, remain objective about the work product and not defend the material.

- Clarify, without trying to justify, techniques that were used and portions of the work that are not readily understood by the inspection team. In general though, the best approach for the author is to "speak when spoken to."

- Be an "active listener"—understand and take notes on comments that help describe defects for your later rework.

- Inspect the work product based on your special understanding, using your increased objectivity of the work provided by the inspection meeting.

3.6.4   Readers' meeting tasks

It is the job of the reader to lead the team through the material in a logical fashion. In preparation, the reader selects a sequence for presentation which allows for clear understanding by the other inspectors. Be sure to read all of the material. Paraphrase the material at a pace suitable for thorough examination.

The reader should

- Not be the author, the moderator, or the recorder.

- Select the most effective sequence for presenting the material. The sequence in which the material appears may not be the most logical for inspecting.

- Rigorously describe, paraphrase, and interpret every part and function of the material. Attempt to "add value" to the inspection via your presentation.

- Answer questions, as possible, posed by the inspectors. Otherwise, ask the author to provide additional clarification.

- Represent a neutral and unbiased focal point for the inspection.

There are a few reasonable questions to ask about the role of the reader.

- *Why not just ask the team for their comments section by section?* Inspection team synergy results from considering all of the details of the work product together. This can only be accomplished by reading the materials completely.

- *Why is there a "reader" role?* There is no other way for the inspection team to examine the material together and remain coordinated than to have someone personally responsible for this function.

- *Why isn't the author the reader?* Although the author is most familiar with the work product and is probably the most fluent member of the inspection team, the author is too close to the material to objectively present it to the other inspectors. In addition, the reader is the first to receive and respond to any criticism, and the author is thereby shielded from potential defensiveness by not presenting the work.

- *Why isn't the moderator the reader?* The moderator needs to focus on the performance of the inspection team, not, primarily, on the technical aspects of the work product.

- *Why isn't the recorder the reader?* Too much busy work is entailed by sharing these roles.

- *Why does the reader paraphrase the material?* The reader provides a detailed, nonbiased interpretation of the work product, which adds additional meaning for the inspection team that goes beyond the literal representation that they are all referring to.

The reader works closely with the moderator in the inspection meeting, and may wish to discuss his or her plans with the moderator prior to the meeting.

3.6.5 Recorders' meeting tasks

The recorder may wish to review the pertinent defect types for the inspection so that he or she can quickly categorize the defects found during the meeting.

The recorder should

- Not be the author or reader, although the moderator may elect to record (the moderator must record if the inspection team consists of only three persons).

- Be familiar with the project defect classification.

- Record all defects on the inspection defect list. This list includes:

    —Line, page, or coordinate number(s) where the defect is noted. If no line numbers or other identification appears in the material, a copy of the material should be attached, with the defect annotated as well as recorded.

—A brief, clear description of the defect (not how to fix it).

—Defect classification, as determined by the project (a sample classification scheme appears in Chapter 4).

- Classify defects as they are detected to preserve their meaning in the context of the work product.

- Turn the inspection defect list over to the moderator to review the defects after the reading of the work product has been completed.

3.6.6 Inspectors' meeting tasks

All members of the inspection team are inspectors, regardless of any other procedural roles they may hold. As an inspector, your foremost task is the detection of defects. An inspection meeting is meant to be highly critical of the work product; it is not intended to offer many compliments. This does not mean that the work product is to be considered inferior. In fact it may be superb, but the focus of the inspection process is to detect defects wherever possible—without inferring a subjective assessment of product quality.

To accomplish this, inspectors must

- Be knowledgeable about the subject area being considered.

- Be prepared, by having individually reviewed the work product for the recommended time.

- Be objective and impersonal, maintaining a technical and a project perspective.

- Be an active participant at the inspection meeting, sharing opinions and views that form the basis of team synergy.

Conversely, inspectors should not

- Assess style issues, except where clarity or maintainability is questioned.

- Use personal pronouns, such as "you" or "yours," but rather address portions of the work product directly, such as "the specification for termination."

- Develop solutions for identified problems. While easy to state, the act of defect detection sometimes requires various alternatives to be considered. Draw the line at exploration and avoid developing corrections.

3.6.7   Prepare inspection meeting reports

At the conclusion of the inspection meeting, or series of meetings, if the disposition of the inspected work product is A, accept, or R, reinspect, the moderator will complete the inspection defect summary and inspection management report. The moderator will certify that the inspection is completed if the product disposition was A. If the disposition was R, reinspect, a reinspection is scheduled by the moderator. The inspection reports are completed, but the moderator does not certify the inspection as complete. A reinspection provides new inspection reports, as for an original inspection, although the meeting type indicates a reinspection.

If the disposition is C, conditional, then the inspection reports are completed insofar as possible, awaiting the further examination of the rework by the moderator. The defects are resolved by the author, and the moderator informed when the material is ready for review. The inspection reports are updated as needed following the review, and if the work product disposition is now A, the inspection is certified complete. The moderator though, may arrive at any disposition at the review of the rework, at times requiring additional rework and, possibly, a reinspection. Chapter 4 provides additional information about inspection data reporting.

Table 3.6 summarizes the inspection meeting stage.

TABLE 3.6   The Inspection Meeting Stage

Inputs	Process	Outputs
1. The work product to be inspected	1. Moderator initiates meeting and verifies preparation time	1. List of identified defects
2. Any necessary references	2. The work product is read	2. Meeting report and defect summary
3. Inspectors' preparation times	3. Defects are identified and recorded	3. Work product disposition
4. Inspectors' preparation notations	4. Defect list is reviewed and product disposition is determined	
5. Inspection checklist	5. Meeting report and defect summary are completed	
6. Inspection meeting recording forms or devices		

3.7 The Rework Stage

Rework is a formal part of the inspection process. Too often, in less formal procedures, no scheduled time is assigned to the rework activity, and the work is considered complete after the product has been examined and the author has agreed to certain changes. In the inspection process though, rework, and its subsequent verification, is explicitly considered and scheduled.

PLANNING
OVERVIEW
PREPARATION
INSPECTION MEETING
- REWORK
FOLLOW- UP

5. REWORK

- Purpose: Meet exit criteria

- Tasks: Resolve all defects

- Roles: Author

During the rework stage, the author is expected to complete the necessary revisions to the work product to eliminate the identified defects, and to then provide the moderator with documentation of how these revisions resolve the defects. The schedule for performing the rework is set by the moderator and the author. In general, succeeding work products are not accepted for inspection until the scheduled revisions have been completed and verified.

3.7.1 Defect resolution

Following the inspection meeting, the author resolves all of the identified defects, regardless of their severity, and brings the work product back to the moderator for follow-up. The term "resolution" is used rather than "correction" because there are at least four possible ways that a defect may be addressed, depending on its circumstances.

1. Most frequently, the defect is corrected and the work product revised.
2. Sometimes, someone other than the author must resolve the defect. For example, this could occur when the source code of a program correctly addresses a questionable requirement. In these cases the re-

quirement defect may not be addressable by the author. The appropriate resolution for the inspection is to enter the defect condition into the project's change-control system, and to provide the moderator with the change-control entry at follow-up.

3. On occasion, a defect is identified that the author later determines is correct. An explanation of the author's judgment is sufficient to satisfy the rework requirement for this condition. If, during follow-up, the moderator still believes that a defect exists, the responsible product manager will resolve the issue.

4. Then, there are rare circumstances which dictate that a particular defect will not be corrected at this time. This must be a decision by project management, not the author. Under these circumstances the defect is entered into the project's change-control system, and the change-control entry is sufficient for defect resolution at the inspection follow-up stage. The inspection has done its job, the defect has been identified, and, as determined by management, appropriately controlled.

The intent is to resolve the outstanding inspection defects expeditiously, and not to burden the inspection process with change-control responsibilities.

3.7.2 Authors' rework tasks

The author's goal in the rework stage is to bring the work product to completion. Specifically, the author

- Resolves all identified defects, regardless of their classification. The author may use whatever resources he or she determines are required, as long as the resolution does not occur as part of the inspection meeting.

- Notifies the moderator of the completion of rework and readiness for the appropriate follow-up procedure if the product disposition was C or R.

TABLE 3.7 The Rework Stage

Inputs	Process	Outputs
1. List of identified defects	1. Author resolves all listed defects	1. Revised work product
2. Work product disposition		2. Moderator notification of completion of rework
3. Schedule for moderator review or reinspection of the rework		

■ Completes the development phase for this work product if the work product disposition was A. It may be entered into the project's configuration control system.

Table 3.7 summarizes the rework stage.

3.8   The Follow-Up Stage

In the follow-up stage of the inspection process, the author's revisions are formally verified. The moderator follows the procedure that was determined by the product disposition at the inspection meeting—either C, moderator verification of the rework, or R, reinspection of the rework. Verification of the revised work product determines whether all the defects identified during the inspection meeting have been resolved, and if the work product now meets the inspection exit criteria.

Follow-up considers

1. The content of the revisions.
2. All interfaces between the revisions and the original work product, on all sides of the affected interfaces.
3. All dependencies between the revisions and the original work product.

Reinspection uses the same procedures as the original inspection, but concentrates on the changes, their interfaces and dependencies.

PLANNING
OVERVIEW
PREPARATION
INSPECTION MEETING
REWORK
- FOLLOW- UP

6. FOLLOW- UP

- Purpose: Certify inspection

- Tasks: Verify all rework
              Report results

- Roles: Moderator
              Author
              (Inspectors)

The reinspection may be either incisive or broad, depending on the scope and nature of the rework. At the conclusion of the follow-up stage, the inspection reports are completed and the inspection of the work product is finished.

Any valid inspection disposition may be assigned as a result of the follow-up procedure, which itself may require additional follow-up. Of course, work products that require no or only very minor revisions will be accepted without requiring further follow-up.

Once the work product revisions have been verified and accepted, the inspection is considered completed.

3.8.1 Moderators' follow-up tasks

The moderator's goal in the follow-up stage is to complete the inspection, if possible. Specifically, the moderator's tasks are

- If the work product disposition was C, reexamine the rework with the author.

- If the work product disposition was R, convene a reinspection of the rework. Follow the tasks that have been previously outlined as for any other inspection.

- At the conclusion of a reinspection, assign any of the three work product dispositions that are appropriate.

- Complete any outstanding inspection reporting. If the work product disposition is now A, certify the inspection management report. If the original disposition was C, mark the original report as completed, but do not revise the original disposition.

Table 3.8 summarizes the follow-up stage.

TABLE 3.8   The Follow-up Stage

Inputs	Process	Outputs
1. Revised work product	1. Moderator verifies that work product meets exit criteria	1. Inspected work product, meeting inspection exit criteria
2. (If a reinspection, refer to inputs for inspection stages 1–4)	2. (If a reinspection, refer to process for inspection stages 1–4)	2. (If the work product disposition is C or R, see outputs for inspection stage 4)
	3. Moderator completes inspection reporting	3. Completed inspection reports

3.9   Inspection Reporting

Inspection reports are part of the administrative control mechanism of the inspection process. They provide information on the progress of the inspections, help focus the participants on their tasks, and record the results of the inspection meeting. These reports may be hard-copy forms, or any other type of media (e.g., on-line and/or computer generated reports) that are appropriate for the project. Table 3.9 describes the various inspection reports. (Examples of these reports are found in Chapter 4.)

3.9.1   The inspection meeting notice

The inspection meeting notice is the formal announcement of an impending inspection. It is sent to the inspectors prior to the meeting, and informs the participants about which work product they are inspecting and what is required of them. If an overview is scheduled, the inspection materials need not accompany the notice, but may instead be distributed at the overview. The inspection meeting notice informs the inspectors of the date, time, and location of the inspection meeting. It includes a complete list of the selected inspectors and their inspection roles. Moreover, if it is known that there will be several inspection meetings, covering various pieces of a work product, this information appears on the inspection meeting notice.

TABLE 3.9   Inspection Reports

Report title	How and when used
1. Inspection meeting notice	To invite participants. Prepared and received prior to the overview, or sufficiently before the inspection meeting for preparation (if no overview)
2. Inspection defect list	By the author during rework. By the recorder to record and classify each problem found during the inspection meeting
3. Inspection defect summary	To report the number of defects found, by classification, at the end of the inspection meeting
4. Inspection management report	To report the inspection statistics to management at the end of the inspection meeting
4(a). Inspection management report (certified)	To inform management that rework is done, provide final data, and certify that the inspection is complete after follow-up

If an overview is not scheduled, the material to be inspected (or reinspected) must accompany the inspection meeting notice. Appropriate references, such as earlier work products, and the results of previous inspections that impact the current inspection should also be included with the distributed materials. The inspection meeting notice may also identify the locations of the material to be inspected if the work is discontinuous or a modification (i.e., a modification may be represented in several places within a work product, and have various interfaces and dependencies which need to be identified).

3.9.2   The inspection defect list

The inspection defect list is a detailed recording of each defect uncovered by the inspection. It documents what is expected to be corrected by the author during rework. It lists, according to project standards

- *Location:* Indicates where the defect is found. If there are multiple occurrences of the defect, project conventions dictate whether the defect will be counted for each incidence. In any case, each location is noted for subsequent resolution. Line numbers, or coordinates for diagrams, simplify determining defect locations.

- *Description:* Succinctly states the problem, but not its solution. Of course, if the problem is best described by simply stating the correct alternative, without the need for any solution hunting, then this is an acceptable alternative. For example, "register HV is used rather than register LV." More than one line may be used for the description, and a space between listed defects is recommended.

- *Defect classification:* Encodes the defect condition, by project and inspection standards. (See Chapter 4 for a sample defect classification scheme.)

The defect list is then distributed: to the author for rework, to the moderator for follow-up, and to the inspection coordinator to keep on file for further quality assurance studies. The defect list is only distributed to the inspection team members if a reinspection has been called for. It is not distributed any further.

3.9.3   The inspection defect summary

The defect summary, unlike the more detailed defect list, only contains a count of the defects by the categories that were determined by the project's defect classification. Descriptions of the defects are not summarized. The defect summary is prepared by the moderator or the recorder from the defect list. It provides a convenient summary of the inspection findings for inclusion in the inspection data base, which contains a count by category of each inspection's results.

3.9.4   The inspection management report

The inspection management report provides performance data to assess how the inspections are being used by a project. It documents the effort involved in the inspection, and provides data that can be used by management to monitor and control the inspection process.

The inspection management report is prepared by the moderator at the end of the inspection meeting. It documents what material was inspected, how much was inspected, who inspected it, how long it took, and what the disposition of the material was. After the disposition is executed, the inspection management report also records the effort required for the author's rework. Inspection management reports can be used to determine whether inspections are following established guidelines, how close to schedule inspections are, and what resources are being devoted to the inspection process.

The inspection management report is not used for evaluating the author, and does not include the number of defects found. Defect counts are too easily seized on as a measure of quality or effectiveness, but in reality provide little information about the quality of an individual work product when used in isolation. Rather, complete defect information is regularly provided to management from the inspection data base, where it can be examined in aggregate, and valid conclusions can then be drawn as to the relative importance of any measures or trends.

After preparing the inspection management report, the moderator sends it to the inspection coordinator, who may then distribute additional copies. The data from this report is fed into the inspection data base. Usually, the immediate development manager receives a copy of the inspection management report for two purposes: to track the progress of the product and its inspections, and to determine whether the inspection conforms to project specifications. The manager should see if the preparation and duration for the inspection was appropriate to the amount of material, and if the assigned disposition agreed with the amount of rework effort. If there is a wide variance with the manager's expectations, the manager may request a reinspection of all or part of the work product.

3.10   Getting the Most from the Inspection Process

Several factors are critical to the success of the inspection process. Among these are commitment, formality, knowledge, support, accountability, and documentation. Each of these is necessary. The extent to which these factors are understood and are present directly affects the success of the inspection process.

3.10.1 Commitment

Inspections do not work if the people involved in them are not committed to making them work. Ideally, all participants believe in the viability of inspections and will therefore contribute their best efforts. This is not always the case. However, it is possible to get maximum commitment, even from doubters, as long as project management demonstrates *its* commitment to the process. Management commitment can be demonstrated in many ways. Among the most useful is the assignment of senior staff members to key roles, such as inspection coordinator and moderators. Additionally, actively use inspection results to direct product development, to build time for inspections into the development schedule, and to reward employees for their contributions to the inspection process (not their inspection results). Although it is necessary for managers to express their dedication to inspections both at meetings and in writing, this alone is insufficient to ensure the full commitment of the project staff.

Management must play a key role to clearly and effectively express the message that inspections are, in fact, a featured part of product development. Inspection planning demonstrates this commitment. Documentation that shows the impact of inspections on successful achievement of schedule and development benchmarks also underscores the importance and criticality of inspections. Use of inspection data, summarized and reported periodically from the inspection data base, underscores the significance of inspections, not only for the improvement of product quality, but also for process control. In other words, when management can demonstrate, rather than just say, that inspections are an important part of the development job, the inspection process is successful!

3.10.2 Formality

A project may be fully committed to inspections, but still fail to run them correctly. Inspections must be defined, executed, and administered to specifications to be effective. The formality of announcements, assigned roles, documentation, and certification of rework must be established and maintained. Inspection meetings must be conducted in accordance with project guidelines. Without this formality, it is too easy for the inspection process to deteriorate into informal review sessions. Such informal processes have their purposes during development, particularly for the individual developer, but they do not serve the project and the development organization as a formal inspection process. Formality keeps the inspections on track and avoids diversions into areas beyond their intended scope. Moreover, formality keeps the inspection team working as a unit for the maximum benefit of the product and the project.

3.10.3 Knowledge

Just as professional knowledge is important for successful development, knowledge of the inspection process is important for successful inspections. Project members must be educated in the purpose and importance of inspections, in inspection procedures, and in the project inspection plan. They must understand what is expected of them in their roles as author, moderator, or inspector. They must be aware of how the inspection process fits into the general project management scheme.

3.10.4 Support

The support that the project establishes for the inspection process is a key factor in its success. This begins with broad education of management and staff. Inspections must then be tailored and documented to project standards, and administered to these standards. Also, an inspection data base must be established and actively used. To accomplish these support tasks, there needs to be an inspection coordinator to define, administer, evaluate, and maintain the process.

Another factor is the support of the project members. Inspections need to be conducted in an atmosphere of teamwork and trust. They should not be seen as a competitive exercise. The focus is on uncovering defects so that the end product may be more successful, therefore reflecting favorably on all project members. Inspections are not an exercise in seeing if one person could have done the job better than another. It is unlikely that all project members will be of equal ability in all areas. But it is equally unlikely that any one member, no matter how talented, would be capable of developing the entire product alone. If the inspection meetings are used as an opportunity to critique the work product without demeaning the author, they provide an opportunity to create team spirit and improve the work environment for everyone.

3.10.5 Accountability

Accountability can be assigned for three types of roles in the inspection process. These are the author, the moderator, and the inspectors. The primary accountability of each can be summed up in a key word:

- Author—for the *product* inspected,
- Moderator—for the *process* of inspection,
- Inspector—for *verification* of the product.

The inspection process does not relieve authors of responsibility for their work. In fact, it often defines an author's responsibilities in more concrete terms than the initial development assignments may have. At the end of an inspection meeting, the author knows exactly what is required in order to have the work product certified complete. Scheduling inspections at development milestones ensures that an author who is having trouble progressing on an assignment has the opportunity to obtain support in order to meet scheduled commitments.

Importantly, none of the other inspection participants, except the author, is accountable for the work product. This is by intent. If all the participants—authors, moderators, and inspectors—do their jobs well, the inspection process, and thereby the development process, will work. There is no need to assign product accountability to any other participant but the author.

It is the moderator's responsibility to be accountable for the inspection process; to follow inspection guidelines and to ensure that all of the other participants follow these requirements. It is then each inspector's responsibility to be accountable for the use of his or her best professional judgment, knowledge of the project, and familiarity with the work product gained through overview meetings and preparation, to identify defects in the author's work. The author retains accountability for the product; but the entire team accepts accountability for the inspection.

3.10.6 Documentation

Documenting an inspection, from the initial inspection meeting notice to the final inspection management report, is a method for helping to ensure that the defined inspection process is being followed, that management is properly informed and involved, and that the resulting inspection data is available for project use. At each stage, the moderator confirms that the reports accurately convey all of the essential inspection information for the other inspectors and for the project. At each stage, this documentation ensures that all of the agreements and findings of the inspection are beyond dispute, and follow the defined project guidelines. What has been committed is delivered, and can be verified. Documentation ensures that the inspection process is uncompromised and consistent with project goals of improved product quality, process productivity, and project manageability.

3.11 Conclusion

The inspection process is not free. It requires commitment, education, planning, control, and feedback. It requires teamwork, and personnel willing to have their work held up to the scrutiny of their peers.

To maximize inspection payoff, inspection teams must work efficiently and effectively. They must follow a consistent set of procedures for each step in the inspection process. When they do so, they become not as good as their members, but better than the sum of their parts. How much better is determined by the effort put into the inspection process, not only by the individuals, but by the project as a whole.

The payoff can be enormous. Properly designed, executed, and administered, an inspections program can lead to tremendously improved product quality, with resulting savings in product test and manufacture time, increased customer satisfaction, and reduction in customer service efforts. Thus the payoff is money in the bank.

4

Implementing Inspections

In previous chapters we described the role of inspections within a quality management process and how inspections are performed. In this chapter we turn our attention to their implementation. The planning that goes into putting an inspection program in place is a major factor in their success. Doing the implementation right sets the stage for doing inspections right.

The goal of the implementation activities is to ensure that the conditions necessary for the successful use of inspections are met. The implementation activities are

1. Commit resources for the inspection process
2. Select initial project(s)
3. Assign an inspection coordinator
4. Determine suitability of the project for inspections
5. Define the inspection process
6. Determine administrative procedures
7. Train management and staff
8. Apply inspections
9. Report inspection results
10. Establish data management tools and procedures
11. Monitor inspections

Implementation begins when resources are committed to define and perform inspections—people, time, and, most importantly, management. The implementation activities are roughly sequential, although some tasks may be performed before or in parallel with others. When a decision has been made to use inspections, project(s) are selected based on their criticality, status, size, schedule, and perceived risk.

A knowledgeable project member is assigned the job of inspection coordinator to perform many of the implementation activities. The coordinator works with project management, project staff members, and possibly an inspections authority. Usually, the first task for the coordinator is to assess the suitability of the project for the use of inspections. Then the coordinator defines and documents the project's inspection procedures. The coordinator also helps to determine appropriate administrative procedures. Once the inspection procedures have been defined, both management and staff are trained in their respective roles and responsibilities, and inspections are then applied.

A system for the storage and analysis of inspection data is installed to keep track of inspection results. The objective is to have the inspection data available on-line to rapidly and conveniently assess the inspection results. These results are used to guide the ongoing development process and track the effectiveness of the current inspection procedures. This information, plus staff perceptions and other qualitative data, is used to evaluate the success of inspections.

4.1 Committing Resources for Inspections

What is needed to implement inspections? From working with a large number of installations, many successful, some not, we have derived a few things that need to be provided to successfully use inspections.

- Management involvement
- An inspection coordinator
- Training
- Scheduled time to use inspections
- Evaluation of inspection results

Probably the most important ingredient in determining the success of inspections is management's desire to use them—their commitment. But commitment is not just belief, it requires contribution. Management's necessary contribution is: first, establishing the goals for the use of inspections, with planned and defined tasks, schedules, and specific responsibilities; then, providing the resources needed to define and execute inspections; and, finally, monitoring and controlling inspections during their use in development. When these elements of management commitment are in place, inspections can then be implemented and applied in a consistent and effective manner within an overall quality management system.

An inspection coordinator needs to be available to assess, define, and document the inspection process. From the lessons that have been learned from successful and failed inspection implementations, there is no substitute for a capable inspection coordinator. Inspections do not succeed without one! Although the role of the inspection coordinator is discussed in more detail subsequently, in general the initial implementation requires a month's time of a knowledgeable staff member.

Training sets the stage for the use of inspections and is a necessary ingredient for their success. Again, there will be a more extensive discussion of inspections training in Chapter 7, but the initial resources are modest, requiring approximately

- One-half day for management
- One day for the staff
- Two days for the inspection coordinator

One overriding reason for some inspection programs producing mediocre or poor results is that not enough time is provided for their use in the development schedule. Given the wide variety of products that are inspected, there is considerable variation in the resources that will be required. But, anticipate that approximately 10 percent of the development effort should be expended for the use of inspections. More specifically, but with greater variance expected, consider the following resources that have produced good results.

- 55 staff-hours per 1000 lines of code (inclusive of preparation, examination, and rework, with an average inspection team size of four)
- 30 staff-hours per 12 pages of architecture (very high level design of hardware or software systems, with an average inspection team size of five)
- 40 staff-hours per electronic circuit board design (each comprising approximately 20 pages of narrative descriptions, schematic diagrams, component specifications, timing diagrams, presumptive layouts, and parts lists, with an average inspection team size of six)

Finally, to capitalize on the investment that has been made in the inspection program, the results need to be evaluated. Evaluation of inspection results requires approximately 1 staff-month. The evaluation report should highlight both the quantitative results of the inspections, and the qualitative responses of the staff to the inspection program.

How well inspections are performed, areas for improvement, and suggested modifications to the inspection program should be included.

4.2 Selecting Initial Projects

When considering the use of inspections, the extent of the implementation needs to be determined—pilot or organization? There are pros and cons to each approach.

As illustrated in Fig. 4.1, implementing inspections widely can provide the greatest benefits for the organization (or organizational unit, such as a large project or a department). It may be opportune in terms of the business situation, when either new work or new methods of development are being initiated. The inspection program will certainly have everyone's interest, and the use of inspections is usually mandated by the corporation. But not all organizations are willing to commit to a full-scale inspection program until they have witnessed their benefits. The resources, time, or risk may be perceived as being too great to be afforded at this time. For these organizations, a pilot inspection program may be the best alternative.

A pilot program selects a small project or one phase of a large project to apply inspections. Following an evaluation of the inspection results,

Both have worked!

- Frequently a local decision
- Depends on extent of corporate guidelines and support programs

	Pilot	Organization
Pro	Establish credibility Provide guidelines Easier to approve Low cost	Large rewards Opportune Mandated High interest
Con	Limited interest Small gain Not representative Might not scale-up	Higher cost Increased risk Added complexity Limited experience

Figure 4.1 Inspection implementation: pilot or organization.

management then decides whether or not to commit to inspections more widely. The pilot method can achieve positive results for a much smaller initial cost and risk than a full-scale inspection program involves. Also, valuable expertise is gained.

However, the results may not always be representative of the larger environment. And opting for a pilot does not demonstrate nor require strong commitment to the program. Therefore, the pilot may show limited results that have little to do with the inspection process itself. Moreover, results may not scale up. Inspection guidelines and procedures used for the pilot may prove unworkable on a larger scale.

For these reasons, even a pilot inspection program must be thoughtfully planned to take into account the characteristics of the broader environment. And the results of the pilot must be evaluated with regard not only to the pilot environment, but to the larger organizational environment as well.

4.3   Assigning an Inspection Coordinator

A critical role to be filled for the effective application of the inspection process is that of inspection coordinator. The inspection coordinator's relationship to inspections is similar to a developer's relationship to a product, where the inspection coordinator has "ownership" of the inspection process for the project. The inspection coordinator facilitates the implementation and use of inspections by performing the following functions:

- Determines the suitability of the project for inspections
- Defines the inspections that will be used
- Customizes each inspection type
- Documents the inspection procedures and report formats
- Facilitates the inspection training and implementation program
- Establishes the inspection data base and analysis reports
- Administers on-going inspection activities
- Evaluates inspection performance
- Maintains the inspection process

There are a variety of documents, procedures, and tools to aid the inspection coordinator, but it is the inspection coordinator's responsibility to see that each of these activities is performed effectively. A few guidelines are suggested for the characteristics of a person who will be performing this role.

- First, although an inspection coordinator can be either a member of management or staff, in general a staff member will have more time available to perform the required tasks and will be more intimate with current development details. With management oversight, a staff coordinator can provide a good balance of technical detail with process management concerns.

- Next, an inspection coordinator must be familiar with the methods and procedures that will be used to develop the product, and must be able to integrate inspections with the other facets of the development procedures.

- An inspection coordinator must also be technically competent. A number of decisions in the definition and use of inspections depend on technical considerations, and the better these are understood by the coordinator, the better inspections are defined and performed.

- An inspection coordinator should be known by and be a respected member of the staff. He or she will be establishing procedures that are used by the project, and the determination of these procedures and their application need to be accepted as "our" inspection process by the other project members.

- Last, an inspection coordinator needs to be interested in development procedures and methodology-oriented work. The coordinator's interest in inspections influences the effectiveness of the quality control process.

The bulk of the inspection coordinator's duties consist of preparing the project for inspections. The coordinator defines and documents the project's inspection process, determines the administrative procedures,

Staff:	Experienced staff member. May reside in QA.
Effort:	10 days
Schedule:	1 month
Tools:	Consultation References Procedural templates Reporting forms Checklists Training programs Database management systems (LIDS)
Continuing:	10%–20% coordinator's time.

Figure 4.2 Inspection coordinator commitment.

provides for inspection training, and otherwise sets the stage for inspection implementation. The inspection coordinator is supported in this effort by project management, other project staff members, and possibly by an inspection authority. It is assumed that the inspection coordinator is knowledgeable of the project procedures, the product being developed, and the development environment. Given this knowledge and reasonable support, the commitment for an inspection coordinator to implement inspections for a project of approximately 30 people is about 10 staff-days, over a month's time, as illustrated in Fig. 4.2.

4.4   Determine the Suitability of the Project(s)

Three sets of factors need to be considered when determining if inspections are suitable for the selected project(s) or organization.

- The state of the project
- The technology employed
- Administrative procedures

At times, the inspection coordinator may initiate development process changes to bring these factors into compliance with inspection requirements. An example may be the incorporation of a change control procedure to the project's administrative structure where none was present before.

Expect that there may be some interaction between inspections and any modifications that may be required to the development process. If the process changes are large, it may be better to delay the use of inspections until after the project adapts to the new procedures, rather than having an unmanageable project. Planning for the use of inspections improves your knowledge and confidence in the development process, and potentially initiates some needed changes.

4.4.1   Project factors

Project factors consist of the sequence of activities (frequently called phases) that define the development life-cycle. These activities are distinguished by what may be called development phase demarcations. [*Phase demarcations* are those points in the development process where the intermediate product changes character—where the intellectual content of the product is enhanced and elaborated (e.g., from requirements definition to the specification of design).] Their completion is used to establish possible inspection points and development milestones. Without a phased development cycle of some form, inspections will not be able to be effectively applied—in-process. Note that appropriate demarcations can also be defined for cyclical or rapid prototype development.

The transitions between development activities (i.e., phase demarcations) determine where inspections are to be used. When applying inspections, each demarcation is evaluated for its importance and visibility. Distinctive product features are controlled at these selected demarcation points by establishing inspections as necessary in-process quality milestones for the verification of the intermediate product, thus controlling its quality prior to flowing to the next project activity.

Analyzing the development model aids in determining what process objectives inspections will be used for, and what measurements and data are necessary to evaluate the effect of inspections.

4.4.2 Technology factors

Technology factors affect how the product is designed, the development methods that are used, and the standards that are to be followed. Inspections work well with a large variety of products and development procedures, given that they are tailored to the environment. However, inspections do place three basic demands on the development process, and require

1. A phased development model (although not necessarily sequential) that uses demarcation points

2. Modular product design, so that activities within demarcations result in inspectable, well-defined work products

3. Basic product documentation standards to ensure that inspectors can understand the work products

Of course, it is assumed that the development environment remains consistent. If it does not, then the inspection procedures need to be adjusted to accommodate to the changes in development practices. In this case comparative measurements are weakened—not always a satisfactory solution, but necessary to keep inspections functioning.

4.4.3 Administrative factors

Administrative factors consider the administrative interfaces between the inspection process and the project, as well as how specific inspection responsibilities will be assigned, activities scheduled, results reported, and evaluations performed. Although mundane, the administrative process acts as the necessary lubricant that keeps inspections running.

At times, administrative procedures for the project need to change to accommodate inspections. For example, when product development assumes verification responsibilities, there may need to be a clarification of the role of a separate quality assurance organization—it is still needed, but in a different capacity. Sign-off patterns, task reporting, modification routing, and milestone criteria can all be expected to need some changes.

4.5   Defining In-Process Inspections

Even though all inspections share a common set of properties, each inspection process must be customized to fit the unique characteristics of the product and the project environment. Once the points in the development process where inspections take place have been identified, the coordinator then defines the inspection.

1. Common properties
2. Types
3. Planning rates
4. Data
5. Product dispositions
6. Roles
7. Documentation (See Chapter 8 for an example Software Inspection Procedures manual.)

4.5.1   Common inspection properties

All inspections, regardless of their more specific type, adhere to the same overall characteristics of the in-process inspection method. Table 4.1 summarizes these common properties.

As can be seen from Table 4.1, an inspection is a formal peer process for the verification of a work product. It uses standardized techniques and produces a recording of defects that are analyzed for the control of the developing product and the development process. All of the participants and their managers are trained in the use and control of inspections. These properties need to be documented in terms relevant to the project. But, having said this, we must still describe what inspections will be used, and how.

TABLE 4.1   Common Inspection Properties

Purpose	Product verification
Organization	Formal peer process
Leadership	Objective moderator
Procedures	Standardized and documented Entry and exit criteria Defect classification Checklists Prescribed roles Defined reporting Controlled follow-up
Roles	Required, with specific responsibilities Author Reader Recorder Inspector
Defect recording	Encoded and stored—for example, by Type Class Severity
Data analysis	Quantitative quality management, of Inspection performance Development effectiveness Product quality
Training	Comprehensive Management Staff

4.5.2   Definition of inspection types

Each inspection needs to be customized for its intended use by the project. This tailoring defines an inspection *type*. For some products, a single type of inspection is defined, while for others several types may be needed. For example, work products in a technical writing project may all be inspected under a single type of "documentation inspection." Alternatively, a software project may define separate inspection types for requirements, designs, and source code. Or a hardware project may include inspection types for component interfaces, circuit designs, and layouts.

Each type of inspection can be defined uniquely and completely by seven parameters. These seven defining parameters and their relationships to the inspection are illustrated in Fig. 4.3. They are specified by the inspection coordinator for each inspection type selected. The following sections describe each of the seven parameters.

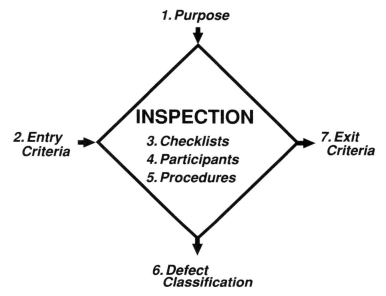

Figure 4.3 Definition of inspection types. Each inspection is defined and documented by the seven parameters shown in this figure.

4.5.2.1 Purpose. Describe what the inspection will accomplish. The overall purpose of the inspection is product verification, but verification can have different meanings for different types of work products. A software module is correct when it performs a function in a stated way, yielding accurate and reliable output for any given set of input. The measure of correctness of documentation is more likely to be based on its organization, comprehensiveness, clarity, and ease of understanding, as well as accuracy.

Therefore, for each inspection type, the purpose is more narrowly defined in terms of its expected contribution. This more specifically reflects the requirements for this work product's verification.

4.5.2.2 Entry criteria. Specify the inputs to the inspection meeting. They include the work product to be inspected, the requirements and specifications relating to the work product, and any required references. The definition of the entry criteria also specifies the condition that is required of the materials to be inspected. For example, minimum entry criteria for code are that it is successfully compiled without error messages and is line numbered; for documentation, the minimum entry criteria are that it pass a spelling checker and is line numbered. (Line numbering is useful for locating a defect found during the inspection meeting.) For inspections of graphical material (such as hardware schematics) the format of the material may be as important as the content.

4.5.2.3 Checklists. Provide guidelines and examples for the defect classifications that are used within the inspection meeting:

- *Global checklists:* An extension or further development of the purpose of the inspection. These are typically at a high level, and elaborate the objective of the type of inspection.

- *Process / representation checklists:* A compilation of hints for finding defects that typically surface when a specific development process and/or interim work product representation is used. For example, they would be the types of defects that typically surface when an electrical design is represented in a schematic format (e.g., common ground conventions); or defects that are frequently encountered when a software unit is represented in a particular programming language (e.g., == versus = in C).

- *Product-specific checklists:* A compilation of hints for finding defects in a particular type of product (i.e., message switching systems, financial transaction systems, data base management systems, etc.). One method for developing product specific checklists is to analyze previous test and/or inspection data and answer the question: How would this defect have been found in an inspection? Describe the circumstances of the defect, and define how the defect would be classified, as an example.

Checklists can be useful at three points in the preparation and inspection of a product.

- By the developer when completing the product, to be sure that all necessary conditions and entry criteria have been addressed

- By the inspectors when preparing for an inspection, to ensure that all meaningful conditions have been studied

- By the inspection moderator at the inspection meeting, to ensure that the product has been completely examined

4.5.2.4 Participants. Identify who will perform this type of inspection. The description of inspection participants specifies the expertise required, and may in some cases include specific names of individuals. Such information is especially useful if a given inspection type requires particular skills, possibly including experts from other projects.

4.5.2.5 Procedures. Explain how each type of inspection is to be conducted. The rate of preparation and examination of the material are defined, as well as the recommended maximum duration of the inspection meeting and the amount of material to be covered. The overall procedures described in Chapter 3 guide the inspection meeting, but there may be circumstances when variations on those procedures are desired. For example, an electronic schematic diagram cannot be examined in the same way as text, or even code, and the logical order of the analysis needs to be specified. The inspection procedures provide guidelines for the participants that ensure that a given class of work products is inspected consistently.

4.5.2.6 Defect classification. Define what things are considered defects, and how they are recorded. Frequently, determining the defect classification depends on the anticipated analysis and use of the data. Usually, three categories are assigned to a defect: kind, circumstance, and degree of impact. These categories are called the defect type, class, and severity. Together, they aid in identifying defects and reporting the inspection results. Defect types can vary in both kind and number across work products. Defect classes and severities, however, are fairly constant for most types of inspections.

The defect classification does not determine the need for rework, as *all* identified defects, regardless of their classification, are required to be resolved. However, the classified defects are crucial for subsequent analysis of inspection results. (Section 4.5.4 discusses defect classifications further.)

4.5.2.7 Exit criteria. Tell inspectors when the inspection is done. The exit criteria define the state of the materials required to complete the inspection. The most common exit criterion is that all of the defects found in the inspection meeting are resolved. Exit criteria generally include the corrected and certified work product, and an inspection report.

When these seven parameters are defined for the inspection types that will be used, along with their common properties, they form the guidelines that will be used by the project in conducting their own "tailored" inspections.

4.5.3 Inspection planning rates

Inspection planning rates are the amount of material that is to be prepared for and then examined at the inspection meeting, per hour. Planning rates for preparation and for examination are usually considered to be identical, as little has been found to distinguish between them in evaluations of inspection performance. The measure of inspection rate is based on the type of work product. For narrative materials "lines" are usually used. For source code, the measure is usually noncommentary source lines, expressed as NCSS or NCSL (noncommentary source statements, or lines, respectively). In this case, comments are inspected with the source code, but they are too variable to reliably contribute to the measurement of the amount of code that is inspected. The rate is expressed in pages when there is a significant graphical component, or where the work product is composed of a number of different types of materials (i.e., an electronic design may contain a narrative description, schematic diagrams, layouts, component descriptions, timing diagrams, and parts lists). In some cases, experimentation may be necessary to establish the appropriate inspection rates.

Inspection rates are used throughout the inspection process. The project manager and the inspection coordinator use them to plan for inspections within the development schedule and to estimate the inspection effort. The moderator uses inspection planning rates to determine how much preparation and inspection meeting time to plan for. At the inspection meeting, the moderator uses the planned inspection rates to decide if sufficient preparation has been done, and then to govern the pace of the meeting. Finally, the inspection results are evaluated to determine the inspection performance characteristics relative to the planning rates.

The inspection process uses a series of relatively short meetings, with a planned maximum duration of 2 to 3 hours (inspections can also be used effectively with much shorter meeting times, e.g., 20 minutes). In this way, the inspection team's effectiveness is maintained and fatigue is minimized. Frequent breaks are also recommended, about every hour for 5 minutes or so, to refresh the inspectors. The entire duration of the inspection meeting(s), including breaks, is used in determining the overall inspection rate.

There is a wide variation of inspection rates that have been found to be effective. Some of the reasons for this variation are

- Type of measurement
- Type of work product
- Format of the work product
- Complexity of the work product
- Size of the work product
- Expertise of the inspectors

For software, surprisingly, the inspection rate for program source code does not seem to be sensitive to the type of programming language used. Both high-level languages, such as Cobol, and assembly-level languages show a similar inspection effectiveness with respect to inspection rate (although the quantity of the logic will vary per statement). With this variation in mind, a starting point for inspection rates can still be given if the environment is defined, and if these rates are then checked against project experience after a few inspections have been performed.

The inspection rates shown in Table 4.2 have been determined to be effective in software system control applications, that is, the programs that are used to access devices, message switching systems, and communications control. The projects that were examined used Pascal, C, PL/1, and various assembly languages.

Note that the preparation rate is estimated as equal to the inspection meeting examination rate. This example should be used only as a guide. For instance, an overview meeting usually proceeds faster than an inspection meeting, but twice as fast (as illustrated in Table 4.2) is only approximate.

If the material cannot be inspected in 2 to 3 hours, schedule more than one inspection meeting, usually on succeeding days, and notify the participants accordingly. Be sure that the materials are distributed to the inspection team sufficiently in advance of the inspection meeting(s) to ensure that there is adequate opportunity for individual preparation.

When the inspection involves changes to existing material, there are three sources to consider when estimating inspection size.

- New and changed material
- Interfaces that are involved

TABLE 4.2   Inspection Planning Rates*

Development stage	Rate		
	Oview	Prep	Insp
Requirements	500	250	250
High-level design	500	200	200
Detail design	500	150	150
Source code	300†	150†	150†
Test plans	500	200	200
Test cases	300	150	150

*Rates are in lines per hour, (a page is ~50 lines) although other measures may be used with nonnarrative materials. An inspection meeting should be scheduled for a maximum of 2–3 hours' duration. Distribute materials sufficiently in advance of the inspection meeting for adequate preparation.

†Noncommentary source lines/hour.

- Dependencies in the unchanged materials that are affected by the modifications.

The sample rates in Table 4.2 have been found to be generally applicable to software inspections. But what rates are applicable for hardware architectures, course outlines, or other narrative materials? Our experience indicates that when the work product is documentation of some type, the rates for software requirements, high-level design, or detail design that are illustrated are appropriate, depending on the level of detail of the work product. When the work product is graphical though, such as state diagrams, experimentation is required to determine the appropriate inspection rates.

4.5.4 Inspection data

Data collection is a required property of an inspection. The type of data collected falls into three categories:

- *Product identification:* Information about the particular work product inspected, including what it is, its size, and where it fits into the product as a whole.

- *Inspection performance:* Indicates the type of inspection performed, the inspection meeting participants, the preparation and examination times, and the product disposition arrived at.

- *Defect characteristics:* The number of defects found and the classification of each. However, since defect characteristics are intended to serve the needs of data analysis, it is ultimately that function that determines the content and structure of the defect classification that is selected.

These categories reflect the several purposes of inspection data collection: to identify defects for early correction, to help to control the development process and to provide feedback on its capability, to measure the effectiveness of the inspection process, and to recognize common defects.

Although there are a limitless variety of classification schemes that can be devised, we have chosen an example of a classification that is both effective and widely used. The form of this example is:

(1)Type /(2)Class /(3)Severity

This three-level defect classification identifies the nature of the defect, the way it is exhibited, and its potential impact on the product. It is at the very least a good starting point for devising a method for your specific project needs. The following three sections describe each component of this classification, and are based on a software project using inspections at the completion of each of three development stages: high-level design, detail design, and code.

4.5.4.1 Type (the kind of defect condition).

A moderate number of defect types are defined for ease of use (see Table 4.3), yet with sufficient discrimination for subsequent root cause analysis. In developing defect types, apply the principal of orthogonality. (*Orthogonality* pertains to being related by right angles—meaning noninterfering, or nonoverlapping definitions.) In this example orthogonality means that each defect *type* is unique, and may be used with any defect *class* and *severity* to clearly distinguish the defect condition. What is desired is a set of defect types where each refers to a unique condition, and each can be of any class or severity. For example, logic (LO) defects are clearly distinguishable from data (DA) defects. Logic refers to the performance of some operation, while data refers to an object, its use, reference, or definition. On the other hand, defect types of logic (LO) and unclear code (UC) are not especially independent. There are questions as to where one applies versus the other. Also, what is missing unclear code? Can there be extra unclear code?

The defect types that are illustrated are intended to represent a middle ground between generality and specificity, and to cover a broad range of defect conditions. They help illustrate a way to think about defects in order to derive a suitable list of defect types for your project.

TABLE 4.3   Sample Code Inspection Defect Types

DA (data)	A defect in internal data use, specification, or description
DC (documentation)	Inadequate, irrelevant, or incorrect product descriptions
FN (functionality)	An incorrect specification
HF (human factors)	A defect in operational procedure or human interface
IF (interface)	A defect in the communication between components
LO (logic)	A defect in procedural, algorithmic, or control logic
MN (maintainability)	The component cannot be maintained by conventional means
PF (performance)	The component is not expected to meet required operational efficiency
SN (syntax)	A defect in language usage
ST (standards)	A departure from procedural or representational standards
OT (other)	A defect condition that has not been defined

TABLE 4.4   Sample Inspection Defect Classes

M (missing)	The product is missing material that needs to be added
W (wrong)	The product contains incorrect or unclear material that needs to be changed
E (extra)	The product contains extra material that needs to be removed

4.5.4.2   Class (the way in which the defect is expressed or addressed).   The three defect classes M, W, and E (Table 4.4) define how a problem affects the work product, and what must be done to correct it—add to the product, change it, or remove material from it. This set of conditions both define how a defect is exhibited and guides its resolution.

There is frequently a concern over how to classify ambiguous or unclear material. Consider that to correct an ambiguity a change has to be made to the work product. Therefore, we recommend that ambiguities be classed as W, "wrong," rather than adding a fourth class, which itself may be ambiguous in its application and rework guidance.

4.5.4.3   Severity (the impact that the defect is expected to have on the work product or development process).   The intent of defect severity is as a *quality assurance* assessment; it is not meant to be used for change control purposes (Table 4.5). The inspection process requires that *all* defects be resolved, regardless of their severity. The two defect severities suggested, major and minor, indicate that for a major defect the product is expected to fail in some visible way, and for a minor defect the product will be misunderstood—not that major defects are more important than minor defects. Operationally, the key criteria that distinguishes major from minor defects is visibility of the resultant failure. If the effect of the defect is potentially visible to the user it is major, regardless of how difficult or trivial the resolution is thought to be!

TABLE 4.5   Sample Inspection Defect Severities

J (major)	A defect that is expected to cause product failure, departure from specifications, or prevent further correct development or manufacture of the product
N (minor)	A defect that reduces the effectiveness, or confuses a product's representation, format, or development process characteristics, but is not expected to impact the operation or further development of the product

The reason for distinguishing between major and minor defects is that major defects are, in a manner of speaking, *testable*. Therefore, the effort expended by inspections to detect and resolve the major defects can be compared to the effort needed to test the product, providing an assessment of the effectiveness of inspections versus testing. Only major defects show the same characteristics as defects found in testing, and provide a common basis for this comparison. Minor defects are not comparable to testing defects and would distort the results if included. On the other hand, minor defects provide a measure of the maintainability of the product and its understandability. They are also an indication of how precisely or negligently the development process is being followed, and of how "dirty" the product is.

During the inspection meeting, the recorder lists each defect detected, using the classification stipulated by the inspection procedures. When the defect data is entered into the inspection data base, it is useful to count each defect that requires individual rework, and to group those defects that are corrected with a single "global" action. In this way, the defect count corresponds to the effort actually required to detect and resolve the defects. However, be sure to record each of the locations of duplicated defects to ensure that all trouble areas are identified for rework.

4.5.5 Product disposition

An inspection product disposition is *not* an opinion by the inspection team of the presumed quality of the product. The product disposition can be thought of as the way that "inspections control product quality without assessing it." It is the procedure that is assigned at the end of an inspection meeting to verify subsequent rework. The most important concept to keep in mind when choosing product dispositions is that they should not be pejorative—they should not in any way comment on the presumed quality of the work or the capability of the producer.

A typical scheme for product dispositions is shown in Fig. 4.4. This set of product dispositions is totally objective to the product and producer, completely controls rework, and specifies an appropriate follow-up method.

Generally, a disposition of A, "accept," can tolerate a few minor defects that are left to the author's discretion as long as the product has met all other inspection exit criteria. If there are any major defects, the product disposition must be C, "conditional," or R, "reinspect." A reinspection should be considered to be similar to an inspection of a modified work product in that the new and changed material, affected interfaces, and dependencies need to be inspected, not necessarily the entire work product again.

> **Accept (A):**
>   Meets the exit criteria.
>   No verification of rework is required.
>
> **Conditional (C):**
>   Does not meet the exit criteria.
>   Limited rework is required.
>   Moderator will verify the rework.
>
> **Reinspect (R):**
>   Does not meet the exit criteria.
>   Rework is required.
>   A reinspection will verify the rework.

Figure 4.4 Inspection product disposition.

The difference between dispositions C and R is frequently subjective, but when the rework is expected to be extensive, to substantially alter the product, or to be complex, a reinspection should be called for. The degree of expertise that the moderator possesses relative to the rework should be taken into consideration in determining whether a disposition of C or R will be assigned. Also, if another inspector has a vested interest in the rework, he or she should attend the follow-up. This would constitute a reinspection, as there will then be a team of three with the author and moderator.

4.5.6 Inspection roles

The roles and responsibilities needed to direct and define the inspection process for the project, and then to perform inspections at the inspection meeting, are defined in Fig. 4.5.

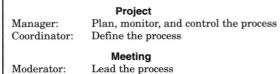

Figure 4.5 Role responsibilities.

At the project level

1. Project management authorizes inspections, specifies them in project plans, controls their use, and monitors their results.
2. The inspection coordinator is assigned by management to define and help implement inspections, provide for inspection data storage and analysis, and maintain the evolving inspection process.

At the meeting level

1. The moderator assures conformance to inspection procedures and keeps the inspection team focused on defect detection.
2. The author prepares the inspection materials to meet inspection entry criteria and resolves detected defects.
3. The reader objectively presents the work product materials.
4. The recorder notes defects for later analysis.
5. Inspectors verify the work product for correctness, conformance to specifications, and compliance with standards.

Management's role is performed from inspection implementation and continues throughout the inspection process. The inspection coordinator is assigned by management and performs his or her role from the definition of the inspection process through its evaluation and maintenance. The role of the moderator is assigned according to project determined procedures, but always before or at the beginning of the inspection The moderator is active during each step of the inspection, except rework, and is responsible for that inspection. The role of author is involved in all phases of the inspection, but only for his or her own work. The roles of the reader, recorder, and inspectors are defined by the inspection moderator, and are only active for this inspection.

The inspection procedures should specify the role selection criteria that are expected to be met. An example is the requirement of one electronic systems project that each electrical design inspection team be comprised of a test engineer, a manufacturing engineer, a circuit layout specialist, and two electrical designers (one of whom is the author). The moderator was required to be the lead project engineer, totaling six persons for the inspection team.

4.5.7   Documenting inspection procedures

The specifications and procedures developed by the inspection coordinator are documented in an inspections procedures manual. This manual typically includes an inspection tutorial, role responsibilities, and specifications for each inspection type. The project inspection manual defines and documents how inspections are implemented for the project. The manual

- Describes the overall inspection process
- Explains the roles of the project manager and the inspection coordinator, and of moderators, readers, recorders, and other inspectors in terms of project specific functions
- Documents the seven parameters defining each inspection type that will be used
- Provides checklists for each type of inspection (one of the seven defining parameters)
- Lists inspection dispositions and their criteria
- Describes and gives examples of the inspection reports that will be generated, and indicates who will receive them

The inspection manual can be considered the blueprint for constructing an inspection process, and the inspection reports are the products of that process—the indicators of its progress and degree of success.

Chapters 8 and 9 provide a comprehensive set of examples of inspection procedures for both software and other types of inspections.

4.6   Administering Inspections

Inspections must be administered. Without an adequate job of administrative planning and execution, even a well-conceived inspection process can fail.

Inspection administration lays the groundwork for the inspection process. It specifies how inspections are scheduled, who is notified, when, and by what methods. Administration provides guidance for running inspections, including recommendations for inspection entry and exit criteria, and for the use and distribution of inspection forms. Administration also defines how inspection results are reported and used, and how inspections are to be maintained.

Inspection administration requires an appropriate commitment of time and effort from the development manager, the inspection coordinator, and the inspection moderator. Their responsibilities for administration are

- *Development manager:* Has overall administrative responsibility. The manager appoints the project's inspection coordinator, who implements their administrative policies. It is management's responsibility to

—Establish guidelines

—Ensure consistency within the project

—Select reporting criteria

- *Inspection coordinator:* Performs what may be thought of as the quality assurance function for the project's inspection process. He or she defines administrative activities, documents the inspection procedures (and any necessary forms), selects the inspection data base management system, analyzes inspection data, and reports on inspection results. The coordinator

—Defines inspection procedures

—Specifies inspection reports

—Analyzes inspection data

—Prepares management reports

—Performs inspection evaluations and audits

Responsibility for specifying administrative procedures falls to the inspection coordinator, who may be part of the project, or may reside in quality assurance and serve many projects. Regardless of the reporting organization, the coordinator's responsibility always lies with the project.

- *Moderator:* Conducts the actual inspections, ensuring that they conform to the established procedures. They have the assistance of the author, reader, recorder, and other inspectors to perform the inspection meeting activities, but responsibility for procedural conformance is solely with the moderators. The moderator

—Applies inspection procedures

—Collects defect data

—Compiles necessary inspection reports

Figure 4.6 depicts a typical structuring of administrative responsibilities.

Administration starts with the development manager, who must incorporate inspections into the development plan. The development manager identifies what is to be inspected and at what point in development. The manager assigns the inspection coordinator, and, possibly, the inspection moderators. The manager also evaluates inspection results with respect to the project and organization, and recommends any necessary modifications to the inspection coordinator.

The inspection administrative procedures are defined and documented by the inspection coordinator. The inspection coordinator es-

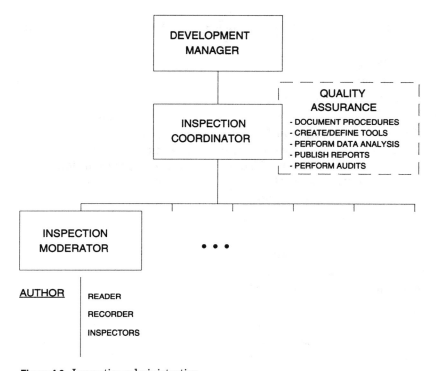

Figure 4.6 Inspection administration.

tablishes inspection scheduling and procedural guidelines, and the administrative framework for each inspection type, which are then documented in the project inspection manual. These procedures are applied throughout the inspection process by the project manager, inspection coordinator, and inspection moderators, and include those for

- Selecting moderators
- Assigning inspection teams
- Scheduling inspection meetings and meeting rooms
- Maintaining the inspection data base
- Reporting and analyzing inspection data

The selection criteria for moderators and inspectors are set by project management, then documented and applied by the inspection coordinator. The coordinator does not initiate project policy, only implements it. The continuing administrative role of the inspection coordinator usually requires about 20 percent of their time.

The administrative tasks that surround each specific inspection are the responsibility of the inspection moderator. These tasks include inspection planning, inspection data collection, inspection disposition, and final certification. The moderator uses inspection forms to document the outcomes of these tasks, then passes the completed forms to the inspection coordinator.

4.7 Inspection Training

Training is an important part of inspection implementation. The inspection training plan is established by the inspection coordinator, possibly in conjunction with a company training specialist. The inspection training plan specifies who will be trained, the training they will receive, and the training schedule. However, inspection training is usually not performed by the coordinator, who most frequently specifies who the trainers will be and establishes the training procedures that will be used. The training plan also provides for continued training as the staff changes, and maintenance of the training program to accommodate updated procedures.

Inspection training is provided for all members of a project, management and staff. Management training is aimed at providing a high-level understanding of the inspection process, its benefits, costs, and the need for management commitment; and then establishing the techniques that will be used to monitor, control, and direct the application of inspections. Inspection training for the technical staff is aimed at teaching the staff inspection procedures and how to perform them.

Both management and staff training are designed to address *all* project members who will be involved in managing, performing, or coordinating inspections. The training program is modular, requiring approximately 1 day of management's time, and 1½ days of staff time. Two days are required for the inspection coordinator.

Although the techniques for managing and performing inspections are necessary and meaningful, the most important ingredient is *attitude*. When the management and staff of a project are committed to inspections, and are then well informed about how to make them work, implementing inspections is easy. A detailed description of an in-process inspection training program is presented in Chapter 7.

4.8 Applying Inspections

When the inspection process has been defined and documented, and the staff trained, inspections are then applied. As in its definition, the application of inspections is not haphazard, but is considered and planned. Inspections are a scheduled and tracked activity within the development plan, and their application is managed equally with other development functions.

4.8.1 Defect detection aids

When using inspections, a few aids to defect detection have proven effective. These are

- Inspection checklists
- Automated tools
- Testing techniques
- Formal proof techniques

Inspection checklists are developed from the project itself, the representation of the product, and the professional discipline involved. Provided as part of the inspection procedures, checklists are useful at three points in the inspection process

1. During work product creation, to ensure that it meets the inspection entry criteria
2. During inspection team preparation, to ensure that inspectors are aware of their responsibilities
3. During the inspection meeting, to ensure that the product has been completely examined

Although few in number, useful automated tools include compilers and syntax checkers, computer-aided software engineering (CASE) tools, documentation tools, library management tools, and tracing tools. (The object-oriented language Smalltalk has a browsing tool called an "inspector" which allows the visualization and verification of data and methods within its object classes.) There are also various types of hardware and software simulators to help verify that required operational specifications are met. In addition, the project may have some of its own tools. When automated tools are used to verify some aspect of the work product, their output should be provided as part of the inspection materials, and may be incorporated into the entry criteria.

The same type of thought that goes into an effective test plan is equally helpful in the manual examination performed by an inspection team. Some testing techniques that may be useful include boundary-value analysis, cause and effect relationships, and equivalence partitioning. When possible, including a tester on the inspection team can help infuse such thinking into the process.

Formal proof techniques, such as mathematical analysis, tend to have more limited application, but may prove effective for evaluating complex algorithms. Their usefulness should be weighed against the relative complexity and lengthiness of the techniques themselves. When applied, formal proofs are best assigned to be performed as part of preparation, to at least two inspectors for consistency (formal proofs are frequently complex, and can themselves be defective), with the results presented at the inspection meeting.

4.8.2 Effective use of inspections

Having evaluated the results from a large number of inspections, we believe that there are a few objective factors that seem to maximize defect detection. (*Objective* items are those that can be quantitatively controlled, versus subjective factors such as the motivation or expertise of the inspection team members.) From our analysis, three "critical factors" appear to determine the effectiveness of inspections. They are

- The *preparation* of the inspection team
- The *rate* of the examination at the inspection meeting
- The *size* of the inspected work product

One study conducted at AT&T Bell Laboratories[1] (Fig. 4.7) illustrates the effect of these factors on inspection performance.

A reasonable interpretation is that inspections with relatively less team preparation that examine the work product faster for larger work products will detect fewer defects. Studies have also shown that inspections are particularly sensitive to the examination rate at the meeting. Further, when work product size increases, preparation effort decreases and examination rate increases, both of which decrease the number of defects found!

Apparently, there is a tendency for people to prepare roughly the same amount of time regardless of the size of the work product, and to conduct a meeting of a fixed length.

The best way of assuring that preparation rate, examination rate, and work product size are satisfactory is to apply the inspection planning rates that have been determined by the project. First, select the appropriate examination rate for the type of work product. Then, determine the meeting time required for each inspection based on this rate and the size of the work product. Consider that an inspection meeting is a maximum of 2 to 3 hours, therefore work products that require multiple meetings should be divided into inspectable units that can be examined in 2 to 3 hours each. Then, determine the preparation time

In this analysis of over 900 inspection results, defect detection increased for:
- increasing preparation effort
- decreasing examination rate
- decreasing work product size

(log-log plots)

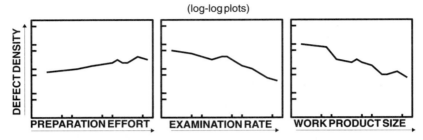

and for increasing work product size:
- preparation effort decreased
- examination rate increased

(log-log plots)

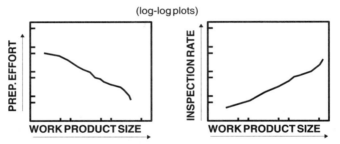

Control limits were established and managed for each of these factors, and resulted in a "...dramatic improvement in inspection results."

Figure 4.7 AT&T Bell Laboratories critical inspection factors.

based on the planning rates for each unit, and distribute the work product with guidelines for preparation and examination.

When planning an inspection program there are a set of "critical actions" that can be taken to improve the effectiveness of in-process inspections. These are

1. Partition the product to allow for adequate preparation time and reasonably short inspection meetings. This may require scheduling a number of inspection meetings to examine large work products. When this is necessary, distribute only the material that will be in-

spected prior to each meeting. If the nature of the work product makes this difficult, distribute a map of the portions to be inspected, with instructions to concentrate on the material required for each meeting during preparation.

2. Staff the inspection with only enough team members to ensure having the necessary expertise. Further restrict the staffing to knowledgeable participants.

3. Encourage adequate preparation to maintain rigorous defect detection. Preparation influences the inspection rate, participant synergy, and the depth of the examination.

4. Control the rate of the inspection meeting to allow for synergy to develop, to maximize defect detection. Allow enough time to consider the materials thoroughly as a team, to increase team interaction and to draw on individual expertise.

5. Inspect effectively, rather than just efficiently. The goal of an inspection meeting is to contribute to product development by detecting the maximum number of defects. It is far better to inspect slowly and thoroughly than to strive to make the most efficient use of inspection resources.

4.9 Inspection Reporting

The inspection coordinator is responsible for the definition of inspection reports, and establishes the procedures for their use and distribution. The inspection coordinator works with management to determine what reports are needed, and oversees the timely collection and entry of inspection results into the inspection data base.

The content, timing, format, and source of inspection reports will vary by project, but the necessity of providing inspection reports is inherent to the inspection process. If the inspection process is not being reported and tracked, it is not being managed, and, in fact, it is not an inspection process.

4.9.1 Inspection meeting reports

The purpose of the inspection meeting reports is to track inspection status and results for control of the inspection process. They provide the data that is used to evaluate inspection procedures, the development process, and product quality. If there is to be no subsequent analysis of inspection defect results, then there is little reason to categorize defects with any more than a rudimentary classification, such as tracking the number of product affecting (content) versus product representation (format) defects. Inspection results can be recorded in a variety of ways: with a variety of forms, through an on-line network, or using some type of notebook computer. At this time, the use of hand-written forms is the most prevalent.

There are four reports that we recommend in the routine scheduling and reporting of inspections. These four forms are the

- Inspection meeting notice
- Inspection defect list
- Inspection defect summary
- Inspection management report

The flow of these forms is shown in Fig. 4.8, and samples of these reports follow. They are derived from a software application composed of three stages of development: high-level design, detail design, and code. These forms coordinate with the preceding sample defect classification.

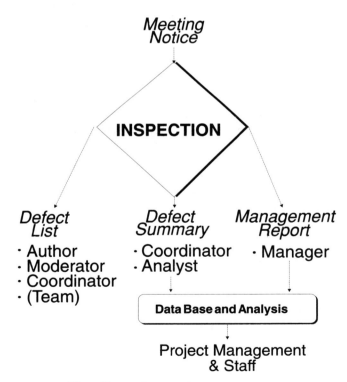

Figure 4.8 Flow of inspection reports.

For each report, the heading information identifies the project and the work product that is inspected. The meeting date applies to the inspection meeting; use a separate meeting notice for an overview when there is to be one. When there are a series of inspection meetings, the meeting date applies to the first. The moderator's is the only name that is stored in the inspection data base to disassociate the defect data from the author, but to retain an association with the moderator.

4.9.1.1 Inspection meeting notice.
The inspection meeting notice (Fig. 4.9) is prepared by the author and moderator to establish the meeting participants, the schedule, tasks, and estimates. It is distributed to all team members, and provides an entry to the inspection data base for scheduling and status information.

Most of the fields on this report are self-evident, although additional information may be helpful for the following:

- *Size of materials:* The size should be the total of all of the materials that will be examined, which may include all the new and changed materials, plus the affected interfaces, and any dependencies that need to be examined in other parts of the work product.

- *Duration and preparation:* These times should be computed by using the project's inspection planning rates for the appropriate type of inspection for the *total* size of the materials that has been estimated.

- *Comments:* This free-form entry should contain an explanation for the computed size of any modified materials, and the locations of inspected materials where they are distributed throughout the work product. It may contain any other information that helps orient the inspectors.

4.9.1.2 Inspection defect list.
The inspection defect list (Fig. 4.10) is filled in by the recorder at the inspection meeting.

- *Location:* Points to the place within the work product that the defect appears. It contains the line number or coordinate of *all* occurrences of the defect if multiple occurrences are being indicated with this one reference.

- *Defect description:* Describes the defect condition. A description of the solution may be indicated (e.g., the name DATAMARTIX_1 is misspelled and should be DATAMATRIX_1), where the solution is synonymous with the defect condition, is self-explanatory, and does not require solution development by the inspection team. Multiple lines may be used when required to describe the defect condition.

Inspection Meeting Notice

Meeting Date: _____

Project: _____   Release: _____

Activity: _____   Document: _____

Component: _____   Moderator: _____

Phone: _____ Location: _____

Meeting Type: ☐ Overview (O)   ☐ Inspection (I)   ☐ Reinspection (R)

Inspection Type: ☐ High-Level Design (HD)   ☐ Detail Design (DD)   ☐ Code (CD)

This meeting has been scheduled for:

Date: _____   Time: _____

Location: _____   Duration: _____

Size of Materials: _____   Preparation: _____

The following persons are scheduled to attend:

Name	Location	Role

Comments: _____
_____
_____
_____
_____
_____

Figure 4.9 Inspection meeting notice.

Inspection Defect List

Meeting Date: _____

Project: _____   Release: _____

Activity: _____   Document: _____

Component: _____   Moderator: _____

Meeting Type: ☐ Inspection (I)   ☐ Reinspection (R)   ☐ Maintenance (M)

Inspection Type: ☐ High-Level Design (HD)   ☐ Detail Design (DD)   ☐ Code (CD)

Location	Defect Description	Type	Defect Class	Severity

Defect Type: DA=Data, DC=Documentation, FN=Functionality, HF=Human Factors , IF=Interface, LO=Logic, MN=Maintainability, PF=Performance, SN=Syntax, ST=Standards, OT=Other

Defect Class: M=Missing, W=Wrong, E=Extra

Defect Severity: J=Major, N=Minor

Figure 4.10 Inspection defect list.

- *Defect classification—type, class, and severity:* These descriptive types are chosen from the project's classification scheme that best applies to the defect. The defect type *other* should be rarely used. Its frequent use indicates that there is a wide disparity between the project's defect classification and the inspected work product.

4.9.1.3 Inspection defect summary. The inspection defect summary (Fig. 4.11) is compiled after the inspection meeting by the recorder and/or moderator, and is a summary of the identified defects by type, class, and severity. In this case, only the summary of defects is intended to be entered into the inspection data base, not the individual defects and their descriptions.

Various standards can be used when reporting the number of defects. In general, we recommend that defects be counted individually for each occurrence, except when they can be addressed with a "global" change by the author (i.e., a misspelled name).

4.9.1.4 Inspection management report. The inspection management report (Fig. 4.12) is completed by the moderator before, during, and following the inspection meeting. Some information on it awaits the completion of the rework and follow-up steps. This form provides the following identification and performance data from the inspection:

- *Product disposition:* Indicates whether the document is A, accepted; C, conditionally accepted, to be reexamined by the moderator; or R, reinspected, which requires a subsequent reinspection.

- *Duration of inspection meeting(s):* The total time used for the inspection meeting(s). Meeting breaks are included.

- *Number of inspectors:* Includes the moderator and the author.

- *Size of materials:* The amount of the inspected materials in the appropriate units of measure (lines, noncommentary source lines, page, etc.). Modified work products (including reinspections) should contain the total of the new and changed materials, interfaces, and dependencies that are examined.

- *Total preparation time:* The sum of all individual preparation times, for all meeting sessions where applicable.

- *Number of inspection meetings:* One for all single-session inspections and more than one when the inspection report covers more than one meeting of a multisession inspection.

- *Overview duration:* The length of time that was spent for any overview meetings that were held.

Inspection Defect Summary

Meeting Date: _____

Project: _____   Release: _____

Activity: _____   Document: _____

Component: _____   Moderator: _____

Meeting Type: ☐ Inspection (I)   ☐ Reinspection (R)   ☐ Maintenance (M)

Inspection Type: ☐ High-Level Design (HD)   ☐ Detail Design (DD)   ☐ Code (CD)

Disposition: ☐ Accept (A)   ☐ Conditional (C)   ☐ Reinspect (R)

Defect	MINOR DEFECTS				MAJOR DEFECTS			
	M	W	E	Total	M	W	E	Total
DA: Data								
DC: Documentation								
FN: Functionality								
HF: Human Factors								
IF: Interface								
LO: Logic								
MN: Maintainability								
PF: Performance								
SN: Syntax								
ST: Standards								
OT: Other								
Total								

Figure 4.11   Inspection defect summary.

Inspection Management Report

Meeting Date: _____

Project: _____   Release: _____

Activity: _____   Document: _____

Component: _____   Moderator: _____

Meeting Type: ☐ Inspection (I)   ☐ Reinspection (R)   ☐ Maintenance (M)

Inspection Type: ☐ High-Level Design (HD)   ☐ Detail Design (DD)   ☐ Code (CD)

Disposition: ☐ Accept (A)   ☐ Conditional (C)   ☐ Reinspect (R)

Duration of Inspection Meeting(s): _____ (hours)   Number of Inspectors: _____ (all)

Size of Materials: _____ (lines)   Total Preparation Time: _____ (hours)

Number of Inspection Meetings: _____   Overview Duration: _____ (hours)

Rework Completed by: _____ (date)   Estimated Rework Effort: _____ (hours)

Reinspection Scheduled for: _____ (date)   Actual Rework Effort: _____ (hours)

Inspectors:

_____   _____

_____   _____

_____   _____

_____   _____

_____   _____

Moderator Certification: _____

Completion Date: _____

Additional Comments:

_____

_____

_____

_____

_____

_____

_____

_____

_____

Figure 4.12 Inspection management report.

- *Rework completed by:* The author's commitment to a completion date for rework. This date is not generally entered into the data base.

- *Estimated rework effort:* The author's estimate of the amount of work required to resolve the defects. This estimate is not generally entered into the data base.

- *Actual rework effort:* The amount of effort that the author has expended to resolve the defects. This field is completed after reexamination by the moderator or after a reinspection meeting. This information is entered into the inspection data base.

- *Reinspection scheduled for:* Used only when the unit disposition is R, reinspect. This date is not generally entered into the inspection data base.

- *Inspectors:* Lists all the inspectors, including the author. The moderator's name appears in the report heading.

- *Moderator certification:* The signature of the moderator given at the completion of the meeting or after the rework is examined, when the product disposition receives an A, accept. The inspection management report will be submitted without moderator certification when the disposition is R, reinspect.

- *Completion date:* The date when the product disposition is an A, accept. The completion date is also filled in when the product disposition is R, reinspect. In this case the inspection is considered completed, but the work product is not yet certified, which will presumably be accomplished by the reinspection.

- *Additional comments:* May be provided to note any conditions, suggestions, etc., that the inspectors wish to record, such as recommended changes to standards, which are not covered by the other items. These comments are not stored in the inspection data base.

Two items should be noted: the author is not specifically identified, and no defect information (even the total number of defects found) is included on this report. In this way, defect data is separated from management consideration during their initial review of the inspection performance data.

4.9.2   Other inspection reports

Inspection data analysis takes place at intervals throughout the application of inspections and is reported to project management, company management, and the technical staff. The following three categories of analysis reports are recommended.

1. *Monthly status and performance reports for project management:* These include inspection effort and results, and statistical process control information where applicable.

2. *Quarterly analysis reports for company management:* These reports include evaluations of the inspection process, and are used for root cause analysis and development process tuning.

3. *Timely inspection evaluations:* These reports indicate the overall performance of inspections, to date, and specify any modifications that will improve the inspection process.

In all cases, inspection reports are never used for personnel evaluation. They provide information about the product, the development process, and the inspection procedures. Chapter 6 provides examples of a number of quantitative techniques that can be used for these reports.

4.10   Data Management Tools and Procedures

Once inspection procedures and the inspection reports have been established, the inspection data management system can be defined. Whether your project develops its own system or tailors an existing system depends on several factors, including

- Resource constraints, such as time, budget, and equipment
- Availability of an existent inspection data base management system, such as Lotus Inspection Data System (LIDS)
- Project data and reporting needs
- The intended integration and compatibility of inspection data with other existing modification and configuration management systems

It is up to the inspection coordinator to recommend the inspection data management system based on these factors. The coordinator's recommendation should provide not only for the initial data base management system, but should also consider continuing operation of the system. The coordinator should establish

1. Who will perform inspection data entry
2. The criteria that trigger inspection data analysis reports

3. The analysis method(s) to be used

4. Reporting and distribution guidelines

By planning for the inspection data base management system up front, the inspection coordinator has the opportunity to build into the system features that support the inspection and development environments on a quantitative, objective basis. Chapter 6 provides suggestions for the types of data to be stored and the types of analysis that can be performed. Also, the appendix to this book includes a sample LIDS Operations Manual that can help guide the selection or development of an appropriate inspection data base system.

4.11 Monitor Inspections

The purpose of incorporating inspections into the development process is to improve the product and the development process. Inspection data provides a built-in system for measuring effectiveness. Finding a significant number of serious defects early in development is one indicator of the success of inspections. Conversely, an inspection program that turns up few defects is less likely to indicate a nearly flawless product than it is a faulty inspection process.

Defect detection is just one of the indicators of the success of an inspection program. The way the staff reacts to the inspection process is another. When the staff perform inspections professionally and find the process useful, inspections deliver results. But if the staff are disenchanted with the inspection process and unwilling to commit themselves to its success, it is likely that the process is flawed.

Finally, management's continuing support is a strong indicator of a successful inspection process. When management makes use of inspection results for product and process control, the staff can clearly see the payback for their inspection efforts. But if management fails to provide them with feedback, the staff may perceive a lack of commitment that can become contagious.

After installing inspections, therefore, you must ask the following questions.

1. Are inspections finding defects?

2. Does the staff find inspections useful and effective?

3. Is management supporting the inspection process and using inspection results?

If the answer to any of these questions is no, then there is a fatal problem in the inspection process as implemented, one that will eventually halt the process if it is not corrected.

4.12 Conclusion

The inspection process is not static; it grows and changes in an effort to attain an ever-better fit with the needs of a project's quality management program. But the nearness of the initial fit is key, and it is the implementation phase that creates this initial fit. A successful implementation program depends on the commitment of management and staff, and on the knowledge and ability of the inspection coordinator.

4.13 References

1. Christenson, D. A. and Huang, S. T., Code inspection management using statistical control limits, *Proceedings of the National Communications Forum,* 1987, pp. 1095–1101.

Managing Inspections

An inspection process is primarily for the control of product quality during development. At the start of a project, the development budget and schedule are highly visible, while product quality becomes visible only toward its end. As a result, many projects "meet" their development schedule and budget goals, only to incur major slippages resulting from product quality—problems uncovered by subsequent testing.

Incorporating an inspection program into a project makes product quality visible from its start and puts quality control on an equal footing with budget and schedule. Better quality control reduces project costs, while improving the project's ability to set and meet realistic schedule goals. But to achieve these results, the inspection process must be carefully managed.

Inspection process management takes place within the broader scope of project management. The most effective way to integrate an inspection program into a project is to make inspections an acknowledged piece of the development pie from project inception.

5.1 The Key Role of Management Leadership

Implementing an inspection program requires up-front management knowledge and commitment. Managers must learn about the inspection process and how it can benefit their project, and then provide endorsements of the program to project personnel. They need to commit some part of the project budget to training and knowledgeable assistance. Most significantly, they then must commit staff resources to key inspection roles, and provide time for staff training. The biggest commitment, though, is to the use of inspections and their incorporation in the development plan. And all of these commitments must be made before a single inspection takes place.

Such commitments of management attention and project resources send a strong message that management considers the inspection process to be important to the success of the project. However, for the inspection process to be effective, the message cannot only be sent at the start of the project. Management must continue to demonstrate commitment through active participation in the inspection process throughout the project life cycle.

5.1.1 Management participation in the inspection process

We have pointed out that management does not attend or in any way directly participate in inspection meetings. How then do they take an active role in the continuing process of inspections? Simply by doing what management does best: managing the process. Like any other development activity, inspections can be broken down into

- Estimating
- Planning
- Staffing
- Directing
- Evaluating

The following sections of this chapter examine management's role in each of these tasks.

5.2   Estimating Inspections

When establishing an inspection process, management requires a realistic estimate of its scope and cost. Although the expected result of a well-designed inspection program is an overall cost savings in product development, it requires the investment of project resources up front. Therefore, management must anticipate these costs and their impact on the project budget to properly allocate project funds and schedule.

5.2.1   Estimating cost

We have found the cost of in-process inspections to range from a low of 2 percent of a project's development budget profile, to as much as 18 percent. This can be generalized, as illustrated in Fig. 5.1, to an ex-

---

Cost:

Typical estimates for in-process inspections range from 5% to 15% of the budget profile.

Range:

- 7% for procedural
- 12% with structural
- 15% including functional

There is approximately 3% variation at each level.

Figure 5.1   Estimated inspection costs.

pected cost of 5 to 15 percent of development, ±3 percent, depending on the extent of use of inspections.

Using generic names for product development stages allows these estimates to be generally applicable. Procedural work products are typified by source code, structural work products by designs, and functional work products by requirements documents.

Budget profile refers to the total cost of development, including inspections. The expectation is that the budget will be significantly less with inspections than without them. Consider the investment in this way. If the total budget is reduced by 10 percent including inspections, then what did the inspection program actually cost? Which is why authors like Phil Crosby[1] have often said that "quality is free!"

The time required for inspections also depends on the extent of their use and on the types of work products inspected. The best way to determine probable inspection rates is to analyze actual project data from previous inspections. This method is not possible if you are installing

Phase	Rate
Requirements	5 pages/hour
External design	4 pages/hour
Internal design	200 lines/hour
Code	150 NCSL/hour
Test plans	4 pages/hour

Notes:
1. Inspection meeting time is planned for 2–3 hours.
2. Preparation rate is approximately equal to the examination rate.
3. NCSL is Noncommentary Source Lines.

Figure 5.2   Sample inspection rates.

an initial inspection program. In this case, the sample inspection rates shown in Fig. 5.2, from representative software development projects, can serve as guidelines.

These inspection rates are derived from a composite technical development environment, akin to producing control software for a communications application. Preparation rates are approximately equal to the examination rates, and for simplicity the two are called the "inspection rate."

Given these approximations, the cost of in-process inspections as a percentage of development budget (for each development stage) can be estimated using the following formula:

$$\text{cost ratio} = \text{average \# inspectors} * \text{individual productivity} * I$$

where individual productivity is in lines/hour and

$$I = \frac{1}{\text{examination rate}} + \frac{1}{\text{preparation rate}}$$

Typical software productivity values for several large development firms is estimated at about 2000 to 5000 lines of code developed and tested per year per programmer. If we assume 4000 lines are produced in a 2000-hour work year, productivity comes to about 2 lines per hour. Then if

$$\text{average number of inspectors} = 4$$

$$\text{productivity} = 2 \text{ lines/hour}$$

$$\text{examination rate} = 150 \text{ lines/hour}$$

$$\text{preparation rate} = 150 \text{ lines/hour}$$

$$\text{cost ratio} = 4 \times 2 \times \left(\frac{1}{150} + \frac{1}{150} \right) = 10.7\%$$

Actual inspection rates vary with the application and must be defined as part of your local inspection procedures. However, these generic averages are a good starting point for software development, and can be reevaluated later as you analyze your inspection results. Unfortunately, hardware development work products are far more variable in size, content, and format, and we do not have representative inspection rates available.

When determining actual inspection rates, there are several environmental factors, listed in Fig. 5.3, that tend to result in higher or lower rates. These differing characteristics reflect different types of projects,

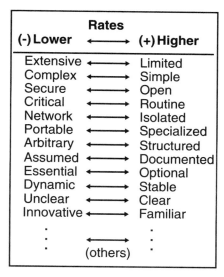

Figure 5.3 Work product characteristics influencing inspection rates.

products, and user needs. They also reflect such things as the complexity and diversity of the development environment, and the familiarity among inspectors of each others' development techniques and the product characteristics. Most projects require some experimentation in setting effective inspection rates.

It is reassuring to know that in our experience it has not required a large number of trial inspections to determine usable inspection rates. Usually fewer than six inspections are enough to provide representative rates that will effectively estimate and guide further inspection performance.

5.2.2 Estimating time

Inspection time estimates depend on the inspection rates your project decides to use. Figure 5.4 shows an example of typical performance estimates for code inspections.

This example is based on the generic inspection rates from the chart in Fig. 5.2. The estimate for rework time of 10 hours per 1000 lines of code [1000 noncommentary source lines (KNCSL)] is based on empirical results and may vary, although in our experience rework has not usually been a dominating factor. If an inspection rate of twice the generic rate [i.e., 300 noncommentary source lines (NCSL)/hour] is assumed, then the estimated inspection time is halved to 27 hours, (the

Item	Guideline
Size of inspection unit	300 NCSL
Inspection team size	4 persons
Inspection meeting duration	2 hours
Staff hours	54 hours/KNCSL (27 for preparation, 27 for meeting)
Meeting rate	150 NCSL/hour
Preparation rate	150 NCSL/hour
Rework	10 hours/KNCSL
Total:	*64 hours / KNCSL*
Expected defects:	*>15 majors / KNCSL* *~ 50 total / KNCSL*
NCSL = noncommentary source lines. KNCSL = 1000 NCSL.	

Figure 5.4 Inspection time estimates—code inspection.

sum of the participants' preparation and meeting times). Given this direct proportional relationship, we recommend that you estimate over a range of inspection rates to establish upper and lower bounds.

Keep in mind that the effectiveness of defect detection also varies with the inspection rate. A higher inspection rate may lead to lower defect detection, which may in turn cost your project time and money correcting defects later in the development process. Again, the reason for determining your own levels of effective inspection rates are to balance development time, development costs, and inspection costs in *your* project.

5.2.3 Adjusting costs to resources

Using the guidelines cited above, managers can determine whether an inspection program fits their schedule and budget. In making this decision managers should keep in mind that, historically, when inspections are well managed and consistently applied, the budget and schedule are met or bettered, management is better informed, and product quality is markedly improved.

Therefore, if the original estimate exceeds available resources, management should consider making some adjustment to enable the project to include an inspection program. There are several possible approaches.

1. Change the development schedule to accommodate inspections.
2. Reduce the test schedule and allocate the time saved to inspections.
3. Prioritize the work to be done and schedule inspections of the most critical work only.
4. Estimate inspection costs based on increased inspection rates.

5.2.3.1 Change development schedule. Obviously, the best of these alternatives for an inspection program is the first. Accommodating inspections within the development schedule gives automatic credibility to the inspection process and indicates to the staff that management considers inspections crucial.

5.2.3.2 Reduce test schedule. The second method is actually a variation on the first. This approach signals that inspections are part of the development process, a part that is expected to significantly reduce the number of defects before the product goes to system test. In our experience, projects that use inspections find and resolve approximately 75 percent of all defects before test.[2] The time saved from system test is often enough to cover the schedule time required for inspections.

Estimating the potential test time savings is based on reducing "marginal" test time by the percentage of defects expected to be found by inspections. *Total test time* consists of the sum of "minimum" and "marginal" test times. *Minimum test time* is that which is needed to exercise a perfect product by the test suite. *Marginal test time* is the additional time required by the defects that are found. For each defect, there is time needed to determine the cause of the failure, correct it, and then retest it. This marginal time is usually far larger than the minimum test time, and a reduction of this time by approximately 75 percent can be significant.

5.2.3.3 Prioritize. Inspecting just the critical parts of the product may be sufficient for some projects. The key to making this option work is to do it right for however much of the product is inspected. In this case, at least the most important elements of the product will be thoroughly inspected. Moreover, the effect on product quality and the resulting inspection data is representative of a good inspection process, and is useful in determining meaningful inspection rates and performance parameters for the project.

We have seen a software project where thorough inspection of design documentation led to such nearly defect-free specifications, that the project chose to selectively inspect their source code and still delivered an essentially defect-free product.

5.2.3.4 Increase inspection rate. Increasing inspection rates is the least desirable of the options, but may still be valuable as long as the rates are within reasonable boundaries. (Note that the authors have not seen effective defect detection of source code at rates greater than 500 lines per hour.) The expected result of increased inspection rates is that fewer defects will be found, and therefore more testing will be required. Any savings in increased inspection rates must be balanced against the probable decrease in test savings.

It should also be noted that in our experience system test procedures are best at uncovering "major" defects, but far less effective at uncovering "minor" defects. This may be reassuring in terms of delivering a product that is unlikely to break, but less reassuring in terms of its probable overall customer satisfaction and future maintainability.

5.3 Planning Inspections

Planning inspections involves determining what will be inspected, when it will be inspected, and who will inspect it. These decisions are documented in an inspection plan, which formally establishes the inspection goals, requirements, and milestones and links them to development. The inspection plan is written by (or certainly for) the project manager, and covers four basic areas.

1. The inspection range—what products will be inspected and at what development stages.

2. The inspection schedule—when inspections will be performed and when inspection results will be evaluated.

3. The inspection resources—the time and people required to carry out the inspection program.

4. An inspection training program—identifies courses, and sets the inspection training schedule.

5.3.1 Coordination with development plan

The inspection process is an integral part of development. If an inspection plan is not established early and integrated with the development plan, inspections are likely to be treated as an afterthought. This can result in a lack of commitment to the inspection program, a lack of resources being applied to inspections, and diminished results.

The inspection plan depends on, and potentially impacts, the development plan. The development plan establishes milestones based on incremental development stages and resulting interim work products. Inspections should constitute a part of these milestones. This allows

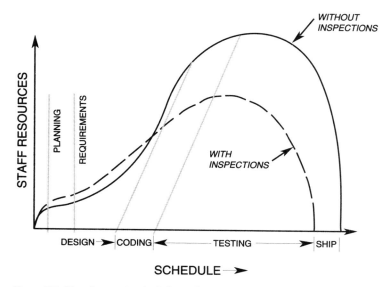

Figure 5.5 Development schedule and resources. From Fagan, M. E., Advances in software inspections. *IEEE Transactions in Software Engineering*, Vol. SE-12, No. 7, July 1986.

the development schedule to incorporate inspections, and the inspection schedule to be coordinated with identified development milestones. Overall, the development plan should reflect a reduction of schedule and budget by the commitment of up front inspection resources, as shown in Fig. 5.5.

Inspection resources are part of overall project resources and the allocation of time and people to the inspection effort must be realistic given the project budget and schedule.

5.3.2   Inspection range

The first task in determining the range of the inspections is to identify the project's work products and evaluate their suitability for inspection. The most appropriate, overall guideline is to inspect *all* of the work products. But when time or resources are limited, not all work products can necessarily be inspected.

To determine the best use of limited resources, first identify the points in the development cycle where it is most important to verify that the work is correct, conforms to specifications, and complies with standards. Critical work products at these key points are the first choices for inspection. Data from previous inspections may indicate that the returns for noncritical work products do not justify the effort. If so, it is better to skip inspection of those work products and risk some errors. On the other hand, it is never wise to skip inspection of critical work products even if resources are limited. In this case, it is necessary to find the resources to ensure that critical work products are as defect-free as possible.

5.3.3 Inspection schedule

The inspection schedule governs two distinct inspection activities: work product inspections and the evaluation of inspection results. For each work product to be inspected, the inspection schedule lists the person responsible for the inspection, and when the inspection is to be completed. Similarly, someone must be responsible for the evaluation of inspection results (generally the inspection coordinator), and when the evaluations are to be completed.

The evaluations of inspection results must be tied to the development schedule. It is expected that inspection results will be assessed at project management meetings and at intervals during the development cycle, and the information used to tune the inspection and development processes. Moreover, when all inspections are completed, a final data evaluation provides estimates of the inspection process for future development. Chapter 6 discusses various techniques for inspection data evaluation.

5.3.4 Inspection resources

The inspection plan establishes initial estimates of two resources: time and people. The time estimate includes the time spent in the inspection meetings, and on preparation, overviews, and rework as well. Allocate staff-hours to each of these activities and include them in development work plans.

Allocating inspection resources involves assigning certain responsibilities to specific staff members. Key among these is the selection of an inspection coordinator. Since the inspection coordinator defines the project's inspection process, the quality of the inspection process is governed by this choice.

We also recommend that the inspection plan identify specific inspection moderators. Choosing moderators during the planning stage establishes responsibility for product verification early in the process, at the same time responsibility for product development is assigned. Pre-assigning moderators enables management to balance expertise and schedule requirements, and helps to ensure the effectiveness of the inspection meetings. In fact, it is a way of management having a direct effect on the conduct of the inspection meeting without being there!

5.3.5 Inspection training

The success of the inspection process depends on the extent of knowledge of all of the participants, both management and technical staff. Project managers need to know how to plan for, monitor, control, and evaluate inspections; developers need to know the principles and practices of in-process inspections, and their roles as participants in inspection meetings. Clearly, to be most effective, inspection training should take place early in the project cycle. To achieve the best results, provide project managers with inspection training before the development staff, and train the staff prior to, or at the start of, development.

Provide not only for initial staff training, but also for continuing training, as needed. Both the project staff and inspection procedures are subject to change. Keep the participants current with up-to-date practices, procedures, documentation, and results.

5.3.6 Monitoring the inspection plan

View the inspection plan as a "living" document, one which may grow and change as the inspection process matures. The initial inspection plan reflects your best estimates of inspection requirements and scheduling. But an inspection process is not static. Changes in the product, the project schedule, staffing, or other areas must be reflected in revisions to the inspection plan, and coordinated with revisions to the development plan. Once inspections are in place, they provide management with feedback on both inspections and development. This feedback enables management to monitor the inspection process and the effectiveness of the development process.

5.4 Staffing Inspections

To staff inspections, management identifies an inspection coordinator, inspection moderators, and, potentially, key inspectors. Early identification of these members helps to incorporate time in their work schedules for inspection activities, including any necessary training.

5.4.1 The inspection coordinator

The inspection coordinator performs several functions crucial to the success of the inspections. He or she

- Defines the initial inspection process
- Prepares tools and aids for implementing and using inspections
- Analyzes inspection data

- Reports the results of the inspection process to management
- Makes any necessary modifications to the inspection process

Select an experienced, highly motivated member of the development team, who is knowledgeable of the project's practices, procedures, products, documents, and schedules. See Chapter 7 for more details about inspection coordination.

5.4.2 Inspection moderators

Inspection moderators are ultimately responsible for the success of the inspections. Moderators

- Verify inspection entry criteria
- Select participants
- Assign inspection meeting roles
- Determine the need for overviews
- Establish inspection rates and meeting times and extent
- Control the inspection meeting for the objective detection of defects
- Verify rework
- Ensure conformance to inspection procedures

Select knowledgeable and motivated project members to act as inspection moderators, usually more rather than less senior. These staff members should be well versed in both the inspection process and the development procedures. Often, an inspection moderator is assigned to a specific phase of a project or to a specific set of development work products. This allows moderators to follow some aspect of the project through several development stages and to establish continuity.

The coordinator and moderators commit their time and responsibility to inspections. Therefore, the choice of appropriate staff members to fill these positions sends a very clear message to the development team of the degree of management's commitment to the inspection process. Strong choices for these positions improve the quality of the inspections, and help ensure that inspections are effective and are taken seriously.

5.4.3 Inspectors

In general, a moderator chooses the members of an inspection team for each inspection meeting, and whenever possible, moderators reconvene the same team for a series of inspections of closely related work products. Inspectors are usually selected from the project staff. In addition to being prepared to technically verify the work product, inspectors must be prepared to take on any of the several inspection roles of reader, recorder, and of moderator, when needed.

Once the inspection process is in place, management may have little involvement in selecting inspectors. However, management must remain informed about the preparedness and knowledgeability of inspectors, and be prepared to bring in subject matter experts or retrain inspectors, if needed.

5.5 Directing Inspections

Having paved the way for the inspection process during the planning stage, management is not then at liberty to sit back and watch the process churn smoothly away. Certainly it would be gratifying if that were the case. But like most project control mechanisms, inspections require continuing attention to ensure that they are followed consistently and correctly.

Inspections are hard work. They require diligence and a considerable commitment of time and energy. Once the technical staff have experienced the benefits of inspections, they not only accept the process, but also often espouse it. But if inspections are mismanaged, or not managed at all, the staff soon become discouraged.

The role of management is to provision inspections—to monitor and control the process, ensure adequate resources, and ensure accurate data reporting. This role falls on the first level of development managers.

5.5.1 Monitoring and controlling the inspection process

The basis for controlling inspections is to assure that the inspection plan is being followed by monitoring that

1. All work targeted for inspection is inspected as planned

2. Inspections are well performed—performed in accordance with guidelines for product size, meeting time, and inspection rates

3. All rework is performed as required and reinspected as necessary

4. Inspection milestones are met as scheduled

5.5.1.1 Adherence to plans.
Development management uses inspection reports to track inspections against the inspection plan. Inspection reports identify what inspections have taken place and when they were

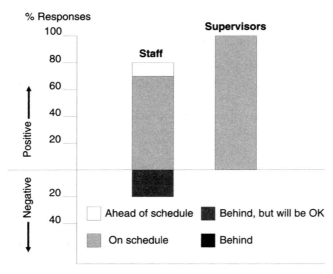

Figure 5.6 Survey of inspection impact on development schedule.

completed. If the reports, or absence of reports, indicate that inspections are not being done or are being done late, development management needs to determine the reason for the problem and take action to get the inspection process back on track. Figure 5.6 shows an example of a qualitative survey of the staff that was performed to assess the impact of inspections on the development plan.

One common reason for inspections being skipped or running behind plan is a slippage in the development schedule. It is never a good idea to attempt to salvage a development schedule by risking product quality. Instead, the schedule should be adjusted or additional resources put into the project. Any "savings" achieved by foregoing quality are sure to result in much higher long-term costs.

5.5.1.2 Monitoring inspection performance. Equally important to following the inspection plan is ensuring that inspections are effective and efficient. The inspection reports provide development management with performance data that can be used to control the adherence of the inspection process to the project's quality goals. Management's job is to ensure that each inspection is well performed. Process control charts, as illustrated by Fig. 5.7, allow inspection performance to be monitored closely during development. Inspections that fall outside the guidelines for preparation and examination are candidates for reinspection, while inspections that fall within the guidelines indicate compliance with the inspection plan. Monitoring mechanisms of this type allow in-process

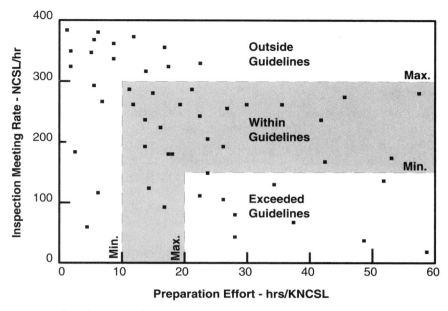

Figure 5.7 Sample control chart for inspection meeting rate versus preparation effort.

inspections to be controlled by meaningful metrics, in real time. (See Chapter 6 for additional methods for monitoring inspections.)

5.5.1.3 Rework and reinspection. A good inspection schedule allocates time for rework and reinspection. Since the purpose of an inspection meeting is to find defects, it is not surprising that many work products need to be revised. Inspection reports inform development management which work products will be reworked and reinspected, and when. Development management uses this information to track rework in the same manner that original inspections are tracked.

Many work products are simply corrected by the author and verified by the moderator. On occasion, some work products must be reworked and reinspected, several times if necessary. In all cases development management is kept informed of the progress of each work product, and is aware of problematic work products. If a work product becomes bogged down, development management determines the cause of the problem and the impact on the overall project, and makes appropriate adjustments.

5.5.1.4 Inspection milestones. Since inspection milestones are closely tied to development milestones, ensuring that inspections, rework, and reinspections are performed smoothly and in a timely fashion is an important part of managing development.

5.5.2 Assuring adequate inspection resources

The inspection plan attempts to anticipate the time and personnel required for all phases of the inspection process. Once the process is in place, it is up to development management to ensure that the time and personnel are allocated and available. Development managers are expected to monitor the time actually being taken by inspections and resolve any discrepancies between the estimated and actual inspection time. If inspections are using significantly more or less time than estimated, either the development or inspection schedule may have to be adjusted accordingly.

A common reason for increased inspection time is an early high rate of defect detection, leading to some extensive rework. There may be a number of causes. The culprit may be that the work product is more complex or different than anticipated. Or there may be inadequate specification of inspection entry criteria. But even if the development schedule needs to be lengthened, eliminating large numbers of defects in the early stages of development will significantly shorten the time required for testing. The result may be no schedule slippage at all, or in fact, an overall improvement.

If inspections are using significantly less time than estimated, development management needs to look carefully at the inspection preparation and examination rates, and the defect detection densities. These areas may indicate that inspections are being inadequately performed. In this case, development management must reinforce the importance of inspections to product and process improvement, and the responsibility of developers to the inspection process. When conflicts arise between a staff member's development and inspection commitments, it is up to management to resolve them. Development management must also consider who is participating in inspection meetings, to make sure that the required expertise is being made available. Where necessary, management should go outside the project to obtain subject matter experts to assist in inspections.

In addition to monitoring participation in the inspection process, development management should also monitor the performance of the staff with regard to inspections. To obtain the maximum benefit from the process, participants are expected to prepare thoroughly and participate actively and intelligently in inspection meetings. Although the results of inspections should never be used in performance evaluation, how well participants adhere to the inspection plan and the effort they expend in inspections should be reflected in their overall evaluations.

It is important that new employees who join the project be trained in the inspection process as soon as possible. Inspections should be presented as simply one more matter-of-fact procedure in the product development process.

5.5.3   Obtaining accurate data

The inspection plan indicates what data is collected during inspection meetings, and how it is recorded. The type of data includes the size of the work inspected, the total preparation time, the duration of the inspection meeting, and the number and types of defects found. Detailed defect information is given to the author and used to direct any needed rework. It is also used to direct a reinspection. A summary of the data is given to the development manager to monitor the effectiveness of the inspection process.

Usually the development manager is not provided with the defect data at this time, only with inspection rates and product information. The performance of the inspections can be assessed without defect information. Defect data is highly variable from one inspection to another, depending on both the nature of the work product and the effectiveness of the inspection. Only the analysis of the defect data from the inspection data base, representing the summary of a number of inspections, is meaningful in the assessment of defect characteristics and trends.

It is management's responsibility to ensure that inspection data is collected regularly and accurately, and reported in a timely manner. Managers make sure of this by monitoring the inspection schedule and asking for any delayed inspection reports. On receiving an inspection report, the development manager checks that the size of the work inspected is reasonable, that adequate preparation time has been invested, and that the length of the inspection meeting is appropriate. Any inconsistencies or seemingly unreasonable numbers should immediately be questioned. Defect data is evaluated from the data base, after the inspection record has been included, to determine the work product's defect characteristics—more or less defects than expected, defect types, and any exceptional or anomalous conditions.

Continued accurate data reporting can be ensured by providing feedback to participants on inspection results. Management should provide the staff with information on such things as the number and type of defects found, the effectiveness of inspections with respect to preparation time and inspection rates (amount of work covered per inspection hour), and the effect of inspections on the development process. When developers know how the data is being used, they are more likely to report it accurately.

5.6   Evaluating Inspections

An effective inspection program requires time to evolve. During the planning stage choices are made about what to inspect and how to inspect it. Evaluations determine how the inspection process is performing.

The responsibility for performing the actual evaluation and making recommendations to management lies with the inspection coordinator. The responsibility for seeing that data evaluation is performed regularly and consistently lies with management. Management must ensure that inspection evaluation is performed in accordance with the inspection plan, provide a method for regular review of inspection data, allocate resources for an inspection data management and analysis system, and establish procedures for adjusting project procedures based on the results of inspection data analysis.

5.6.1   Ensuring inspection evaluation takes place

Inspection reports provide a trail that indicates, at any time, what percentage of the developed product has been inspected. However, an analysis of the project's cumulative inspection data is necessary to assess the effectiveness of the overall inspection process. This is why management makes sure that reasonable milestones are included in the planning process. Data evaluated too early in the process is too sparse to provide an accurate measure of effectiveness. Data evaluated too late in the process cannot be used to adjust it. It is management's job to find the right balance.

Having established data evaluation milestones, make sure that they are met. Begin this process by ensuring that inspection data is used by development management as it is reported. Then, review the summarized inspection data as an integral part of the periodic (usually weekly) project management meetings. Percolate these results up through broader management review of the project, as they represent the first in-process indications of product quality and development performance. Like many processes, inspections are most successful when carefully tended and adjusted to suit their environment. Inspection data provides the means for adjusting both the inspection and development processes in real time—if it is used (see Chapter 6).

5.6.2   Management review of inspection results

An effective way of dealing with inspection data is to create a schedule and a forum for management review of inspection results. This review can take many forms. The inspection coordinator may provide management with an inspection evaluation report, which includes the data analysis and the coordinator's recommendations. Or the inspection coordinator can meet with the appropriate managers and present the evaluation. This review of inspection results should depend on the style that management and the inspection coordinator are most comfortable with.

Whatever the form, the content of the review is specific. The evaluation must clearly provide data that establishes the relative effectiveness of the inspection process in uncovering defects. This includes

1. *The percentage of the product inspected relative to the inspection plan.* Helps management judge how well the inspection plan is being followed. When combined with information on the percentage of the product developed relative to the development plan, it gives management a good, timely picture of the product's progress.

2. *The percentage of major defects found by inspection, at each stage, versus those found by subsequent testing.* Measures the effectiveness of the inspection process. If major defects are slipping through the inspection process, some adjustment needs to be made. The types of de-

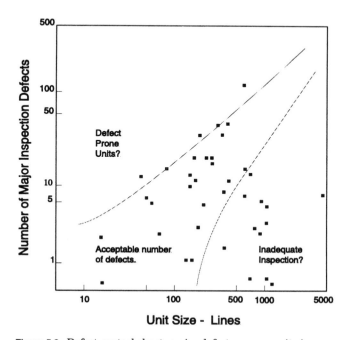

Figure 5.8   Defect control chart: major defects versus unit size.

fects being missed may fall into identifiable categories, or may be attributable to some other weakness in the inspection process.

3. *Inspection performance based on inspection rates, size of work, and number of reinspections.* Measures efficiency of the inspection process. This data can be used to determine the most effective work product size to inspect, the most effective amount of time to dedicate to inspecting some quantity of work, or payback of reinspections. Figure 5.8 illustrates a sample relationship between inspection defect density and unit size. This sample indicates that there are few defect-prone units, but a number of the inspections are questionable when compared to predetermined project guidelines.

4. *The number, distribution, and density of defects found.* Measures effectiveness of the development process and product quality. Each defect found and corrected is one less error passed on to the customer. When this data indicates that certain types of defects occur frequently, that information may be useful in identifying ways to avoid those errors to begin with.

5. *The cost of inspections versus total development and test costs.* Measures the payback for inspections. Experience has shown that inspections lead to reduced development and testing costs and improved quality. Thus the real cost of doing inspections is usually negative—a net development savings.

5.6.3 Allocating a data analysis system

The best way to make use of inspection data is to keep an accurate and cumulative record of the results of all inspections. The cumulative data can be used to determine the overall success of the inspection process in achieving product quality, and to detect trends that may impact development procedures. The data can also be used to determine the initial inspection procedures for new projects. A data management system facilitates accuracy, completeness, and accessibility, and is probably the only way such an analysis can be accomplished.

Although inspection data is likely to vary for each project, the overall inspection measures, such as inspection rates and defect densities, remain fairly uniform for an organization. Therefore, the actual data is more likely to vary in detail, rather than in kind, and the procedures for analyzing and reporting the results should not vary greatly. For example, although defect types may vary from project to project, each project collects data by defect type. It is thus possible to define a generic inspection data management system for the organization that can then be tuned to a specific project's needs.

One such system, described in the Appendix, is used for the data analysis results illustrated in Chapter 6. The system is called Lotus

Inspection Data System (LIDS), and makes use of a personal computer. Other systems may be on-line in a centralized system. Regardless of which approach is taken, a data management system should not be looked on as a luxury but as a necessity. Not only does the system provide an effective means of data collection and analysis, but it can also save the project resources. Manual analysis of inspection data takes more time and is more prone to errors. Moreover, unless regression analyses and other sophisticated statistical techniques are performed, data trends may be missed.

Of course, resources must be allocated to creating and maintaining such a system. Funds and/or personnel for developing the system must be provided. Someone must also be responsible for entering the inspection data and producing standard analysis reports. When a data management system is used, an administrator can perform these activities, relieving the inspection coordinator of that portion of the workload.

5.6.4 Adjusting project procedures

The results of the analyses of inspection data may show that inspections are performing exactly as desired, in which case the process should continue as initiated. They may reveal that inspections are not being applied according to the inspection and development plans, and therefore management intervention is required to get the process on track. They may show that the process is being properly applied, but that the desired results are not being achieved, indicating a need to tune the inspection process. They may even point to a flaw in the development process itself, indicating a need to reassess the development plan or procedures.

Whatever the results, management must be prepared to respond appropriately. Should the results indicate that the inspection process is proceeding swimmingly, management is certainly justified in giving itself a pat on the back, but not in becoming complacent. Management must continue to monitor the inspection data and analyze the results.

Should the data indicate that inspection procedures are not being followed, management must determine why not, and what actions to take to get the inspection process on track. If inspections are being performed properly and diligently, but the results are disappointing, management must reassess the inspection process and be prepared to make whatever revisions are needed to make the inspections effective, even if this requires a major overhaul of the inspection process and reinspection of several units. If the inspection process is not right for a project, it must be corrected as early as possible—or eliminated.

But sometimes seemingly disappointing results can have a positive meaning. For example, a low defect rate per inspection hour across a given class of work product may simply mean that such work products are reasonably defect free and need not be inspected, or could be inspected in larger units. There are indeed times when the return for the inspection effort is measured in increased confidence in the product for the developer and the user.

Management's biggest challenge comes when the inspection data reveals a possible problem in the development process itself. The decision to revise project procedures after development has begun is not an easy one. However, going to the field with a fatally flawed product is never a desirable outcome of development.

Possibly the most difficult case is when the inspection data reveals not so much a project flaw as a design that makes it difficult to ensure the product's quality. Quality that cannot be adequately defined and measured cannot be ensured. When quality is included as one of the goals of a product, the measure of that quality must be quantifiable. The inability to do so should be viewed as potentially fatal. Good managers require a design change when the products quality cannot be coherently described, quantified—and inspected.

5.7   Management Do's and Don'ts

Clearly managers have a lot to keep track of. The following checklist highlights the key points to keep in mind.

DO:

1. Schedule adequate time and resources to conduct inspections.
2. Ensure that inspection entry and exit criteria are established and used.
3. Choose a strong inspection coordinator and provide him or her with support.
4. Provide complete training for the staff.
5. Assure the staff of objective analyses and confidential results.
6. Emphasize product and process improvement.
7. Evaluate inspection data.
8. Share the inspection evaluation results with the staff.
9. Allow for the process to develop.

DON'T:

1. Schedule inspections if the product and staff are not both ready and prepared.

2. Use inspections as a substitute for requirement or design reviews.

3. Plan to inspect more material than can be adequately accommodated.

4. Defer inspections when schedule pressure arises.

5. Use inspections for performance appraisal.

6. Allow management to participate in inspection meetings.

7. Allow inspections to degenerate into confrontations or personal attacks.

8. Imply inspections are used because of a lack of confidence in the staff.

5.8 Conclusion

When inspections are thoughtfully planned, and quality management procedures are consistently adhered to, quality can be free—but it is never a gift. Only through close attention to the inspection process can management be assured that inspections will run smoothly and meet their quality goals.

The inspection process has been used successfully by many project managers working on many types of products and has a good track record. The key to the successful application of in-process inspections is commitment. When management is committed to making inspections work, and demonstrates that commitment by actively managing the inspection process, inspections do indeed work. The choice is clear.

5.9 References

1. Crosby, Phil, *Quality is Free: The Art of Making Quality Certain,* McGraw-Hill, 1979.
2. Bell Northern Research (BNR) reports finding 80 percent of all defects prior to test by the inspection of 2.5 million lines of code. See: Russell, Glen, Experience with inspections in ultralarge-scale developments, *IEEE Software,* Vol. 17, No. 1, January 1991.

6

Inspection Data Analysis

Inspection data analysis provides the ability to measure and control the performance of the inspection process, the quality of the emerging product, and the effectiveness of the development process. Accomplishing this depends on the collection and analysis of data about the identity of the work products that are inspected, the performance of the inspections, and the defects that are found.

Collecting, analyzing, and reporting this data is vital to the success of the inspection process over time. They help manage the project based on objective, quantitative quality measurements made by the inspections. Further, conditions and people change; products and projects must change with them. Processes that are not constantly measured and adjusted tend to erode. It is the analysis of in-process inspection data that can provide insight into our products, development processes, and procedures—in real time.

In this chapter we offer guidelines for quantitatively evaluating the inspection process, and for providing indicators of where problems or weaknesses may lie.

6.1 Data Collection

During an inspection three types of data are recorded as an integral part of the process: project identification data, inspection performance data, and product defect data. This data provides a profile of the work product inspections, and is composed of

- Project identification data
  —Project name (and any other relevant organizational information)

—Work product name (this may also include items such as release, account, etc.)

—Work product status (new, tested, modified, etc.)

—Moderator

—Meeting type (inspection, reinspection, overview)

—Inspection type (e.g., requirements, code, test plan)

- Inspection performance data

—Size of the work product (e.g., lines, pages)

—Date of the meeting

—Preparation time (hours)

—Examination time (hours)

—Number of inspectors

—Estimated rework (hours)

—Actual rework (hours)

—Rework completion date

—Work product disposition (e.g., accept, conditionally accept, reinspect)

- Product defect data: Defect data classifies the problems identified in the product by the inspection meeting. In this chapter, we have used the sample defect classification scheme defined in Chapter 4. This data is composed of

—Location of the defect (e.g., line #)

—Description of the defect

—Defect type (documentation, interface, logic, etc.)

—Defect class (wrong, missing, extra)

—Severity (major, minor)

When this information is collected and stored for each inspection, the result is a base of cumulative knowledge about the project, the product as a whole, each product component, and each inspection type.

The desirability of having an inspection data base of some type cannot be overemphasized. The actual mechanism of the data base is not important. It can be constructed using spreadsheet technology, one of many commercial data base management systems, or may be custom written, so long as it does not remain a collection of paper records. Although paper records require little effort to collect, they are tedious to use. Manual analysis rapidly becomes overwhelming as the number of inspections and products increase. Two salient characteristics of an inspection data base system are its input and its output; data entry should be straightforward so that they not encumber the inspections, and the most common forms of analysis should be automated and fairly easy to perform so that they are done frequently and in-process.

Additionally, other data is useful to ascertain the effect of inspections on the project. For example, to determine the effects of inspections on testing effort, or delivered product quality, or maintenance costs requires a history of these factors that both precedes and follows the inspections. Therefore, a complete, accessible, and well-maintained inspection data base is necessary, but by itself is not completely sufficient for monitoring and controlling all of the attributes of product quality.

6.2   Uses of Inspection Data

Information available from the analysis of inspection data includes

1. Inspection process performance
2. Defect-prone components
3. Poorly inspected components
4. The number, type, and location of defects
5. Defect costs
6. Defect trends
7. Development performance
8. Comparisons of releases, products, procedures, etc.
9. Metrics and models
10. Action items

6.2.1   Performance of the inspection process

We recommend evaluating the performance of inspections first in order to provide an opportunity for early adjustments to the inspection process and to furnish guidelines for subsequent use of the inspection data.

The performance of the inspection process is evaluated by

- The number of defects found, both overall and distributed by type of inspection and work product

    —Inspection preparation rates, examination rates, and work product sizes

    —Inspection effort, by type of work product

    —Required rework, distributed by defect category and work product

A few basic questions should be answered by this information.

- What is the defect content of the product?
- Were the preparation rates, examination rates, and work product sizes consistent with standards and expectations?
- What resources were used?
- Was the effort reasonable with respect to the quality gains?

Inspection performance should be analyzed continuously, using small sets of inspection data, in order to maintain in-process control of the inspections. Compare the inspection results with specifications, expectations, and experience to assess their reasonableness. Only perform more detailed data analysis when the overall performance results are understood.

6.2.2   Identifying defect-prone components

Perhaps the most significant result of inspection data analysis is the identification of defect-prone components within or close to each development phase. This ability is provided by using statistical process control (SPC) techniques, developed within the discipline of industrial engineering. SPC has evolved from the measurement and analysis of tangible hardware products and their manufacturing steps, where the development stage is substantially controlled and the measurements are reliable.

In-process inspections, however, are used when the product is often intangible and the development process is intellectual. Here, the development process cannot be controlled. Also, the measurements cannot be considered unquestionably reliable. There is an inherent variation in the measurements made by in-process inspections, which involve applying the human intellect to uncover problems in its own products. This is why it is imperative to first establish that inspections are performing satisfactorily before using SPC.

A translation of SPC techniques for the analysis of inspection data is then possible using suitable approximations and interpretations. The premise is to identify and control the quality of those components that show an exceptional propensity for defects, while they are still in the process of development. In this way, potential problems that are very costly later can be avoided. The application of SPC techniques for software inspections are illustrated later in this chapter by the PBX200 project.

6.2.3   Identifying poorly inspected components

Recognizing components that have been poorly inspected provides the ability to control the application of the inspection process; to identify those components that have received only cursory in-process quality control. Performing this analysis within the current development stage allows those components to be reinspected before they move forward, reducing the propagation of defects to following development activities, and decreasing the cost and time required for subsequent testing.

SPC analysis concurrently identifies those components that have been poorly inspected as well as defect-prone components.

6.2.4 Increased knowledge about defects

Awareness of the occurrence of defects is an important piece of our total knowledge; the more we know about our products and processes, the better they can be. Defect analysis reveals information about the nature of product weaknesses. Determining the ways in which defects occur and the processes they occur in can help determine appropriate remedial actions. There is abundant data about the effects of undetected defects, but there is still much to learn about the interactions among types and classes of defects, and between defects and processes.

Identifying the major contributors to defects within the project leads to eliminating them. One of the quality methods emphasized currently is root cause analysis. Root cause analysis identifies defects with the highest frequency and attempts to find their causes. Inspection data can provide invaluable input to an analysis effort aimed at root causes, and because the data is analyzed in-process, it can be applied to achieve improvements within the product life-cycle.

6.2.5 Understanding defect costs

The clearest understanding of what defects cost comes from analyzing project data. By calculating the cost of defects and the cost benefit of eliminating defects early, the impact of in-process quality control becomes concrete. With this understanding, project resources can be more effectively estimated and allocated to quality control processes.

Inspection data provides the number of defects found and the effort used to identify and remove these defects within the development stages. Testing furnishes comparative results for determining quality cost allocation following the development stages, and allows the relative comparison of effectiveness and cost between testing and inspections. This information allows us to balance quality control among various procedures to obtain the best results for the project.

6.2.6 Process tuning

The results of inspection data analysis can be used to continuously tune the inspection and development processes. The key characteristic of inspection data is that it informs us about the state of the product in-process, when decisive actions can substantially alter the course of continued development, and improve product cost-effectiveness within this development cycle.

6.2.7 Trend analysis

Inspection data analysis provides indicators that can reveal possible process flaws. By analyzing defect trends, such as their distribution with respect to several factors (i.e., defect type, project phase, type of work product, etc.) it is often possible to detect patterns where these factors are particularly sensitive to defects.

Inspection defect data may need to be sliced several ways to determine whether a pattern exists. Patterns that are identified can lead to quality improvement within the product, and also within the inspection and development processes.

6.2.8 Release comparisons

Accumulating inspection data for several products or product releases enables us to compare them. When the inspection process is working correctly, each product release should be "better" than the last. That is, it should have fewer defects. Inspected products would be expected to have a better quality scorecard than those that are not. If these results are not confirmed by comparison, the inspection process needs to be revised.

6.2.9 Improved metrics and models

One result of inspection data analysis is that project personnel become attuned to collecting and using quality data. At the very least, this leads to decisions based on reality, not on assumptions. Often it leads to suggestions of additional data to be collected or requests for data to be analyzed in new ways. As the person analyzing the inspection data becomes more knowledgeable, he or she can improve the data analysis methods. Thus, the reliance on metrics leads to improvements not only in the development process, but often in the metrics themselves.

Inspection data analysis also indicates the state of the development or quality management model being used. Even when there is no explicit development model, there is still an implicit concept of the "form" of the development process in use. This model can be evaluated against real, in-process results from the inspections. It can be compared against expectations and previous data. Depending on an assessment of its overall effectiveness, the model can be adjusted to better match the reality revealed by the data. The result is an improved model to apply to future projects.

6.2.10   Action items

A key use of inspection data analysis is to develop action items. Recognizing defect trends or causes is only useful if something is done about them. One way to ensure that something is done is to create action items, assign them to project personnel, and publicize them.

This first-hand knowledge is a strong motivation to collect and record the data carefully at its source—the inspection.

6.3   Analysis of Inspection Data

Inspection data analysis can be performed in a variety of ways, with the only limitation being the creativity and motivation of the analyst. This section illustrates a few, fundamental analytic approaches that can be applied and built on. Five examples are used that are derived from actual project inspection records, although the names and identification of the projects are fictitious. (The name of one case, Fix Transmittals, is not fictitious. Our appreciation for this data is accorded to Bull HN Large Systems development that has permitted its use and their attribution.) The projects illustrated, with a brief summary of their use, are

- TACK—evaluation of inspection performance
- PBX200—SPC techniques
- Dispatcher—defect analysis
- MCOS—process inferences
- Fix Transmittals—assessment of product performance

6.3.1   TACK project

The TACK project, undertaken in an international electronics firm, examined the data for a large number of inspections of C code. The results of their analysis are shown in Table 6.1.

These results are disappointing. The density of the major defects found is particularly low, while the preparation and examination rates are very high. The inspection specifications called for preparation and examination rates of 200 lines per hour or less. By comparison, another large project within the same company adhering to these same inspection guidelines, identified 15 to 20 major defects per 1000 lines of code (KLOC) of C for 250,000 lines of code. It was obvious that the TACK

TABLE 6.1   TACK Project C Code Inspections

Factor	Result
Number of inspections	904
Total size inspected	92,375 lines of C source code
Preparation rate	1014 lines per hour
Examination rate	913 lines per hour
Major defect density	1 per 1000 lines of source code

project's 400 percent greater examination and preparation rates had significantly reduced their ability to detect major defects. Because their defect detection rate was so low, they did not pursue any further inspection data analysis, but rather sought to identify why the inspection process was allowed to operate uncontrolled.

The TACK project demonstrates that process control can be lost by delaying inspection performance analysis. This evaluation is simple to perform and informative. In truth, a number of earlier, informal, inspection performance evaluations by TACK were performed, but the attitude of project management did not support the active use of the data. Opportunities were missed to adjust the inspection process, to gain better control of product development, and to obtain valuable insight into the development process.

As a result of this analysis, the TACK project implemented a series of remedial management and staff seminars that emphasized inspection performance guidelines and management process control techniques. In addition, new estimating and project planning procedures giving greater emphasis to inspections were instituted.

Were the inspections worthwhile? Interestingly, the project thought so despite their relatively poor performance. But their conclusion is not quantitatively substantiated. The TACK project demonstrated, more by their disregard than by their observance, these principles of inspection performance analysis.

1. Analyze inspection performance continuously, on small sets of inspection data.
2. Compare the results with specifications, experience, and expectations to assess their reasonableness.
3. Use the results to actively control the inspection process, and to make modifications as needed.
4. Perform more detailed data analysis only when the performance results are acceptable and understood.

6.3.2 PBX200 project

In contrast to the large number of inspections considered by the TACK project, this example evaluated 25 inspections of detail design and code modules. These modules were enhancements to the software features of a local office telephone switching system, or PBX, required by an upgrade to the hardware. The results of the inspections of both the detail designs and source code (in C) were analyzed together, as their inspection characteristics were very similar. A listing of the 25 PBX200 inspection records, without the detailed defect data, is shown in Fig. 6.1. The inspections were conducted over the 5 months February through June 1988.

6.3.2.1 Performance analysis.
The inspection performance analysis (Fig. 6.2) shows that there were 23 new inspections and two reinspections. Overall

- Approximately 7500 lines were inspected
- The density of the major defects that were detected was 13 per 1000 lines (KL)
- The cost was 42 staff-hours per KL
- The average inspection rates were 250 lines per hour for preparation and 195 lines per hour for examination
- The average size of the materials inspected was 300 lines
- Three people comprised the inspection teams

The density of the major defects that were detected, 13 per KL, is somewhat lower than expected for detail design and code inspections. The examination and preparation rates exceeded the guidelines of 150 lines per hour established by the PBX200 inspection standards. This may explain the somewhat lower defect density.

The defect density, shown in Fig. 6.3, is inversely proportional to the examination rate, increasing as the examination rate decreases. At an examination rate of 150 lines per hour, the defect density is estimated to increase to approximately 20 major defects per KL, using linear regression, which matches expectations.

Three factors known to affect the density of the defects that are detected and the performance of the inspections are the examination rate, preparation rate, and the work product size. The examination rate determines how much time the inspectors spend inspecting the materials as a team, which affects the level of detail of their coverage and the time for team synergy to develop. Preparation rate affects how knowledgeable the inspection team is, while the work product size tends to negatively affect both the examination and preparation rates.

NUM	COMPONENT	INSP-DATE	MOD	MEET	INSP	DSP	LINES	DUR	TEAM	PREP	RWRK	EFFRT	RATE	DEF	MAJ	DENS	COMP-DATE
1	DISP FUNCTION	02/16/88	CLYD	I	FE	C	280	1.25	3	3	1	7.8	224	9	3	10.7	02/17/88
2	TRANS TYPE 1	02/26/88	MACH	I	FE	R	280	2	3	2.5	30	38.5	140	14	4	14.3	03/02/88
3	TRANS TYPE 1	03/04/88	MACH	R	FE	C	280	1.5	3	1.5	2	8.0	187	5	2	7.1	03/07/88
4	PROG KEYS	03/14/88	CLYD	I	FE	C	414	2	3	5	3	14.0	207	15	14	33.8	03/15/88
5	STATUS DISP	03/31/88	MACH	I	FE	C	520	2.25	3	3.5	7.5	17.8	231	17	10	19.2	04/11/88
6	TRANS TYPE 2	04/04/88	MACH	I	FE	C	1200	2.25	3	3.5	10	20.3	533	10	4	3.3	04/07/88
7	OPS	04/07/88	MACH	I	FE	C	240	1.5	3	2	7.5	14.0	160	8	1	4.2	04/12/88
8	LCD - SERVICE	04/12/88	PITT	I	FE	A	80	0.5	3	1.5	0	3.0	160	2	0	0.0	04/12/88
9	STATUS BUS	04/13/88	MACH	I	FE	R	440	2	3	3	30	39.0	220	18	10	22.7	04/27/88
10	LCD - TERM	04/14/88	PITT	I	FE	C	85	0.75	3	1.5	0.5	4.3	113	2	2	23.5	04/14/88
11	OPS	04/15/88	CLYD	I	FE	C	81	1	3	1	1	5.0	81	8	1	12.3	04/15/88
12	STATUS DMA	04/21/88	MACH	I	FE	C	330	2.5	3	3	10	20.5	132	10	8	24.2	05/18/88
13	LCD - USER	04/22/88	DARE	I	FE	C	250	1	3	1.5	0.5	5.0	250	4	1	4.0	04/22/88
14	STATUS BUS	04/26/88	MACH	R	FE	C	440	1	3	1.5	15	19.5	440	9	3	6.8	05/18/88
15	WAIT DISPLAY	05/02/88	CLYD	I	FE	A	350	1.5	3	2	0	6.5	233	3	0	0.0	05/02/88
16	ACTIVE DISPLAY	05/05/88	DARE	I	FE	C	240	1	3	2	0.5	5.5	240	4	4	16.7	05/16/88
17	STATUS DISK	05/18/88	MACH	I	FE	C	570	2.5	3	3.5	8	19.0	228	16	2	3.5	06/08/88
18	TRANS TYPE 4	05/26/88	MACH	I	FE	R	400	3	3	2.25		11.3	133	18	4	10.0	05/27/88
19	AUDIBLE ALERT	06/14/88	CLYD	I	FE	A	80	0.5	3	1.3	0	2.8	160	0	0	0.0	06/16/88
20	CHAN HANDLER	06/16/88	MACH	I	FE	C	200	1.8	4	4.5	9	20.7	111	13	8	40.0	06/17/88
21	DIAL_0 AND LDN	06/18/88	MACH	I	FE	C	36	0.5	3	1.7	1	4.2	72	5	2	55.6	06/20/88
22	DIRECTED RECAL	06/22/88	DARE	I	FE	C	370	2	3	4	5	15.0	185	13	5	13.5	06/23/88
23	DMA HANDLER	06/23/88	MACH	I	FE	C	40	0.3	3	1	0.5	2.4	133	2	2	50.0	06/23/88
24	ALERT/CON	06/24/88	DARE	I	FE	C	120	1	3	3	0.5	6.5	120	7	3	25.0	06/24/88
25	DO NOT DISTURB	06/30/88	MACH	I	FE	C	140	0.8	3	2	0.5	4.9	175	8	5	35.7	07/10/88

Figure 6.1 PBX200 inspection records (summary data).

```
***** PBX200 FEATURE ENHANCEMENT INSPECTION DATA ANALYSIS ******

****************** INSPECTION RECORD TOTALS ******************

    Records:   25  Total Effort:   315.3      Total Lines: 7466

Exam. Effort: 109.2      % Exam:   35%   Effort/1000 Lines: 42.2

Prep. Effort: 61.25      % Prep:   19%      Def/1000 Lines: 29.5

Rwrk. Effort: 143        % Rwrk:   45%      Maj/1000 Lines: 13.1

    Total Maj:   98       % Maj:   45%   Rework/1000 Lines: 19.2

     Defects: 220  Rework/Maj:    1.46      Rework/Def:   0.65


   Inspections:   23  Reinspections:    2     Overviews:    0

****************** INSPECTION RECORD AVERAGES ****************
     Duration:    1.5       Effort:  12.6            Lines: 298.6

    Team Size:    3.0      Defects:   8.8    Effort/Defect:   1.4

   Exam. Rate: 194.7          Maj:   3.9       Effort/Maj:   3.2

   Prep. Rate: 248.6  Prep/Person:   1.2    Effort/Person:   4.1

                         Rework:   5.7
```

Figure 6.2 PBX200 feature enhancement inspection data analysis.

Figure 6.4 indicates that the examination and preparation rates are directly proportional. Reducing the preparation rate from 250 to about 150 lines per hour corresponds to an examination rate of 150 lines per hour. Further, Fig. 6.5 shows that the preparation rate is directly related to work product size, decreasing as work product size decreases.

Therefore, as a strategy to increase defect detection, the PBX200 project should inspect less than 200 lines of material at a time, prepared at a rate of 150 lines per hour, and then examined at 150 lines per hour.

Figure 6.6 shows the effort for detecting major defects (rework effort is not included) in staff hours versus examination rate. Although definitive conclusions cannot be drawn, the region of lowest cost per defect appears to occur at an examination rate of approximately 125 to 250 lines per hour. Looking at the inspection records in Fig. 6.1, the highest per defect costs were incurred by those work products that are considered to be of high quality (low density of major defects). As the quality of a work product cannot be determined prior to its inspection,

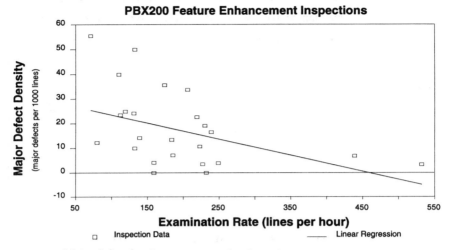

Figure 6.3   Major defect density versus examination rate.

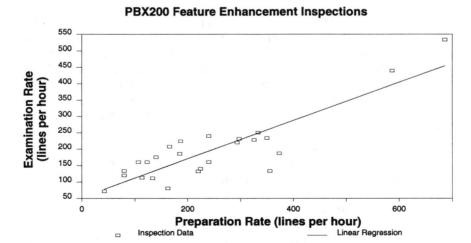

Figure 6.4   Examination rate versus preparation rate.

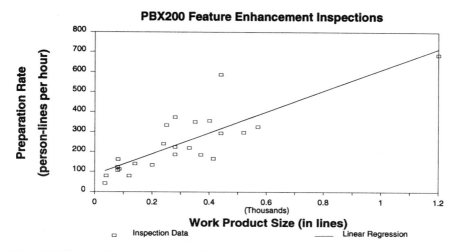

Figure 6.5 Preparation rate versus work product size.

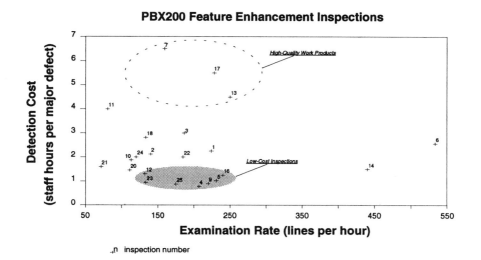

Figure 6.6 Cost per major defect versus examination rate.

the data indicates that following the inspection guidelines for examination rate, preparation rate, and work product size helps assure both high product quality and the best inspection performance related to cost.

The cost of following these guidelines is more than offset by saving the far greater time and effort otherwise required to find and remove these defects in subsequent testing and in later operation of the product.

6.3.2.2 Defect analysis. The results of the performance analysis of the PBX200 inspections appears to be reasonable and understood, and further analysis of the defects and then of process control characteristics are warranted.

Using Pareto analysis (where the highest percentage occurrences are considered first) the dominant type and class of the major defects were Logic (LO) and Wrong, shown by Figs. 6.7 and 6.8. There can be many interpretations of this data, depending on the project. Environmental and product factors all influence the meaning of the analysis. For PBX200, this analysis indicated that the specifications were satisfactory, but that there were problems encountered implementing the feature enhancements in the detail design and code. (In this and many cases, Functionality/Missing would indicate problems with the specifications.)

The ratio of defect severity for most projects whose inspection results we have reviewed has been approximately 20 percent major to 80 percent minor defects. (We define *major* defects as "operational" within the

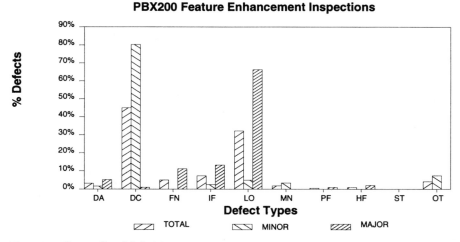

Figure 6.7 Composite of defect types.

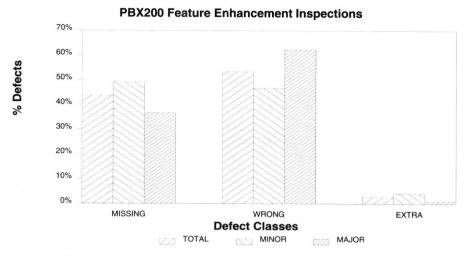

Figure 6.8 Composite of defect classes.

product, and *minor* defects as "representational" of the product.) For PBX200, the relatively high proportion of major defects of 44 percent, shown in Fig. 6.9, seems to indicate that either the implementation standards were fairly well defined and followed, or that minor inconsistencies in representation were not actively sought during the inspections. A review of the work products by the project manager would quickly determine which was the case.

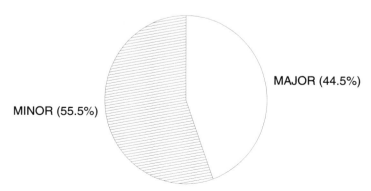

Figure 6.9 Defect severity as major and minor (%)

6.3.2.3 Process control. Looked at from the perspective of using the data to control the quality of the work product, the analysis of overall inspection performance masks the underlying diversity of the individual inspection results. It is just this diversity that is the measure of control. To reveal the diversity of the data and to achieve some ability to manage the quality of the work products within each development phase, we recommend the use of SPC[1] techniques. SPC can identify both defect prone and poorly inspected work products, and uses graphical techniques, called "control charts," to recognize those inspections whose results are "anomalous," meaning significantly different from the norm.

The technique we suggest for using SPC control charts for inspection data is approximate, as SPC presupposes that measurements are made of a process that is substantially under statistical control to identify those few instances where control has varied. SPC also considers that the measurements themselves are reliable. This is not wholly true for the PBX200 project, or for any other inspection results where an intellectual process, the inspection, is being used to measure an intellectual product. However, we believe that approximate SPC methods can be applied to inspection data sufficient to identify specific work products for further quality control actions. Three steps are used for this analysis.

1. First, a control chart is prepared for the major defect densities found by the inspections in the sample set (in this case, the 25 PBX200 inspections). The inspections that have defect counts that are unusually large or small are respectively identified as potentially "defect-prone" or "poorly inspected."

2. Then, the "dispersions" (difference from the mean) of the work product sizes, preparation rates, and examination rates for the inspections in the sample set are charted and examined to confirm or deny the initial determination from Step 1.

3. Finally, any work products having some sort of identified anomaly not resolved in the preceding two steps are further checked with the detailed inspection results to substantiate their anomaly.

Step 1.   To prepare a control chart of the major defect density, using the 25 PBX200 inspections as an example, first consider the major defect density of each work product to be "attribute" data (counts of defects per unit inspected). Next, determine the mean defect density, $\bar{\mu}$, of the set of inspections. Then, the upper control limit (UCL) and the lower control limit (LCL) are established using $\bar{\mu}$. The work product size is expressed in this case as KL, and the defect density as defects per KL.

However, because the size of the inspected work products vary, the UCL and LCL for each inspection also vary, depending on the size of each inspected work product (called the "area of opportunity"). To simplify these charts, the UCL and LCL are held constant over the set of inspections analyzed. The average work product size is used to determine the UCL, and the maximum work product size is used to determine the LCL (where the LCL is never taken as less than zero). This is an approximation. However, we believe that these simplifying assumptions provide sufficient sensitivity for this analysis of admittedly approximate data.

Using these assumptions, the equations (derived from Wheeler and Chambers[1]) for the mean defect density, $\bar{\mu}$, the UCL, and the LCL for the control chart of major defect density are

$$\bar{\mu} = \frac{\displaystyle\sum_{i=1}^{n} \text{defects}_i}{\displaystyle\sum_{i=1}^{n} \text{work product size}_i}$$

$$\text{UCL} = \bar{\mu} + 3\sqrt{\frac{\bar{\mu}}{\text{average work product size}}}$$

$$\text{LCL} = \left| \begin{array}{c} \bar{\mu} - 3\sqrt{\dfrac{\bar{\mu}}{\text{maximum work product size}}} \\ 0 \end{array} \right| \text{ the greater of}$$

The major defect density of each inspection, μ, the mean defect density of the set, $\bar{\mu}$, the UCL, and the LCL are then charted. We have chosen to sort the inspections in ascending order by their inspection date, but other sequences can be used.

From the resulting control chart, shown in Fig. 6.10, inspections number 4, 20, 21, 23, and 25 are identified as potentially "defect-prone." This means that their major defect density equals or exceeds the UCL. Inspections 6, 8, 15, 17, and 19 are identified as potentially "poorly inspected," as their major defects are equal to or less than the LCL. This completes Step 1.

Step 2.   Next, for those inspections identified in Step 1, distinguish apparently well-inspected work products from those that are poorly inspected. A well-performed inspection is considered to be one whose

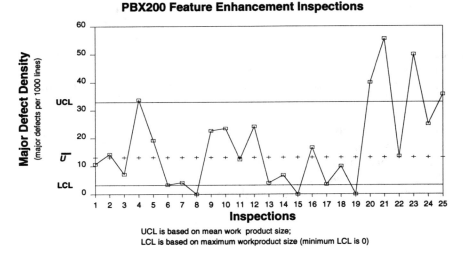

Figure 6.10 Control chart of major defect density.

preparation and examination rates are reasonably close to project standards. The work product is usually of moderate size as well. On the other hand, a poorly inspected work product has few defects detected, high preparation and/or examination rates, and may be large.

The dispersion of the examination rates, preparation rates, and work product sizes are plotted for the set of inspections. An upper limit of two standard deviations from the average, called the "+2 sigma level," is then determined and used to indicate excessive departure from the average. The reason for this is that 90 to 98 percent of the data is usually within 2 standard deviations of the mean. Inspections that exceed the "+2 sigma level" are considered anomalous. Other values for sigma may be used, depending on the variability of these factors and the degree of sensitivity desired. Figures 6.11, 6.12, and 6.13 illustrate the resulting dispersion charts for the 25 PBX200 inspections.

From these charts, we see that of the defect-prone candidates, inspections 4, 20, and 25 were all examined and prepared at a moderate rate, and were of moderate size, between 150 and 500 lines. These work products are therefore considered well inspected and classed as defect-prone. The other potentially defect-prone work products, 21 and 23, are both small; each less than 50 lines. Defect density is magnified for small work products (one major defect in 50 lines would produce a density of 20 defects per KL), and these work products are therefore considered acceptable, although if either were critical they would warrant further investigation.

Of the potentially poorly inspected work products, only inspection 6

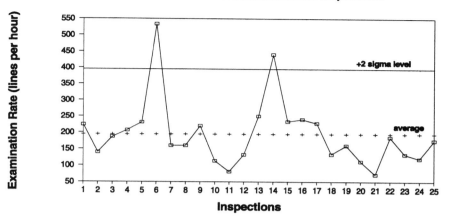

Figure 6.11 Dispersion of examination rate.

stands out. It has unusually high preparation and examination rates, and is very large. Inspections 8, 15, 17, and 19 were apparently adequate inspections of "high-quality" work products.

Be aware, though, that this assessment is subject to personal judgment and is not exact. A high-quality work product will have few defects even though it is well inspected, and conversely, a defect-prone work product may show defects despite being poorly inspected. This completes Step 2.

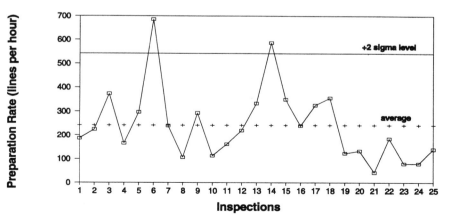

Figure 6.12 Dispersion of preparation rate.

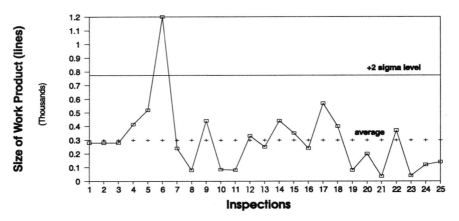

Figure 6.13 Dispersion of work product size.

Step 3.   Although the major defect density of inspection 14 was acceptable, both the preparation and examination rates for this inspection are very high, and it is considered as anomalous in Step 2. When the detailed characteristics of inspection 14 are examined in the inspection records, listed in Fig. 6.1, we see that it was a reinspection. A reinspection can be adequately conducted at higher preparation and examination rates because the inspection team has prior experience and familiarity with the work product, and inspection 14 is therefore considered acceptable.

This completes the three steps recommended for the SPC analysis of inspection data.

As a result of following these three steps, four work products have been identified for special action to control their quality. This is about 20 percent of the feature enhancements. This corresponds to the "80/20 rule" of conventional wisdom, where 80 percent of the problems are often attributable to 20 percent of the components. A variety of actions may be taken for the work products identified as being defect-prone. Depending on the project and circumstances, these work products may be redesigned, reworked, reinspected, or scheduled for more stringent testing. The work product in inspection 6 was clearly poorly inspected, and should be reinspected, with tighter control of the preparation and examination rates. This work product may also be divided among a few inspection meetings because of its size.

Through the use of SPC analysis, in-process inspection data can provide us with the ability to quantitatively control product quality during development, if a few actions are taken.

1. Collect and store inspection data in an inspection data base.

2. Use a tool that can easily perform statistical analysis of the inspection data [this analysis was performed using Lotus Inspection Data System (LIDS), incorporating SPC techniques].

3. Analyze the inspection data in a timely manner to facilitate process control close to the point of origin of any anomalies so that they can be corrected before they can propagate.

4. Evaluate the inspection results in small batches to simplify the analysis, and to produce timely results. Do this by using the concept of a "moving average" as necessary. Batches are formed from the current inspections and the most recent past inspections, dropping older inspections when the batch size exceeds a workable and/or meaningful limit. This may be approximately two dozen inspections.

5. Apply controls to maintain work product size, preparation rates, and examination rates consistent with project guidelines. Christenson and Huang (Chapter 4, reference 1) found that inspection effectiveness was improved by establishing and managing work product size, preparation effort, and examination rate to recommended limits.

6. Review the averages of the inspection performance factors over time, and revise the guidelines as necessary from analysis of the inspection data and perceived results.

6.3.3 Dispatcher project

Dispatcher is designed to distribute various types of messages and transactions among subsystems, and consolidates a number of previously disparate systems. In the previous analysis of the PBX200 inspections, we focused on using inspection performance measurements to control product quality within the development process. In the Dispatcher example, we describe some of the ways inspection defect data can be used to characterize the product and the project.

6.3.3.1 Defect density.

Defect density was the primary measurement used in Dispatcher, and is expressed in terms of the number of defects detected per unit inspected, in this case defects per KL, and for code as per 1000 noncommentary source lines (KNCSL). A reasonably high overall defect density usually indicates that the inspection process is working well, while a consistently low defect density is more likely to reflect an ineffective inspection process than a fault-free product.

This is not to say that a high defect density is desirable. One goal of the inspection process is to continually identify and eliminate as many

TABLE 6.2 **Defect Density by Phase for Dispatcher Project**

Phase	Major defects per KL
Project plan	1.5
Requirements	2.2
High-level design	1.3
Low-level design	0.7
Documentation	2.0
Code	27.7 (per KNCSL)

causes of defects as possible. If this goal is achieved, it is expected that the defect density will continually lower throughout product development. Therefore, high and low defect density are relative terms with ever-changing definitions. But whenever the defect density falls significantly below the established average, you should suspect a problem in the inspection process.

A useful breakdown of defect density is by development phase. This was done for Dispatcher as shown in Table 6.2.

This breakdown helps to pinpoint one or more areas of trouble. When the defect density indicates that there is a significant disparity between phases, as it does here, a number of questions arise.

- Is the code defect-prone?

- Do some unusual conditions surround the coding phase?

- Are the earlier inspections being performed properly?

- Can defects be recognized in the earlier phases?

We are alerted to these potential problems with the product, the development process, or the inspection process.

A further useful breakdown of defect density is by components. This is particularly true for the Dispatcher code inspections, illustrated in Table 6.3, where the defect distribution is far from uniform.

The difference in defect density between Comp-1 and the other components bears further investigation. In this case, Comp-1 contains a disproportionate number of standards defects. Greater familiarity with project standards would have eliminated this class of defects and reduced the defect density to 26.3.

When defect density is consistently well above the average for specific types of components, it is possible that those components are defect-prone. Conversely, a low defect density may indicate components that are more defect-free than the others. Any significant deviation from the mean defect density should be investigated. It is a good idea to

TABLE 6.3   Defect Density by Component for Dispatcher Project

Component	Defects per KNCSL
Comp-1	52.1
Comp-2	19.5
Comp-3	16.1
Comp-4	20.8
Comp-5	15.7

require a reinspection of defect-prone components after rework. The tendency to introduce new defects is likely to be greater in these components than it is in most.

It is wise to spend more time testing defect-prone components and products. Testers are advised to plan extra test cases that specifically look for the types of defects that most frequently occur in these components.

6.3.3.2 Distribution of defect types. A distribution of defects by their types is likely to show clustering. It is typical of defect data that a large number of defects arise from a small number of causes. By further breaking down defect categories into narrower classifications, it is possible to isolate problem areas. For example, Fig. 6.14 shows the defect distribution for the Dispatcher high-level design phase.

Note that the data demonstrates the clustering effect, with the largest numbers of defects ascribed to documentation (DO), functionality (FN), syntax (SN), and logic (LO). The other defect types, standards (ST), human factors (HF), interface (IF), requirements (RE), and data (DA) are of far lower significance. The remaining defect type, other (OT), is used for unanticipated conditions, and should always be small. If it is ever large, then the underlying conditions should be investigated immediately.

The analyst manually broke the documentation and functionality defects into greater detail, using the defect descriptions from the inspection defect reports, and selected appropriate subordinate defect types. This process was performed at two levels, providing considerable detail, although subjective, about these two defect types that dominate the distribution. Figure 6.15 shows a breakdown of the documentation defects. The majority of defects are description (DE), either missing or wrong. The other defect types, clarity (CL), grammar (GR), logic (LO), human factors (HF), content (CN), and format (FT) were less significant.

These again can be further expanded, as shown in Fig. 6.16. The description defects are refined into seven areas: sparseness (SP), defini-

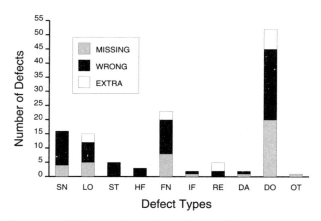

Figure 6.14 High-level design inspections—distribution of primary defect types.

tion (DF), misleading (MI), terminology (TM), labels (LB), verbosity (VB), and explanation (EX). This breakdown shows that the document contains wrong terminology, misleading descriptions, and missing explanations. This may indicate a lack of understanding of some portions of the product. The missing information may indicate a problem with the requirements or with the flow of information within the project.

A similar analysis of the functionality defects, shown in Figs. 6.17

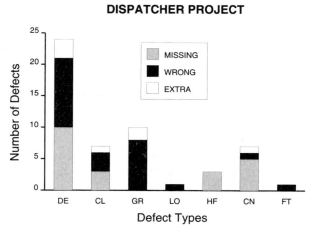

Figure 6.15 High-level design inspections—distribution of documentation (DO) defects.

DISPATCHER PROJECT

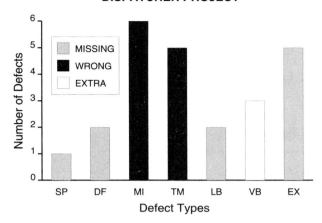

Figure 6.16 High-level design inspections—distribution of description (DE) defects.

and 6.18, indicates that they are concentrated in the feature (FE) and definition (DF) categories, versus dependency (DP), contention (CT), and validation (VL). The most significant feature problem is missing information, with either an entire feature not considered (NC), or some case (CS) overlooked, with extraneous information (EX) and the implementation (IP) of lower significance.

Clearly there is some requirements-related disconnect. Further in-

DISPATCHER PROJECT

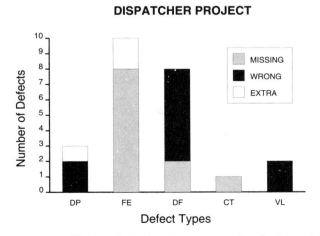

Figure 6.17 High-level design inspections—distribution of functionality (FN) defects.

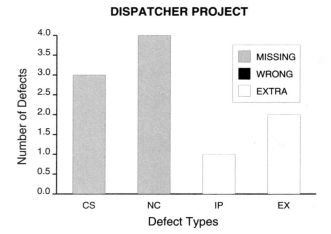

Figure 6.18 High-level design inspections—distribution of feature (FE) defects.

vestigation may show that the requirements are unclear, or that the development team is working from outdated requirements, or that development is not appropriately familiar with the requirements.

By breaking the defects down into ever-narrowing categories, it is often possible to isolate and eliminate a defect source. In this way, we can improve the product and often the development process in the same step. Furthermore, we may discover that our data classifications are too broad and need to be refined to provide more useful information, thus improving the inspection process as well.

6.3.4 The MCOS project

The microcomputer operating system (MCOS) project demonstrates how inspection data analysis can be used to derive inferences about the development process. In this example, the results of 23 inspections of Pascal source code for a new microcomputer operating system were evaluated. The overall performance of the 23 inspections is shown by Fig. 6.19, and is satisfactory. The average preparation and examination rates were approximately 150 lines per hour, and the average work product size was about 200 noncommentary source lines (NCSL). Fourteen major defects were detected per KNCSL, and about 1 hour of rework was required per major defect.

Not surprisingly, the performance of the MCOS inspections is similar to that of the PBX200 project. Inspection performance has been found to be reproducible for similar types of work and environments. In this

```
*************** MCOS CODE INSPECTION  DATA ANALYSIS **********

******************** INSPECTION RECORD TOTALS *****************

   Records:    23  Total Effort:196.4           Total Lines: 4549

Total Exam: 105.4        % Exam:   61%  Effort/1000 Lines:   43.2

Total Prep:  73.94       % Prep:   38%      Def/1000 Lines:   57.2

Total Rwrk:  69.75       % Rwrk:   36%      Maj/1000 Lines:   14.3

       Maj:  65          % Maj:    25%  Rework/1000 Lines:   15.3

   Defects: 260      Rework/Maj:    1.07       Rework/Def:    0.27


  Inspections:   23    Reinspections:   0      Overviews:     0

****************** INSPECTION RECORD AVERAGES *****************

  Duration:   1.5         Effort:  8.5             Lines:  197.8

Team Size:    3.4        Defects: 11.3     Effort/Defect:    0.8

Exam. Rate: 162.7           Maj:  2.8         Effort/Maj:    3.0

Prep. Rate: 149.7   Prep/Person:  1.3      Effort/Person:    2.5

                         Rework:  3.5
```

Figure 6.19 MCOS code inspection data analysis.

case, both projects involved inspecting detailed software logic for system control applications with experienced developers. Despite being produced by different companies and with different programming languages (C and Pascal), inspection results were comparable.

The relationship of inspection performance factors is also similar between MCOS and PBX200. For instance, Fig. 6.20 shows that the major defect density decreases as examination rate increases. This seems to be universal among inspections, regardless of project or work product.

The distribution of the MCOS defect types and classes, shown in Figs. 6.21 and 6.22, shows a pattern that is significantly different from that of PBX200 and from expectations. The expected distribution for code inspections is that the majority of major defects would be wrong logic, with some contribution of data (DA), interface (IF), and a few other types. But the predominant major defect category of the MCOS inspections is missing functionality. Also meaningful is the very broad array of significant major defects—LO, FN, DA, and DC. This pattern

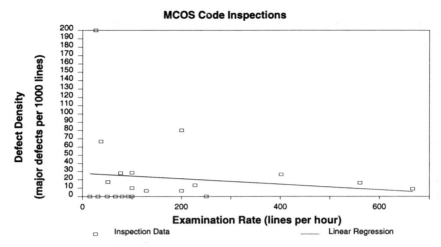

Figure 6.20 Major defects versus examination rate.

of defect types, and the predominance of missing information, indicates that design problems are surfacing at the code inspections.

The probable reason is that a detail design specification was not prepared by MCOS. Design decisions made during coding are more hurried, poorly coordinated, and are made at the wrong development level. Coding is more concerned with the application of logic rather than with the specification of function and consequently does not accomplish design particularly well.

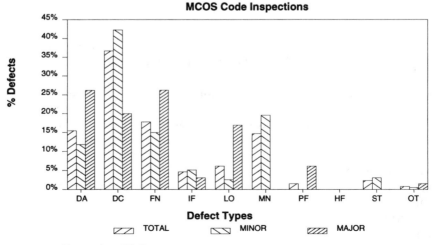

Figure 6.21 Composite of defect types.

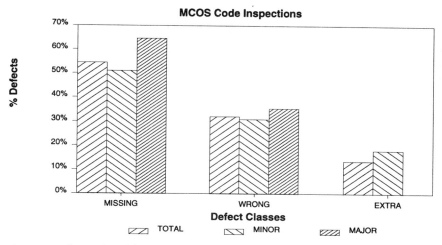

Figure 6.22 Composite of defect classes.

The recommendation from this analysis was to incorporate a detail design phase to reduce these problems, with inspection of the design prior to coding. This example shows how inferences about the development process can be derived from the analysis of inspection data.

6.3.5 Fix transmittals

The ultimate assessment of inspections, however, lies in the reduction of defects experienced by the customer. Our last example uses measures other than those provided by inspections, in this case reports of operational failures (bugs), to evaluate the effect of inspections on the software maintenance process at Bull HN Large Systems Software Products.

6.3.5.1 Bull HN. Bull HN is an international manufacturer of computer hardware and software, and has been using in-process inspections in many phases of their systems development. The Large Systems project began applying inspections during 1990 in the corrective maintenance process for their operational software. They call these corrections "transmittals."

As with many projects, Bull HN measured the problems found in the use of their software. Problems in any product are a problem, but are especially troublesome when they are intended to fix previous problems. Aside from the cost and disruption to the product, these second-order problems (bugs in bug fixes) can result in further deterioration of user confidence which is already diminished, creating considerably more difficulties. From 1989 through 1991, Bull HN measured more than 600 of these transmittals for second-order failures. The results of these measurements are illustrated by Fig. 6.23, where the density of the reported failures of the transmittals is compared on a relative scale from 0 to 6.

Prior to August 1990, the average relative level of failures for the transmittals was 4. At that time inspections were introduced into the maintenance process, and from August 1990 through May 1991, the average level of failures was 1. In the case of transmittals this fourfold improvement in failure density is a very significant improvement in product quality.

6.3.5.2 Other metrics. The final evaluation of the effectiveness of inspections is not found directly in the inspection data, but in other measures of product development and performance. As the Bull HN example demonstrates, inspection data is only one part of the information associated with any development project. And it only tells a part of the story. To better assess the effect of inspections on the product and development process, inspection data is most useful when combined with other process and product measurements. Some of these other measures are

- Operational failures, by type and cost (both to resolve the initial problem and those incurred by the user)
- Product complexity, both internal and related to interfaces

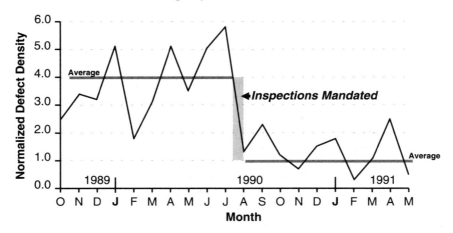

Bull HN Large Systems Software Products

Figure 6.23 Relative defect density of "Fix Transmittals."

- Development process costs, by phase and function
- Test failures, test effort, and cost of testing

When used with inspection data, these other measures determine how to best employ inspections to control the quality of the product. Although this is not a complete listing of all possible product and development metrics, these few examples provide useful data about the product and the development process. This data helps put inspection results into perspective.

6.4   Failures Versus Defects

Finally, it is important to distinguish between product failures and defects. Failures and defects are not synonymous. The most serious result of defects is product failure. The absence of identified defects provides only a partial measure of product quality and does not guarantee the absence of failures, nor does the absence of failures guarantee the absence of defects.

A *defect* is a problem with the product that is detected sometime during its development. A *failure* occurs when a product does not perform the task the user requires and expects of it during operation. This can occur when the product stops working, when the product works but in a way the customer is uncomfortable with, or when the product works as required, but does not do what the customer wants.

A good example of a product failure that is unrelated to defects is the story of the wrench at the First Annual Conference on Software Reliability in 1974. The wrench is clearly a simple tool that has worked reliably for generations. Then came the space age. In one of the early space explorations, a bolt came loose in a space capsule. An astronaut took a wrench, tightened it on the bolt, then tried to turn the bolt. Instead of the bolt, the astronaut turned. The wrench had failed—not because of any defect in design or manufacture, but simply because of an unforeseen change in the environment in which it was asked to operate.

Not all failures can be avoided. There are always circumstances we can't predict. It is important that our data analysis distinguish between failures that could have been avoided and those that probably could not. Just as the analysis of defects can improve our processes, the analysis of failures can improve our vision. Studying the things that seemed difficult to predict in the past can give us some insight into the scope of future problems.

This is not to say that all failures are unpredictable—far from it. We are only saying that they are in a class apart from defects and subject to different rules. One such rule is that they carry a very high customer cost and therefore a very high cost to product developers. Defects that do not lead to failure are still costly, but far less so than those that do. It is important, therefore, when setting quality goals, that we give highest priority to eliminating defects that are potential sources of failure.

One possible predictor of failure is the number of major defects found by inspections as a percentage of the total defects. *Major defects* are defined as those that are potential sources of failure. Since it is unlikely that even a rigorous inspection program will find all defects, when a large number of major defects are detected, this increases the probability that there is an undetected major defect in the final product. Robust testing and exercise of modules that contain a high percentage of major defects reduces the probability of failure in the deployed product.

When failures do occur, and a failure analysis identifies one or more defects as the cause, this information should be fed back into the inspection process. By analyzing failures versus defects, you can learn more about the interaction between defects and failures, modify the defect categories, and improve the detection of failure-producing defects in your inspections. Keep in mind that this is an iterative process, and that quality is a long-term commitment. Many of the steps you take today will have their results further down the road.

6.5 Conclusion

We are accustomed to thinking of defects in a negative sense, as a partial measure of the distance we need to travel to attain quality. But information about defects is also one of our assets. Through appropriate analysis, inspection data tells us things about our products and processes that we could not otherwise know. When inspection data is put to use, it can provide us with keys to controlling and improving our products and processes.

In this chapter, we have tried to give you a flavor for the ways inspection data can be employed, particularly in the use of SPC analysis of inspection results for the control of product quality during development. We do not profess to have learned all that inspection data analysis has to offer. But we have found that the more we collect, collate, and analyze inspection results, the more we learn about product quality, the inspection process, the development process, and the data itself. This, after all, is the objective of inspection data analysis.

6.6 References

1. Wheeler, D. J. and Chambers, D. S., *Understanding Statistical Process Control,* SPC Press, Knoxville, Tenn., 1986.

Inspection Education and Support

In this chapter we discuss the education and support needed for a successful inspection program. Foremost is an education program of fundamental courses that we have found to be necessary. We emphasize the need for complete and timely education because an inspection program is only as good as the people who employ it. These people, no matter how talented they are, are only as good as their knowledge of inspections.

Additionally, we specify two other types of support: what we call "coordinating" activities, and the tools and media that aid the implementation and use of inspections. We also explain how education can be administered and how the support elements can be customized for a project's needs.

7.1 Characteristics of an Inspection Support Program

An inspection support program focuses on corporate quality objectives, in terms of the quality needs of the development project. Therefore, to be most effective, the inspection support program is oriented not to individuals, but to the project. It is modular and structured, involving courses, coordinating activities, and supporting tools and aids. The program that we suggest is shown in Fig. 7.1.

The support program addresses all project members, both management and staff, and concentrates on providing them with information that is immediate, complete, and relevant to their needs and those of the project. Therefore, different levels of education and support are provided for each of the project responsibilities—managing, applying, and coordinating inspections. By "coordinating," we mean the activities performed by the inspection coordinator to assess, implement, administer, evaluate, and maintain inspections.

7.2 In-Process Inspection Education

Comprehensive education is the most significant part of inspection support. We have found a combination of courses, such as those summarized in Fig. 7.2, to be effective for establishing the necessary in-

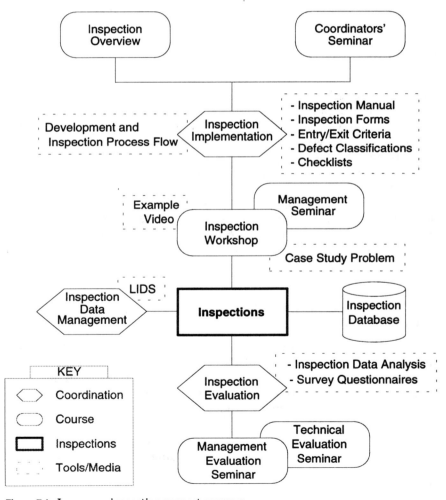

Figure 7.1 In-process inspection support program.

Activity	Participants	Purpose	Length
Inspection overview	Project managers Senior staff	Provide knowledge for project use of inspections	4 hours
Inspection coordinators' seminar	Inspection coordinators	Develop inspection coordination techniques	4 hours
Inspection workshop	Project staff	Provide the ability to perform inspections	1 day
Management seminar	Project management	Provide guidelines for managing inspections	2–4 hours
Management and Technical evaluation seminars	Management Staff (Client) (Others)	Present inspection results and recommendations	2–4 hours each

Figure 7.2 In-process inspection education program.

spection knowledge among management and staff that has resulted in highly effective inspection programs.

Experience has shown that the best method for educating employees about inspections is on a project basis. One reason is the need to have all project members knowledgeable about inspections so that they can contribute to the process together. The need to tailor the education to the project's needs is equally important.

The sections that follow describe each course, and some conditions for possible variations.

7.2.1 Inspection overview

The inspection overview, outlined in Fig. 7.3, is a general description of in-process inspections, what to expect from them, and what they require. It is designed to provide project management with the information they need to make an educated decision about whether or not to implement an inspection program.

The inspection overview answers the following questions:

- What are process management and quality control?
- How are inspections performed?
- How are inspections directed?
- What are the benefits?

Objective:
- Establish an understanding of the inspection process by project leadership
- Define the necessary project costs and the expected benefits
- Obtain a commitment to initiate the program

Length:
- 2 to 4 hours

Audience:
- Project management and key staff--from a few to many

Content:
- Process management for quality control
- Description of the inspection process
- Directing the inspection process
- Inspection data and results
- Inspection costs
- Implementation requirements
- Support programs

Modifications/adaptations:
- Specific project development process, quality, and cost data

Figure 7.3 Course outline—inspection overview.

- What are the costs?
- What resources are required?
- How do I start?

Our experience has been that half a day allows ample time to present the seminar and answer questions. The most successful inspection overviews include key technical personnel as well as project management. When they both understand the benefits and purpose of the inspection process, they are in a better position to decide together whether inspections fit the project's managerial and technical needs, and to support the use of inspections should they choose to go ahead.

The objective of the overview is for management to determine if inspections should be used. The overview should therefore relate the concepts of managing development quality to the inspection process, and how inspections contribute to the project. The cost and effort required by inspections need to be compared with their expected benefits, and the steps necessary to implement inspections should be defined.

The best way to tailor the inspection overview is to present data from the project itself (if available) or from a similar project that successfully implemented inspections. Project data might include

- A review of the project budget, including the estimated impact of inspections. Even if this is an educated guess it helps management to assess the cost impact of incorporating inspections.

- An examination of the project's past error statistics. Past performance problems provide an estimate of the project's weaknesses and help show how inspections might benefit the project.

- An appraisal of the project's past development cycles, including time spent in testing and redevelopment. If the appraisal shows that actual development schedules have been drawn out by extensive testing and redevelopment clearly some in-process verification procedure is warranted.

When data from similar projects are used, they should demonstrate how inspections benefited those projects. Such information might include

- The number of defects found and corrected before the project went to system test.

- The relative number of user detected errors for releases that were not inspected versus those that were inspected.

- The total development time required without inspections versus the time required with an inspection program in place.

7.2.2 Inspection coordinators' seminar

The inspection coordinators' seminar, outlined in Fig. 7.4, describes the tasks required of the inspection coordinator to implement, administer, maintain, evaluate, and modify a project's inspection process. The seminar is held when there are a few new coordinators who will be performing this function for a number of projects. If there are only one or two coordinators, this same information would usually be provided using individual consultation with either an experienced coordinator from within the company or an inspection consultant. The inspection coordinator should also attend these other courses:

- Inspection overview
- Inspection workshop
- Inspection management seminar

The inspection coordinators' seminar should be adapted to the procedures and techniques that will be used by the company and the projects that are being considered.

Objective:

- Introduce the characteristics of the inspection support program
- Establish the role and responsibilities of the inspection coordinator

Length:

- 4 hours

Audience:

- Inspection coordinators

Content:

- Structure of the inspection support program
- Implementation responsibilities
- Training resources
- Inspection data management requirements
- Inspection data analysis techniques
- Inspection evaluation

Modifications/adaptations:

- The course should be adapted to company specific techniques, standards, and procedures

Figure 7.4 Course outline—inspection coordinators' seminar.

7.2.3 Inspection workshop

The central course of an inspection education program is the inspection workshop. Its objectives are to train and motivate project personnel to participate in inspection meetings. The workshop can have many formats and lengths, which can vary in our experience from 1 to 3 days. The advantages of a 1-day inspection workshop are that it is easier to schedule and requires fewer resources than a longer course. Of course, a 3-day workshop can provide much broader coverage of inspection and related topics, but we have found that a 1-day course is frequently satisfactory. Other topics, such as special moderating techniques or methods of preparing inspectable work products, can be covered in separate sessions when required.

The 1-day inspection workshop outlined in Fig. 7.5 has been very effective in many circumstances. This workshop first describes the principles of inspections and quality control, and then details all of the steps necessary to perform an inspection. It covers the roles and responsibilities of each inspector, and includes a case study inspection during which the participants practice these roles and procedures.

The 1-day workshop also discusses the performance of the case study inspection teams, the quantitative and qualitative factors that affect the effectiveness of the inspection process, and the personal interac-

Objective:
- Establish the ability to successfully perform inspections
- Clarify when and when not to apply inspections
- Motivate the participants to want to use inspections

Length:
- 1 day

Audience:
- ALL development personnel who will perform inspections
- Limited to a maximum of 25--a recommended lower limit is approximately 8

Content:
- Inspections and quality control
- The inspection process--in detail at an implementation level, featuring all roles, steps, and procedures
- Inspection case study
- Case study discussion
- Inspection performance factors
- The dynamics of inspection meetings

Special requirements:
- Video monitor--if a demonstration inspection is slow
- Case study problem, inspection reporting forms
- "Break-out" rooms--for the case study inspections

Modifications/adaptations:
- Unique project development procedures, and how they relate to inspections
- Related project or corporate inspection data and experiences
- Plans for the implementation of inspections
- Project specific standards or administrative procedures

Figure 7.5 Course outline—inspection workshop.

tions among inspectors that can influence the inspection meeting. Finally, the workshop discusses any project-specific procedures that will be used.

7.2.4 Inspection management seminar

The success of in-process inspections is dependent on the management of the inspection process. Put directly, we have never seen a successful inspection process that was not properly managed. Although the seminar presents procedures that are useful to manage the process, its principal message should be that inspections must be a managed activity to flourish!

The inspection management seminar provides guidelines for managing the project's inspection program to realize its potential. The seminar is presented to project managers, second- and third-level managers, the inspection coordinator, and possibly development team leaders. As outlined in Fig. 7.6, the seminar describes how to

- Apply inspections to control product quality
- Estimate the scope and cost of inspections
- Develop and administer the inspection plan
- Staff inspections
- Control and monitor the inspection process
- Direct inspections toward project and company goals
- Evaluate inspection results
- Support inspections

Objective:
- Establish management understanding of the inspection process
- Define the expected inspection costs, benefits, and data
- Specify the techniques necessary to plan, monitor, and control inspections
- Outline inspection implementation and support needs

Length:
- 4 hours

Audience:
- Primarily first- and second-level managers, although technical project leaders may be included
- Include the project inspection coordinator (IC)

Content:
- Relationship of inspections and quality management
- Inspection process description
- Inspection data and results
- Management techniques for inspections
- Requirements for inspection implementation and support

Modifications/adaptations:
- Unique project development procedures, and how they relate to inspections
- Related project or corporate inspection data and experiences
- Plans for the implementation of inspections
- Project specific standards or administrative procedures

Figure 7.6 Course outline—inspection management seminar.

The inspection management seminar applies generic management principles to specific procedures for running an inspection program. Although the management procedures may vary between different projects and companies, the goal of the seminar must be clear and consistent—to manage the inspection process to ensure its success.

7.2.5 Inspection evaluation seminars

The purpose of the inspection evaluation seminars is to present the results of the quantitative and qualitative evaluation of the inspection process to management and staff, along with an interpretation of these results and recommendations. The format of the inspection evaluation seminar, outlined in Fig. 7.7, is strongly influenced by a number of factors. These include

1. *The results of the quantitative and qualitative data analysis.* Clearly, if the inspection data indicates that everything is going ex-

---

Objectives:

- Provide recent quantitative and qualitative inspection results for the project
- Evaluate the results with expectations and general inspection experience
- Make recommendations for inspection process improvements

Length:

- 2 to 4 hours

Audience:

- Project managers
- Project technical staff

Content:

- Inspection objectives for the project
- Quantitative inspection results--with evaluation
- Qualitative inspection results--with evaluation
- Overall assessment and recommendations
- Inspection tutorial--as needed

Modifications/adaptations:

- The entire course is governed by the immediate project experience
- Partition the audience by management and staff--the issues will be somewhat different
- There may be another audience--the user or contractor may be vitally interested in the inspection results
- Involve the inspection coordinator
- Produce a formal report!

Figure 7.7 Course outline—management and technical inspection evaluation seminars.

tremely well, a relatively perfunctory and informal feedback session suffices. Major findings, however, require a formal seminar and a thorough presentation of the data analysis.

2. *The development environment.* Considerations such as how the project is organized—whether it is relatively self-contained or part of a cross-development effort, how tightly or loosely managed—can each have an impact on the format of evaluation seminars and the type of information presented in them.

3. *The person or persons presenting the evaluation.* A project may choose to make the inspection coordinator solely responsible for evaluation seminars, or may choose to have either an inspection consultant or management share in or conduct the sessions. Each of these persons brings different experiences and perspective to the evaluation seminars.

4. *The audience.* Evaluation seminars should be presented to both management and staff. Presentations made to higher levels of management would likely tend to be more formal and general. Presentations made to development managers tend to be more detailed and action-oriented. Those presented to the staff are the most technical and procedural.

The seminars are used to present the project's inspection data and surveys of the staff and management. They make recommendations for improvements in the inspection process, and discuss any other inspection issues. If only minor changes are indicated, a less formal forum is more likely to be used. But if significant changes in the inspection process are indicated, formality of the evaluation seminars is useful in underscoring their importance. Any changes that are required to improve the effectiveness of the inspection process must be communicated at the seminars.

Evaluation seminars typically last 2 to 4 hours for either management or technical personnel. If the proposed changes are extensive, reeducation may also be necessary.

7.2.6 Inspection education administration

To be effective, the inspection education program requires guidance and coordination. Administration of inspection education is particularly important because of the relatively large number of people that may be involved, the diversity of the courses, and the coordination required between various project groups. Administration of the education program is frequently provided by the inspection coordinator, although it may also be done by another member of the project team, or even by someone from outside the project, such as from a quality assurance or a training group. The main requirement is to make sure that inspection education is properly carried out for the project.

The project's inspection education administrator must decide what type of inspection education program best fits the project's needs. It is essential that all project members receive inspection education, and that they receive it early in the project cycle. It is also essential that inspection education be developed and delivered by someone fully knowledgeable of the inspection process. While use of an inspection consultant is strongly recommended, the first place to look for such a consultant should be within your company. Your organization may already have in-house expertise, and it may even have courses available that can be customized to your project's needs. An in-house inspection education program has an edge in producing inspection education that works well for your environment.

In arranging inspection education, the administrator establishes a series of class dates and schedules project members. The administrator should work not only with class size and schedule issues, but also with the work assignments of the project members.

7.2.6.1 Monitoring inspection education. A successful inspection education program achieves two goals: it provides project personnel with the knowledge they need to manage and to participate in the inspection program, and it instills an understanding of inspection benefits and a positive resolve to obtain those benefits. However, the "best" inspection education program is of no use whatsoever if it doesn't work for your project, and the only way to know whether or not it works is to monitor the inspection data.

Among the things inspection data can reveal are how well the inspection procedures are being followed and how effective those procedures are. If project members are not applying inspection procedures correctly, either they are not sufficiently knowledgeable about those procedures, or they are not sufficiently committed to the inspection process. Whenever the data reveals a problem in either the application of inspections or the effectiveness of the inspection procedures, it is time to reeducate your staff.

7.2.6.2 Reeducation. In the best of all possible worlds, employees who are new to a project, whether through hiring or transfer, would be trained in inspections as soon as they joined the project. But this is often not practical; many new employees will first be introduced to inspections by participating in an inspection meeting. As a result, it is likely that over time a project will have members who have never taken an inspection course. The inspection skills of these project members will be uneven. They are candidates for reeducation. Project procedures can also change, and any change in project procedures is likely to effect a change in the inspection procedures as well, requiring reeducation.

7.3   Coordinating Activities

Although projects may be similar in several respects, no two are ever alike and use exactly the same inspection procedures. A close analysis of each project generally reveals differences that are significant enough to affect the inspection procedures. Inspection coordination activities tailor the inspection process to the project's development procedures and are comprised of

1. Inspection implementation
2. Inspection data management
3. Inspection evaluation

7.3.1   Inspection implementation

Implementing inspections can be thought of as a two-step process, as illustrated in Fig. 7.8. First assess the project's potential use of inspections, then define the inspection process for the project.

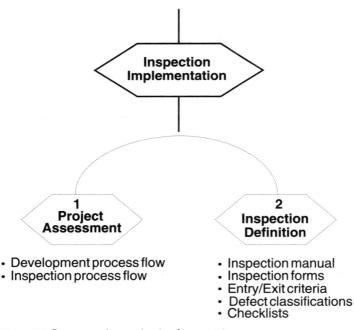

Figure 7.8 In-process inspection implementation.

7.3.1.1 Project needs assessment. When project management decides to implement an inspection program, the applicability of inspections to the project must still be assessed. A needs assessment is typically the first activity conducted by the inspection coordinator, who interviews project personnel and reviews project plans to determine to what extent inspections are suitable for the project. This process, outlined in Fig. 7.9, generally requires a week or two for data collection. This is followed by another week for analysis to determine what aspects of the project are suitable for inspections.

The project needs assessment is inherently a unique procedure, since it is based on an in-depth look at a particular project and its plans and personnel. The format of the needs assessment may be varied to fit a project's style. The inspection coordinator will want to interview all key project personnel, including project management and lead technical staff members. For some projects no other interviews may be needed; others may require additional interviews. A project that consists of

---

Objective:
- Establish the feasibility of using inspections for the project--at this time!
- Derive the necessary inspection implementation tasks
- Estimate the effort and schedule to accomplish inspection implementation--including training
- Obtain project commitment of necessary resources

Project members:
- Inspection coordinator
- Management
- Staff members
- (Others)

Time:
- From 1 to 4 weeks

Considerations:
- Project schedule and current stage of work
- Project resources--personnel, time, funds
- The structure of the project's development plan
- Product technology
- Interfacing organizations
- Administrative procedures

Results:
- Preparation of a project inspection implementation plan

Figure 7.9 Outline of project needs assessment.

many diverse parts or that interacts with other projects may even necessitate interviewing people outside the project.

Whether or not project plans exist and how complete existing plans are can also affect how the needs assessment is conducted. When a project has done comprehensive planning, the inspection coordinator can extract much of the information he or she needs from the project planning documentation. If little or no documentation exists, the inspection coordinator must rely more heavily on input from persons involved in project planning decisions.

A lack of good project planning may even be taken as a signal that inspections would not be a good fit for the project. The inspection process requires complete and consistent planning and documentation of inspection procedures and inspection meetings. Unless the project is willing to provide this, an inspection process has little chance of succeeding.

Thus, the recommendations of the needs assessment must be based not only on the appropriateness of the development process to inspections, but also on the coordinator's assessment of the organization's ability to apply inspections effectively.

7.3.1.2 Inspection definition. If the recommendation of the needs assessment is to implement inspections, the project's inspection coordinator prepares an inspection implementation plan. This requires approximately 1 month, and is outlined in Fig. 7.10.

One of the keys to producing a successful inspection process is to tailor inspections to the specific needs of the project. Most of the tailoring takes place in the project inspection manual which provides a custom road map for conducting the project's inspection meetings. Preparing this manual is usually a case of tailoring an existing procedures manual, a "template," to the project's inspection requirements. (Templates are provided in Chapters 8 and 9 for a variety of in-process inspection types.)

Specifically, the inspection procedures define the entry and exit criteria, error classifications, and each of the other seven defining parameters for each inspection type that will be used. They also include general and administrative procedures as well as the technical procedures. These procedures include

- General inspection procedures and any project-specific modifications
- Inspection roles and participants
- Inspection types and use
- Administration
- Change control

Objective:

- Prepare the necessary procedures for the project's inspection process, including administration
- Define inspection parameters
- Establish the necessary training requirements
- Determine an inspection evaluation plan

Project members:

- The inspection coordinator
- Members of project management, staff, and interfacing organizations as needed

Time:

- Approximately 1 month
- Custom case study development may be overlapped, or will extend the time by ~1 month

Considerations:

- Development phase demarcations
- Contractual, corporate, and project requirements and standards
- Development technology
- Interfacing organizations
- Security considerations

Results:

- Inspection manual
- Management and administrative procedures
- Training program
- (Case study problem)

Figure 7.10 Outline of inspection definition.

7.3.2 Inspection data management

One reason for the success of inspections is its emphasis on data collection and analysis. Inspection data analysis helps track defect trends and identify defect-prone components and procedures. Feeding the results of inspection data analysis back into the development and inspection processes leads to improvements in both.

Storing, retrieving, tracking, and analyzing defect data requires a data base system and data analysis tools. Fortunately, generic tools exist [e.g., Lotus Inspection Data System (LIDS)], and the inspection coordinator can provide one or more alternatives to meet project requirements.

The coordination of inspection data management essentially involves identifying an appropriate data base system, and then tailoring it to the project's inspection data collection and analysis needs. Tailoring the data base management system requires defining project-specific information, such as defect classifications, inspection types, dispositions, and naming conventions. In addition, the type of reports and their distribution reflect the project's data reporting needs and inspection procedures. The data management process is outlined in Fig. 7.11.

If an established inspection data base management system is tailored to fit the project, the coordinating effort requires approximately 1 week. During this time the inspection coordinator sets up the initial data base system and trains the inspection administrator in its use. This effort can be concluded before any inspection meetings take place, resulting in an established data base skeleton. It is important that the inspection data base system be established early in the inspection cycle so data collection and analysis procedures become routine activities from the start.

Objectives:

- Define the data that will be obtained for each inspection
- Prepare inspection data collection procedures
- Install the inspection data base software
- Specify inspection data administration

Project members:

- The inspection coordinator
- Data base management expertise

Time:

- Approximately 1 week, overlapped with training, to implement the data management system

Considerations:

- Inspection identification, performance, and defect data formats
- Reporting requirements
- Data management systems available--(LIDS)
- Time and effort available for data management
- Forms design
- Data collection, entry, maintenance, and reporting procedures
- Technical and administrative documentation and training

Results:

- Inspection data management procedures
- Installed inspection data management system
- Inspection data collection forms, reports, and documentation

---

Figure 7.11 Outline of inspection data management.

Developing a new data base management system obviously requires additional time. In some cases, a project may justify the cost and time required to build a completely project-specific data base system. However, we strongly suggest that the possibility of tailoring an existing system be investigated before considering such a step.

7.3.3 Inspection evaluation

The evaluation of the inspection program is an ongoing process. The inspection coordinator conducts the evaluation, using data collection and analysis techniques (such as those described in Chapter 6) to monitor the cost, benefits, and overall performance of the project's inspections.

The inspection evaluation reports

1. The performance of the inspection process
2. The effect of inspections of the development process
3. Recommended changes (if any) to current inspection procedures

Although certain generic statistics are collected for all inspection programs, much of the data collected is project-dependent. Figure 7.12 provides guidelines that are generally indicative of the effectiveness of the current inspection process. The way data is analyzed can be strongly influenced by the type of project and the environment it is developed in. The inspection coordinator must use his or her judgment and experience in evaluating the project's inspection procedures.

7.4 Tools and Media

Inspection tools and media are all of the objects that assist the education, implementation, and use of inspections. These tools and media are illustrated as accompanying items in the diagram of the support program in Fig. 7.1, and include

- Development process analysis techniques
- Inspection procedure manuals, defect types, forms, and checklists
- Video examples
- Case study problems
- Data management systems (e.g., LIDS)
- Survey questionnaires
- Analysis and evaluation techniques

- Compare inspection metrics with target values
- Observe relationships between variables
- Decide on the major inspection parameters
    Unit size
    Inspection/preparation rates
    Defects—density, type, class, severity
    Number of reinspections
    Effort for defect detection, rework
- Key indicators for monitoring
    Inspection performance
    Cost/benefit ratio
    Defect densities
    Dominant defect categories
    Defect-prone components
    Attitudes
- Consider data validation
- Determine inspection modification plans

Feedback analysis to project staff members, as well as to management!

Figure 7.12 Inspection evaluation guidelines.

Three of these tools—inspection procedure manuals, data management systems, and evaluation techniques—are illustrated in Chapters 8 and 9, the Appendix on LIDS, and Chapter 6, respectively. The others, outlined in this section, provide an introduction to the objects that help to support an inspection program.

7.4.1 Process analysis

A variety of process analysis techniques help determine where inspections can be profitably applied. One analytic approach that has been frequently and effectively used is data flow analysis. This technique is depicted in the data flow diagram portrayed in Fig. 7.13. Data flow analysis is a straightforward method for quickly and graphically determining the types, number, and placement of inspections in the project's development flow, and identifying any special considerations. Data flow analysis is not further discussed in this book. The subject is well treated in publications by Ed Yourdon,[1] Tom DeMarco,[2] Gane and Sarson,[3] and others.

For example, the diagram in Fig. 7.13 shows that department S51 (an actual case, but fictitiously named) is made up of a systems engineering group and a product development laboratory, each having re-

Department S51

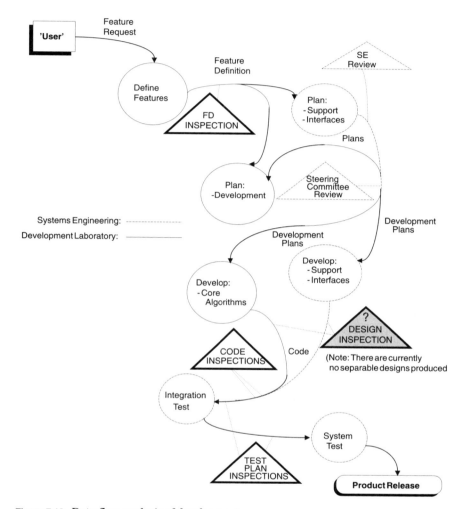

Figure 7.13 Data flow analysis of development process.

sponsibility for a part of the development process. The development laboratory wants to perform four types of inspections, while the systems engineering work is reviewed at two stages. The design inspection is shown to be problematical because no separable design documents are currently produced.

The decisions that will affect how and where inspections are employed are guided, not determined, by the data flow analysis and any other form of process analysis used. For example, the preceding example identified the absence of necessary design documents, but any decisions about what to do are left to project management. Process analysis techniques provide the necessary information for helping make these early and crucial decisions.

7.4.2 Video examples

The advantages of having video media available for various inspection overview, instructional, and reference purposes are substantial. Video examples are highly portable, present a consistent message, and can be economical when broadly used and reused. We recommend that video media be considered as a part of inspection support, rather than constituting the whole of it.

A fundamental concept of inspections is *group synergy*—the cumulative interaction that occurs among a small group of people working together on a common problem. The media is often an intrinsic part of the message. Therefore, we caution that media not be used unless it is part of group interaction. Video may be used to introduce the process, exemplify its use, or provide technical reference. Figure 7.14 summarizes video in all three of these modes.

Our use of video media has always taken place in the context of a

---

Objective

Instructional:

- Only a part of a process of training—not the whole
- Inspections are based on synergy, which is dependent on people interacting in groups—without this interaction, just viewing a tape is counter to the inspection process

Form

1. Overview of process:
- Can stimulate interest
- Must be followed up by a support program
2. Example inspection:
- Provides a graphic demonstration of instructional points
- Short, and very portable
- Use with interactive discussions—not in place of them
3. Taping of workshop:
- Long—good only for reference
- Does not encourage personal interaction
- Demonstrates a limited commitment to inspections if used for training

Figure 7.14 Video tape media.

discussion of the various inspection issues relevant to the audience and meeting. We have employed a number of different video production methods which have included video taping of

- Actual inspections, in whole or in part
- Instructor presentations and classes
- Prepared, scripted presentations and inspections
- Prepared, scripted, and professionally portrayed situations and roles within and surrounding an inspection program

Each of these techniques has produced overview and instructional videos of varying quality, but all have been useful.[4] Of course, the effort invested in video technology is proportionate to the size and extent of the inspection support effort, and to the degree of organizational commitment to inspections.

7.4.3 Case study

The centerpiece of the inspection workshop is the case study problem. Its presence is implied by the term "workshop" which means that active participation is expected of the attendees. In a 1-day class, 3 hours, or 40 percent of the class, is devoted to preparing for, performing, and discussing team inspections. Such a large percentage of class time is devoted to the case study because we believe that personal experience best teaches inspection principles and procedures, not just listening to a lecture.

Keep in mind that the purpose of the case study problem is to foster learning about inspections, rather than the development process or the material. Thus, because of the relatively short time frame, the problem should be easily understood by all of the members of the class, and should only challenge their inspection skills, rather than their technical expertise.

Development of a new case study problem is not a trivial task, and requires about a month. The task requires someone with the technical skill to simplify a problem and present it in an easily understood way. The problem may involve code (which is by far the easiest form of case problem to develop, although the most restrictive), designs (in a variety of formats), requirements, schematic diagrams, or any representation of a work product that is meaningful to the class.

Make sure that the case study is complete. The problem should be accompanied by an appropriate specification and have a known defect content, although this is not revealed. Inspection forms, procedures, and defect descriptions should also be part of the case study material.

The discussion that follows the case study inspections should involve each member of each team, and both the qualitative as well the quantitative inspection results should be discussed. Our suggestion is that the team's actual defect performance be rated against their expectations, not those of other teams. To accomplish this, we ask each team to estimate their performance before the actual results are revealed.

Figure 7.15 summarizes our method. We believe that case study problems are very useful, provided that they focus on inspection, not technical issues, and that the KISS principle is rigorously applied—Keep It Small and Simple.

7.4.4 Survey questionnaire

When evaluating an inspection program, it is important to consider qualitative as well as quantitative data. You should measure not only the performance of inspections, but their perceived effects on the project. Even if all of the quantitative data is positive, inspections may

---

Objective:

- Provide *inspection* exercise and experience
- *Not* an example of development procedures
- *Not* a subject for work-product content analysis

Selection:

- May be a general, nonwork related problem
- Major categories exist: software; hardware; documentation; etc. . . . .
- Project specific material works well--BUT requires development and must be "sanitized"

Length--one day class:

- 3 hours
- Preparation--1 hour; Inspection Meeting--1 hour; Discussion--1 hour

Development:

- Is difficult! Usually requires simplification
- Must have a predecessor specification
- Provide a known defect content
- Requires approximately one month to prepare
- Rigorously apply KISS--Keep It Small and Simple!

Discussion:

- Both quantitative and qualitative
- Collect both inspection performance and defect data
- Involve each inspection team--discuss human factors
- Rate teams on the basis of their own estimate of their effectiveness, rather than absolute performance, as optimistic, realistic, pessimistic

---

Figure 7.15 Outline of inspection workshop case study.

still present a problem if an attitude of discontent is prevalent. To obtain complete and concise qualitative data, a survey questionnaire is needed.

This questionnaire may be distributed and be self-administered, or may be administered by an interviewer, depending on whether you desire breadth or depth of the inquiry. If an interview mode is chosen, make sure that the interviewer is seen as objective, is not directly associated with the inspection program, and is not a member of management.

Management and staff should have different questionnaires since their goals and experience with the inspection process are different, and consequently the information obtained differs. For management, the basic areas to question are

- Inspection education and experience
- Overall perceptions of inspections
- Inspection costs/benefits
- Role in inspection planning
- Techniques employed to manage inspections
- Techniques employed to administer inspections
- Schedule, budget, and quality impact of inspections
- Assessment of group's inspection skills
- Effect of inspections on group
- Assessment of inspection education
- Recommendations for inspection program
- Comments

For the staff, the basic areas to questions are

- Inspection education and experience
- Overall perception of inspections
- Personal inspection skills—types and roles
- Perception of group's inspection skills
- Perception of inspection management
- Perception of inspection administration
- Adequacy of inspection scheduling and of preparation time
- Objectivity of inspections
- Effect of inspections on development schedule
- Effect of inspections on product quality

- Cultural effects of inspections
- Adequacy of inspection education
- Revisions to the inspection process
- Comments

These questions represent broad areas of inquiry. They are meant to assist in the development of your own project's questionnaire which will explore these questions, and/or others, in more or less detail depending on the needs and style of the particular project.

7.5   Conclusion

Education is the most important factor in inspection support. Education comes first because we need to understand a process before using it. Understanding means not only technical comprehension of the process and the steps necessary to apply it, but also knowledge of the objectives and benefits of the process, and of how it fits into the overall project goals.

Support means that the infrastructure needed to implement, use, and evaluate inspections has been planned and is actively available. The staff is assisted throughout all phases of the inspection process. Procedures for continuous evaluation are stressed, as well as using the results of evaluation to further fine-tune the process and increase our knowledge of it. An effective inspection process continues to improve both the product and the inspection process itself. This makes inspections the natural choice for product verification where the product and development environment continuously evolve.

The program outlined in this chapter has been successfully used by many projects over several years, and we believe it will assist you to establish a successful inspection program.

7.6   References

1. Yourdon, Edward, *Managing the System Life Cycle,* Yourdon Press, Englewood Cliffs, N.J., 1988.
2. DeMarco, T., *Concise Notes on Software Engineering,* Yourdon Press, Englewood Cliffs, N.J., 1979.
3. Gane, C. and Sarson, T., *Structural Systems Analysis: Tools and Techniques,* Prentice Hall, Englewood Cliffs, N.J.
4. For an example of the extensive use of video media for inspections education, refer to Russell, Glen, Inspection in ultralarge-scale development, *IEEE Software,* Vol. 17, No. 1, January 1991.

Software Inspection Procedures Manual

This chapter provides a sample version or "template" of a software inspection procedures manual. It includes a general description of inspections and the roles and responsibilities of the participants, and addresses 11 software inspection types that have been derived from a variety of projects.

Inspections are a predefined process and, as such, an inspection procedures manual should be prepared by each project using inspections. The sample manual furnished by this chapter is generic and is intended to be selected from and modified as project needs dictate. It attempts to set a standard for structure and form that is workable in many circumstances. Individual projects that implement inspections are expected to develop tailored versions of these procedures that satisfy their particular needs.

The first nine sections of this manual summarize the inspection process that has been described in detail in Chapter 3 of this book, and provide the definition and use of project-specific terminology and procedures. These sections document the expected inspection activities for the project staff.

Sections 10 to 20 document 11 types of software inspections which describe how the procedures are to be applied for each type of inspection, and cite the parameters to be used.

The remaining sections define the defect types and inspection forms that are used by the project.

Software Inspection Procedures Manual

Contents

8.1   Introduction

During the SOFTWARE_PROJECT, formal in-process software inspections are held for all newly developed products. The purpose of these inspections is to detect and correct defects at an early point in development, to ensure the quality of the software. Formal inspections allow defects to be detected and fixed early in the development process when repairs are inexpensive, rather than in the later stages when such repairs are very costly. This is part of our overall goal of meeting the customers' quality needs and improving our development productivity.

This document outlines an inspection process that can be tailored to the needs of many types of software projects. This process consists of a set of formal inspections whose objectives are to find defects during the development phase. Their scope ranges from requirements to test documentation. The entities to be inspected, along with an inspection-type abbreviation, are listed below.

- Requirements (RE)
- Architecture (AR)
- High-level design (HD)
- Detailed design (DD)
- Code (CD)
- Unit test plans (UTP)
- Unit test cases (UTC)
- Integration test plans (ITP)
- Integration test cases (ITC)
- System test plans (STP)
- System test cases (STC)

It should be noted that these are peer inspection procedures, with all members of the software development team participating in their implementation. This ensures a uniform level of quality in the software.

8.1.1 Document organization

This document begins with a description of the inspection process which includes

- General overview
- Inspection roles
- General procedures
- Procedures for participants
- Inspection coordinator's procedures

Finally, the document describes each of the inspection types. Each description includes the following items:

- Purpose
- Materials to be distributed
- Entrance criteria
- Reference materials
- Coverage rates
- Participants and roles
- Inspection meeting procedures
- Exit criteria
- Checklists
- Defect types

8.1.2 How to use this document

Section 2 provides a tutorial on general inspection procedures and therefore should be read first. The remaining sections describe the procedures for each participant role and inspection type; they should be referred to throughout the project's duration. The last sections contain samples of the reporting forms which will be used to collect data for the monitoring and analysis of inspections.

8.2 General Overview

8.2.1 Definitions

- *Inspection type:* A category of inspection associated with a distinct development phase. The development phase is such that its completion is necessary before going on to the next phase. An example of an inspection type is the detailed design inspection (DD).

- *Work product:* A product that is produced by the development activity of one phase of a project, and is verifiable by inspection.

- *Inspection meeting:* A formal meeting of a small group of participants who assume certain roles in order to find, classify, and report defects. Inspections are *not* the proper forum for debating engineering judgments, suggesting corrections for defects, or educating project members; these functions are performed in reviews and overviews.

- *Entry criteria:* A description of the materials and events that are necessary before an inspection meeting is initiated.

- *Checklist:* A list of guidelines to check for in examining the materials.

- *Defect classification:* A means by which defects found during an inspection meeting are classified. These defects are recorded onto a detailed inspection defect list and are classified according to the following criteria:

  —Location: Where the defect occurs in the work product.

  —Description: What the defect condition is.

  —Type: The different defect conditions that are identified for each type of inspection (see the consolidated list of defect types at the end of this manual).

  —Class: The way the defect is manifested, such as:

    - *Missing:* Information is needed, but is absent
    - *Wrong:* Information that is present is incorrect or unclear
    - *Extra:* Unnecessary information is present

  —Severity: The presumed effect the defect will have on the work product, such as:

    - *Major:* A defect which results in an observable departure from specifications or intended operation of the work product or prevents its successful development in subsequent stages.
    - *Minor:* A defect in description, format, or representation of the work product, which does not affect its specification, operation, or development.

- *Exit criteria:* The conditions that must be met before an inspection can be certified as complete.

- *Inspection coordinator:* The person responsible for defining, implementing, administrating, and maintaining the inspection process. The functions of the coordinator are described more fully below under inspection coordinator's procedures (Section 8.9).

- *Inspection data collection process:* Analytical tools and procedures used to monitor the inspection process itself. Quantitative data associated with the inspection process of an inspectable entity is stored in a data base. This allows the usefulness of the formal inspection process to be evaluated, and provides guidance for future design process improvements.

- *Inspection database:* A data base storing the input from the inspection data collection process. The data base may be accessed to provide statistical information about the inspection process, design processes, and the product.

8.2.2 Purpose

Software inspections are a rigorous and formal technique for the peer examination of work products. Inspections are conducted with the intent of reducing the number of defects transmitted from one development stage to the next, thereby reducing the cost of removing defects found in later phases or after a product has been released. Another goal of software inspections is to assure adherence to project coding and documentation standards to make the inspected work products as maintainable and modifiable as possible. To best achieve these goals, it is important to remember that *the results from software inspections are not used to evaluate the author's performance,* but are only used to improve the quality of the inspected product.

There are two groups served by a set of standard procedures: the users and the developers.

- The user, whether external or internal to the developing organization, needs the software product. Further, the user needs the software product to meet identified specifications. Thus, the user cannot afford to rely solely on tests at the conclusion of the software development effort. Should the software product fail to meet requirements at that point, the user's need still exists and a major portion of the development time has been lost. The user, therefore, needs to have a reasonable degree of confidence that the product is in the process of acquiring required attributes during software development.

- The developer needs an established standard against which to plan and to be measured. It is unreasonable to expect a complete, clear, and consistent product from each development phase without the application of a standard measure. Also, cost-effective project improvements cannot be made unless there exists a stable framework for measurement and evaluation.

8.2.3 Software inspection process overview

The inspection process consists of six steps (Table 8.1).

During the *planning* step, the author collects the necessary materials and selects a

TABLE 8.1   Software Inspection Process Overview

Step	Description	Objectives
Planning	Establish schedules. Choose inspectors. Obtain materials	Ensure that schedules and participants are established and materials are available
Overview	Presentation by author of work to be inspected	Provide educational background to understand inspection materials
Preparation	Individually study inspection material	Prepare participants to identify defects at the inspection meeting
Meeting	Formal process of inspecting distributed materials	Find and record defects as a team
Rework	Resolve problems identified at the inspection meeting	Revise product
Follow-up	Verify satisfactory resolution of all problems found during inspection	Certify author's revisions and complete inspection reporting

moderator. The moderator consults with the author to determine the other inspection participants, and reviews the material against the inspection entry criteria to verify its readiness for inspection. The moderator then schedules the inspection and sends the materials, along with an inspection meeting notice, to each inspector.

The *overview,* when applicable, is a presentation by the author of the materials to be inspected to educate the other inspectors about the material's functions and functional relationships as well as to give them a detailed description of the materials. The overview is attended by all inspectors. The moderator arranges and conducts the overview session.

Preparation is an individual exercise performed by all the inspectors to allow them to become thoroughly familiar with the materials so that they can better find defects during the inspection. Using the information provided at the overview, and guided by the appropriate checklists, each inspector is responsible for his or her own adequate preparation of the materials and is required to record the preparation time.

The inspection *meeting* is attended by the author of the material to be inspected, the moderator, and other inspectors. Since the meeting has as its objective looking for defects and not education, no one else should be present. At the beginning of the meeting, the moderator reviews the agenda for the inspection meeting. The moderator, not the author, conducts the meeting. The reader, who is selected by the moderator and the author in the planning phase, leads the other inspectors through the materials by paraphrasing them, not reading them verbatim. As all the materials are "read," each inspector looks for defects. As defects are recognized, they are recorded and classified on the inspection defect list. At the conclusion of the inspection meeting the moderator seeks the inspectors' agreement with the correctness of the inspection defect list and arrives at a disposition for the inspected materials.

During *rework,* the author revises the materials according to a copy of the inspection defect list supplied by the moderator.

After the defects have been resolved to meet the exit criteria, the moderator *follows-up* by verifying the author's revision. When the inspection has met the exit criteria and is certified complete, the moderator submits an inspection summary report and an inspection report to the software inspection coordinator.

8.3   Inspection Roles

Inspectors shall have the following roles:

- Author
- Moderator
- Reader
- Recorder

The minimum size of an inspection team is three people. When an inspection team is composed of only three people, the moderator acts as recorder.

8.3.1   Author

The role of author is assumed by the individual who is responsible for effecting changes to the work product (who is not necessarily the same as the person who wrote it). The author's role at the inspection meeting shall be to detect defects based on his or her special understanding of the product and to answer specific questions which the reader is not able to answer.

The author must not serve as moderator, reader, or recorder.

- The moderator's role is to run the meeting and to ensure that comments are not directed to the author or made about the author.
- The reader specifically takes the onus of receiving the comments on the work product.
- The recorder must be impartial, so as not to reinterpret the defects before recording them.

8.3.2 Moderator

The moderator's task is to ensure that the other members of the inspection team complete their functions for each step of the inspection. The moderator must ensure that during the inspection meeting the inspection team concentrates on finding defects and does not bog down in disagreement, discussing trivial issues, in solution-hunting, or in seeking alternate solutions. The moderator must be unbiased regarding the area under inspection and must be sensitive to each participant. During the inspection, the moderator is the key to ensuring that resources are efficiently utilized and maximum effort toward finding defects is achieved.

After the inspection, the moderator follows up on the resolution of defects from the inspection defect list and provides the inspection report to the inspection coordinator.

8.3.3 Reader

The reader leads the team over the work in a complete and logical fashion. The reader is prepared to describe the various parts and functions of the work, reading and paraphrasing the material at a moderate pace suitable for thorough examination. Because the order in which the material appears in the work product may not be optimal for inspecting, the reader must select an appropriate order of presentation. During the meeting, the reader paraphrases and interprets the material, describing every part and function of the material in detail, and answers any questions posed by the inspectors. (Additional clarification may be required by the author, but only after the reader's response.)

8.3.4 Recorder

The role of the recorder is to record all the defects on the inspection defect list for this inspection.

8.3.5 Viewpoints

It is often useful for individuals with specific viewpoints or interests in the work product to participate in an inspection to sharpen the group's collective understanding of the work to improve defect detection.

- Requester: Represents the customer or someone responsible for an earlier phase of development.
- Receiver: Uses the work product in the next phase of development.
- Validator: Ensures testability of the product.
- Standardizer: Is especially familiar with standards to which the work product must adhere.
- Maintainer: Will have to be able to understand the material on a long term basis.
- Peer: Is especially familiar with the techniques used by the author.

An inspection team should be a small group with an appropriate balance of these points of view. Requesters and receivers should participate in inspections whenever possible.

8.4   General Procedures for All Inspectors

An inspection meeting is a cooperative activity. The meeting brings together professional software developers with differing viewpoints and levels of experience. The purpose of the meeting is to work together to improve the product being inspected by uncovering its discrepancies, i.e., the points at which the product does not meet the specifications. Your participation in an inspection begins when you receive the inspection meeting notice and the materials to be inspected. Participation ends when consensus is reached at the end of the meeting on the disposition of the inspected material.

8.4.1   Overview

At the overview meeting, if held, the author presents whatever information is necessary for a complete understanding of his or her work by the other inspectors. This might be a general review of an overall design so that the function of a particular part may be understood, or it might be a general tutorial on some special techniques that are applied in the material to be inspected. An overview is not a review, and hence not an appropriate place to discuss design or implementation alternatives.

8.4.2   Preparation

An inspection meeting cannot be held unless all the inspectors have prepared by studying the material to be inspected. Note preparation time on the inspection meeting notice.

The total preparation time of all the inspectors is one item of data that is collected from an inspection meeting. The inspections coordinator uses this data to continually evaluate the effectiveness of the inspection process in the project. Each inspector may note any questions and defects that are noticed during preparation directly on the materials.

During preparation, while each inspector should first be interested in thoroughly understanding the material, secondary emphasis may be placed on finding defects. Without a thorough understanding, inspectors are not able to contribute effectively to the meeting. If checklists for finding common defects are available, use them at this time.

8.4.3   Meeting

The inspection meeting is narrowly focused on looking for defects. It is the responsibility of all the inspectors, especially the moderator, to keep the meeting focused on this purpose.

Classify all defects reported by class, severity, and type. Inspectors should be familiar with the defect classification. Describe defects as crisply as possible, but avoid the temptation to correct the defects during the meeting. Also, be aware that it is easy for the meeting to drift into discussion of "good" programming practice, alternative techniques, special coding tricks, etc. If there is interest in conducting such discussions, a separate review may be held.

The author should leave the meeting with a clear understanding of the specific defects that need correction before the inspection is complete.

The inspection meeting starts promptly, but not until all the participants are present. If, by 10 minutes after the scheduled start of the meeting, the moderator, reader, or author is not present, the meeting must be rescheduled. If other inspectors are absent after 10 minutes, the moderator decides whether to begin the meeting or to reschedule it.

The meeting follows a specific agenda.

- Introduction
- Establish preparedness
- Read work product and record defects

- Review defects
- Determine disposition

8.4.3.1 Introduction. For an inspection meeting to be successful, it is important that all participants feel comfortable with the process. To start the meeting, the moderator introduces the inspectors, describes their roles, and acknowledges the work of the author. The moderator states the purpose of the inspection and asks the inspectors to focus their efforts toward defect detection, not solution hunting. The moderator reminds the inspectors to direct their remarks to the reader and to comment only on the product, not the author.

8.4.3.2 Establish preparedness. It is pointless to have an inspection unless the inspectors are prepared. The moderator verifies preparedness by asking each inspector to state the total time they recorded on their log. If the moderator feels that the inspectors are not well enough prepared, he or she stops the meeting and reschedules it. A guideline for minimally acceptable team preparation is one half of the total time that is expected.

8.4.3.3 Read work product and record defects. The reader is responsible for choosing the most effective way to present the document to the inspectors. The order in which the material appears in the document may not be the best order for inspecting.

Defects that were discovered during preparation and any others that come to light as the team systematically examines the work are noted by the recorder. Address any comments on categorizing the defects to the recorder, not the author. The inspection meeting must objectively address the contents of the work product, and the moderator focuses this part of the meeting on creating the inspection defect list.

If an issue is raised during the meeting that is unclear as to whether or not it is a defect, the recorder records the issue on the inspection defect list as a defect. After the meeting, the author makes the determination and, if appropriate, the correction. If the unit disposition is conditional, the moderator reviews the author's resolution of the issue at the time of the reexamination.

The recorder records all defects by class, severity, and type on the inspection defect list.

8.4.3.4 Review defects. At the close of the inspection, the moderator reviews the inspection defect list with the team to verify its completeness and accuracy. The inspection defect list records what items the author needs to correct and is a factor in determining the disposition of the product.

8.4.3.5 Determine disposition. Each inspection team must decide whether to

1. Accept the author's material as is. Further verification of rework is not required. The material meets the exit criteria.
2. Conditionally accept the author's materials contingent on the moderator's verification of the author's corrections.
3. Reinspect to verify the material after rework.

Although it should be made with the other participants' advice, it is the moderator's responsibility to determine the disposition.

8.4.4 Meeting synergy

A good inspection meeting is one in which the total effect is more than the sum of each individual's contribution. It is one in which the group joins together cooperatively in objectively discovering as many defects as possible in the work. A good inspection meeting unfolds like a detective story in which each person's remarks are picked up and developed by other members in the group in a vigorous search for defects.

When the proper atmosphere is created, the author can be the most helpful person in the meeting. It is important to remember that the author's work is the subject of the inspection, not the author.

8.5 Procedures for Authors

Authors have special responsibilities in the following steps of the inspection process:

- Planning
- Overview
- Preparation
- Meeting
- Rework
- Follow-up

8.5.1 Planning

The author reviews the materials to be inspected with the moderator, and provides him or her with a copy. Verify that the work product satisfies the inspection entry criteria. The moderator schedules the time, place, and duration of the inspection meeting. If the moderator decides that the work product does not meet the entry criteria, the inspection may have to be postponed until the author can bring the work product into compliance with these criteria.

8.5.2 Overview

If the moderator determines that an overview meeting is necessary, prepare as for any technical presentation. The purpose of the overview is educational and attendance is open to others, but all inspectors must attend. The author presents the work product and discusses any special techniques used or other issues that aid in understanding the material.

8.5.3 Preparation

After the moderator has accepted the inspection material, the author's next responsibility is to prepare for the meeting. As a check, you should receive a copy of the inspection material. The author usually does not have any extensive preparation for the meeting but should at least go over the material to verify that it is complete and in proper order.

8.5.4 Meeting

The author's next responsibility is to be present at the inspection meeting. This role is a difficult one since the focus of the meeting is to uncover defects in work for which the author is responsible. The author should not be defensive, but should rather focus on helping find defects and understanding inspectors' comments.

8.5.5 Rework

The author resolves all identified defects, regardless of their severity. This may be done by

1. Correcting the defect
2. Explaining why the defect condition is correct
3. Entering the defect into the change control system for resolution by another party
4. Obtaining management approval to enter the defect into change control for later resolution

8.5.6   Follow-up

If the disposition of the inspected materials is accept or reinspect, the moderator signs the inspection report and your participation in this inspection is completed.

If the disposition is conditional, the author informs the moderator when the document is ready for his or her final certification. When the moderator approves the revision by signing the inspection report, the author's participation in this inspection is completed.

8.6   Procedures for Moderators

All moderators must have received training in software inspections at an inspection workshop.

These instructions, therefore, assume that the moderators are familiar with inspections in general and concentrate on specific instructions.

Moderators have special responsibilities in the following steps of the inspection process:

- Planning
- Overview
- Meeting
- Follow-up

8.6.1   Planning

8.6.1.1   Determine the need for an overview. The moderator's first task is to determine whether or not an overview should be held. The purpose of an overview is educational. Whenever the moderator thinks that the inspectors do not have enough information about the material to be inspected or that an overview would decrease the participants' preparation time, schedule an overview.

8.6.1.2   Overview planning. If the overview must be held, it should be held at least 3 days before the inspection meeting. The moderator may distribute the inspection materials before, during, or after the overview, provided all inspectors have adequate time to prepare for the inspection meeting.

8.6.1.3   Verify materials. For each inspection, verify that the material meets the entry criteria. If the criteria are not met, the moderator works with the author to bring the material to the point where it can be effectively inspected. All work products must be capable of being understood with no further background than that which may be obtained at an overview meeting.

8.6.1.4   Schedule meeting. After consulting with the author, the moderator selects the other inspectors, appoints a reader and recorder, schedules the meeting, determines the preparation and meeting duration, reserves a meeting room, and sees that the materials are distributed to the other inspectors far enough in advance of the meeting to allow for adequate preparation.

The moderator should obtain a quiet room, large enough to comfortably accommodate the inspection team, equipped with a (preferably round) table. If the reader specifies a need for visual aids, arrange for the appropriate equipment to be present. An inspection team should be composed of a small group of people with an appropriate balance of points of view. Requesters and receivers should participate in inspections whenever possible. When choosing the inspectors, keep in mind that at least one of the participants should be familiar with the subject matter of the inspected material; this helps prevent the meeting from degenerating into a training session.

8.6.1.5 Prepare meeting notice. The inspection meeting notice requires that the moderator estimate the inspection meeting duration and the average preparation time expected of each participant. You may choose to adjust these estimates, based on the complexity of the work product to be inspected.

An inspection meeting should be scheduled for no more than 2 hours. If the material cannot be inspected in this amount of time, schedule more than one inspection meeting and notify the participants accordingly.

When the material to be inspected involves changes to modified material, the moderator and the author decide how much of the old material needs to be inspected. Be particularly aware that the size of the materials to be inspected, and consequently the required preparation and examination time, is the total of the

1. New and changed lines

2. All interfaces, on both sides of the interface

3. Any dependent materials

8.6.1.6 Appoint a reader. The reader must not be the moderator or the author. The reader must have enough appropriate experience to be able to understand and effectively paraphrase the material.

8.6.2 Overview

The moderator's responsibility at the overview meeting is to guide discussion toward providing the information necessary for a successful inspection. Remember that an overview is not a review, and hence not an appropriate place to discuss design or implementation alternatives.

8.6.3 Meeting

The moderator's responsibilities during the inspection meeting are to

- See that all the physical needs for the meeting are satisfied.
- Start the meeting on time and move it along so that it finishes on schedule.
- Follow the outlined inspection meeting agenda.
- Keep the synergy of the meeting high by being aware of and correcting any conditions, either physical or emotional, that are draining off any participant's attention. This includes everything from calling a stretch break to repairing the effects of inappropriate personal remarks.

Before the meeting, make copies of the inspection defect list, inspection defect summary, and inspection report. Bring to the inspection meeting any references that may be useful (e.g., standards references, programming language references, etc.). At the end of the meeting make a copy of the inspection defect list for the author.

8.6.4 Follow-up

At the completion of the meeting, complete the inspection defect summary and inspection report forms. If the inspected document receives a disposition of either accept or reinspect, submit the paperwork to the inspections coordinator and the inspection is complete. If the material inspected receives a disposition of conditional, your examination of the author's corrections is required. When this examination is complete, submit the inspection defect list, inspection defect summary, and inspection report to the inspection coordinator.

When multiple meetings are required to complete an inspection, follow-up on the entire multisession inspection after all the material has been covered.

8.6.4.1 Prepare inspection defect summary. Tally on the inspection defect summary form the defects reported on the inspection defect list.

8.6.4.2 Prepare inspection report. Fill out the inspection report as follows:

- *Number of meetings* is one for all single-session inspections and more than one when the inspection report covers more than one meeting of a multisession inspection. Multisession inspections for which follow-up is done separately for each meeting are treated as separate single-session inspections.
- *Inspection duration:* The total time used for the inspection meeting(s). Meeting breaks are included.
- *Overview duration:* The total time used for the overview meeting(s).
- *Number of inspectors* includes the moderator and the author.
- *Total preparation time:* The sum of all individual preparation times.
- *Size:* The length of the inspected materials in the appropriate units of measure (lines, noncommentary lines, pages, etc.).
- *Unit disposition* indicates whether the work product is accepted, is to be reexamined by the moderator (i.e., conditionally accepted), or requires a subsequent reinspection.
- *Estimated rework effort:* The author's estimate of the amount of work required to correct the defects.
- *Rework to be completed by:* The author's commitment to a completion date.
- *Actual rework effort:* The amount of effort that the author has expended to resolve the defects. This field is completed after reexamination by the moderator or after a reinspection meeting where the resultant disposition is accept.
- *Reinspection scheduled for:* Used only when the unit disposition is reinspect.
- *Other inspectors:* Lists all the inspectors except the moderator.
- *Moderator certification:* Given at the completion of the meeting or after the rework is examined if the unit disposition was conditional.
- *Additional comments* on inspection process may be provided to note any conditions, suggestions, etc. that the inspectors wish to record, but are not covered by the standard items.

8.7 Procedures for Readers

Readers have special responsibilities in the following steps of the inspection process:

- Preparation
- Meeting

8.7.1 Preparation

The reader receives the material at the same time as the other inspectors. However, extra preparation may be needed so that the reader will be able to

- Select the most effective sequence for presenting the material. The sequence in which the material appears may not be the most logical for inspecting.
- Paraphrase and interpret the material.
- Rigorously describe every part and function of the material.
- Answer questions posed by the inspectors.

In the inspection meeting the reader works closely with the moderator, and may wish to discuss the above points with the moderator prior to the meeting.

8.7.2 Meeting

The reader leads the team through the material in a logical fashion. In preparation, the reader may have selected an alternate sequence for presentation which allows for a clearer understanding by the inspectors. Be sure to read all of the material. Paraphrase the material at a pace suitable for thorough examination. The moderator assists in maintaining an appropriate pace.

8.8 Procedures for Recorders

Recorders have special responsibilities in the following steps of the inspections process:

- Preparation
- Meeting

8.8.1 Preparation

The recorder may wish to review the pertinent defect types for the work product to be inspected to be able to quickly categorize the defects found during the meeting.

8.8.2 Meeting

Record all defects by class, severity, and type on the inspection defect list. In filling out the inspection defect list, the following apply:

- *Date:* The inspection meeting date.
- *Line number(s):* The first line number where the defect is noted. If no line numbers appear in the material, a copy of the material is attached with the defect annotated as recorded.
- *Defect description:* A brief, clear description of the defect (not how to fix it).
- *Defect type* characterizes the defect condition, and is defined for each inspection type. Refer to the consolidated list of defect types in Section 8.21.
- *Defect class* and *severity* are discussed in the following sections.

Turn the inspection defect list over to the moderator to review the defects after the reading of the work product has been completed.

8.8.2.1 Defect class. The software inspections require that each defect be assigned to one of the following three classes which indicates the way in which the defect is manifested:

- *Missing:* For material that should be in the work product, but is not
- *Wrong:* For material that is and should be present, but is incorrect or unclear
- *Extra:* For material that should not be present since it is gratuitous, exceeds the specifications for the product, or would cause unnecessary testing and/or maintenance effort

8.8.2.2 Defect severity. The presumed effect the defect will have on the operation or representation of the work product, that is,

- *Major:* Produces an observable departure from requirements and specifications, or produces a failure in operation, or prevents successful further development of the product.
- *Minor:* Defects of format and representation, or those that do not cause failure or departure from requirements.

8.9 Inspection Coordinator's Procedures

The inspection coordinator is responsible for the initial installation and on-going use of software inspections.

8.9.1 Initial installation of inspections

The initial installation of software inspections involves

- Arranging, scheduling, and participating in inspection workshops
- Preparing the initial version of the inspection procedures for the project
- Answering questions about, and making dynamic adjustments to, the inspection procedures
- Arranging for any special inspection consulting activities
- Receiving and filing an inspection defect list, inspection report, and inspection defect summary for each completed inspection
- Arranging for initial evaluation and review activities

8.9.2 Ongoing use of inspections

As the inspection program matures, the inspections coordinator

- Draws on the resources of the inspection program to extend the software inspection procedures manual to inspections of all types of development material.
- Administers changes to the software inspection procedures manual based on modification requests received.
- Issues a periodic coordinator's report describing the project's inspection activities and their results.
- Establishes a project inspections data base to contain the information received on the collected inspection reports and inspection summaries.
- Periodically analyzes the information in the inspections data base to determine ways of improving the software development process and inspection procedures.

8.9.3 Inspection data

Since inspection data is a record of developer defects it needs to be treated with special sensitivity. The inspection coordinator is responsible for maintaining the confidentiality of individual inspection results and for distilling from these results the summary and trend information that is useful for overall process management.

8.9.4 Administrative procedures

The inspection coordinator is responsible for setting up a general plan and schedule for inspections and providing for its administration. The inspection coordinator may recommend a moderator for each inspectable entity to management. Moderators are selected from members of the software team, with more experienced people selected more often.

8.9.4.1 Forms. In order to carry out the inspection process, as well as aid the data collection process, the following four forms will be used:

- The *inspection meeting notice:* To inform participants of the date, time, place, and reason for an inspection meeting and possible overview.

- The *inspection defect list:* To provide a detailed list of all defects found during the inspection meeting for use in rework and follow-up stages.

- The *inspection defect summary:* Summarizes the number of defects along each classification dimension in order to provide an input to the inspection data collection process.

- The *inspection report:* Provides a summary of the work effort, participants, and disposition of the inspection process for a particular entity. It is used as input to the inspection data collection process and may be used for project tracking.

8.9.4.2 Administrative flow. The following administrative transactions occur for each inspectable entity:

1. The moderator decides whether or not the entry criteria have been met. If not, the author corrects whatever aspects fail the criteria. Once the entry criteria have been met, the author and moderator, with possible consultation from the inspection coordinator, decide when the inspection meeting(s) should be held. Notices of such meetings are distributed to the participants and departmental supervision by the moderator using the inspection meeting notice.

2. After the inspection meeting the moderator distributes an inspection defect list to the author.

3. The author reworks the areas indicated by the defect list, and then prepares a summary of how each defect is resolved.

4. If the inspection disposition is accept or reinspect, then the inspection defect summary and inspection report are prepared by the moderator and submitted to the inspection coordinator as soon as possible after the original inspection. The inspection report is also distributed to departmental supervision. When required, the reinspection is scheduled after the rework phase, like a regular inspection, through use of an inspection meeting notice. The reinspection participants should be from those that were present at the original inspection meeting; e.g., the moderator, author, and at least one other original inspector. The preparation material should be the inspection defect list, the inspection defect summary, and the updated pages of the original inspection materials. During the reinspection, these resolutions are verified against the exit criteria. Note that a reinspection is similar to a modification inspection, in that the new and changed material, its interfaces, and any affected dependencies are inspected.

5. If the inspection disposition is conditional, then the moderator awaits the end of the rework phase. Then, the moderator verifies the resolution of the defect contained on the inspection defect list against the exit criteria.

6. After the exit criteria are met, the moderator submits the inspection defect summary and inspection report to the inspection coordinator. The moderator or coordinator also distributes the inspection report to departmental supervision. When the exit criteria are met and the inspection is concluded, the moderator signs the moderator certification on the inspection report.

7. The inspection coordinator enters the data from the inspection report and inspection defect summary into the inspection data base.

8.9.4.3 Location in entry criteria. In order to identify defect locations, it is required that all work products have some form of line numbering.

8.9.4.4 Changes to this document. Since many of the procedures break new ground, change activity to these procedures is anticipated. Thus, sectional updates will be issued as appropriate.

8.9.4.5 Effect of changes to previously inspected entities. Project change-control procedures should be invoked when previously inspected levels are changed.
Changes to such levels can occur for three reasons.

1. Changes in the requirements
2. Defects which slipped by the inspection process
3. Changes in higher levels

The procedures used in handling changes should mimic those used in synthesizing the original design materials. Thus, as a change filters down through the various development phases, inspections must be held for each affected entity in each phase. The same moderators used for the original inspections are assigned to these "change" inspections. For practical reasons, inspections may be combined for small changes, where separate inspections would be very inefficient.
Subsequent sections of this document describe each of the types of inspections selected for use by the SOFTWARE_PROJECT.

8.10 Inspections of Software Requirements

8.10.1 Purpose

1. To ensure that the requirements meet customer needs
2. To ensure that the requirements can be implemented
3. To detect omissions, defects, and ambiguities in the requirements

8.10.2 Materials to be distributed

Distribute the following materials 5 working days prior to the inspection:

- Requirements document
- Requirements checklist
- All applicable modification requests

8.10.3   Entrance criteria

- The requirements document is line-numbered.
- The requirements document has been run through a spelling checker.
- The document conforms to the standard requirements document format.
- The document contains all information types required by project standards (e.g., input, output, performance requirements, etc.).

8.10.4   Reference materials

- Technical prospectus
- Requirements standards

8.10.5   Coverage rates

- Preparation: five to seven pages per hour
- Inspection: five to seven pages per hour

8.10.6   Participants and roles

The following functional roles are required for a requirements inspection:

- Moderator who is a lead technical staff member with systems engineering experience
- Author of the requirements
- Reader
- Recorder (this role may be performed by the moderator)

It is effective for the materials being inspected to be looked at from various viewpoints. For a requirements document the following viewpoints are recommended:

- Customer
- Designers
- Developers
- Validator (unit, integration, and system)
- Maintenance staff member
- Installation and field staff member
- User documentation author

It is acceptable for a single inspector to take more than one viewpoint. When possible these roles should be filled by the people who are actually responsible for the effort. Be sure that the inspection team has at least one peer systems engineer.

8.10.7   Inspection procedures

The requirements should be examined against all known customer needs. Emphasis should be placed on detecting missing or incorrect features. Be sure that the requirements are not so detailed that the designer and coder are restricted to a single implementation. Be sure that there is enough detail for the designer to work without consulting the author of the requirements. Ensure that all modification requests have been addressed.

8.10.8 Exit criteria

- All defects found have been corrected or placed under modification request control.

8.10.9 Checklist

The following checklist should be used to verify that all relevant areas of the requirements document have been examined.

- Have all materials required for a requirements inspection been received?
- Are all materials in the proper physical format?
- Have all requirements standards been followed?
- Is the requirements document complete, i.e., does it implement all of the known customer needs?
- Does the human interface follow project standards?
- Has all the infrastructure been specified, i.e., backup, recovery, checkpoints, etc.?
- Are the error messages unique and meaningful?
- Have all reliability and performance objectives been listed?
- Have all security considerations been listed?
- Do the requirements consider all existing constraints?
- Do the requirements provide an adequate base for design?
- Are the requirements complete, correct, and unambiguous?

8.10.10 Defect types

See the consolidated listing of defect types (Section 8.21).

8.11 Inspections of Software Architecture

8.11.1 Purpose

1. To ensure that the architecture conforms to the requirements
2. To ensure that the architecture can be implemented
3. To detect omissions, defects, and ambiguities in the architecture

8.11.2 Materials to be distributed

Distribute the following materials 5 working days prior to the inspection:

- Architecture document
- Requirements document
- Architecture checklist
- All applicable modification requests

8.11.3 Entrance criteria

- The architecture document is line-numbered.
- The architecture document has been run through a spelling checker.
- The document conforms to the standard architecture document format.

- The document contains all information types required by project standards (e.g., input, output, performance requirements, etc.).
- The requirements have been inspected and finalized.

8.11.4 Reference materials

- Architecture standards

8.11.5 Coverage rates

- Preparation: five to seven pages per hour
- Inspection: five to seven pages per hour

8.11.6 Participants and roles

Functional roles required for an architecture inspection are as follows:

- Moderator who is a lead technical staff member with architecture experience
- Author of the architecture
- Reader
- Recorder (this role may be performed by the moderator)

It is effective for the materials being inspected to be looked at from various viewpoints. For an architecture document the following viewpoints are recommended:

- Requirements author
- Designers
- Developers
- Validator (unit, integration, and system)

It is acceptable for a single inspector to take more than one viewpoint. When possible these roles should be filled by the people who are actually responsible for the effort.

Be sure that the inspection team has at least one peer who has been responsible for architecture, i.e., someone other than the author.

8.11.7 Inspection procedures

The architecture should be examined against the requirements. Emphasis should be placed on detecting missing or incorrect specifications, logic, interfaces, and infrastructure (the technical elements not apparent to the user, but necessary in a system, in order to implement the requirements, e.g., backup, recovery, checkpoints, sorts, spoolers, etc.).

Be sure that the architecture is not so detailed that the designer and coder are restricted to a single implementation. Be sure that there is enough detail for the designer to work without consulting the author of the architecture.

Ensure that all modification requests have been addressed.

8.11.8 Exit criteria

- All defects found have been corrected or placed under modification request control.

8.11.9 Checklist

The following checklist should be used to verify that all relevant areas of the architecture document have been examined:

1. Have all materials required for an architecture inspection been received?
2. Are all materials in the proper physical format?
3. Have all architecture standards been followed?
4. Is the architecture complete, i.e., does it allow for an implementation of all of the requirements?
5. Are all interfaces clear and well defined?
6. Is minimum data passed at each interface?
7. Is minimum global system data added or impacted?
8. Has all the infrastructure been specified, i.e., backup, recovery, checkpoints, etc.?
9. Has the architecture been adequately decomposed?
10. Have all reliability and performance requirements been addressed?
11. Have all security considerations been addressed?
12. Does the architecture consider all existing constraints?
13. Does the architecture contain unnecessary redundancy?
14. Does the architecture provide an adequate base for the high-level designs?
15. Have maintainability issues been addressed?
16. Is the architecture complete, correct, and unambiguous?
17. Is the architecture feasible?

8.11.10. Defect types

See the consolidated listing of defect types.

8.12 Inspections of High-Level Design

8.12.1 Purpose

1. To ensure that the high-level design conforms to the requirements and architecture
2. To ensure that the design can be implemented
3. To detect omissions, defects, and ambiguities in the design

8.12.2 Materials to be distributed

Distribute the following materials 5 working days prior to the inspection:

- High-level design document
- Requirements document
- Architecture document
- File layouts (if applicable)
- High-level design checklist
- All applicable modification requests

8.12.3 Entrance criteria

- The high-level design document is line-numbered.
- The high-level design document has been run through a spelling checker.
- The document conforms to the standard high-level design document format.
- The document contains all information types required by project standards (e.g., input, output, performance requirements, etc.).
- The requirements and architecture have been inspected and finalized.

8.12.4 Reference materials

- Design standards
- Hardware/software configuration

8.12.5 Coverage rates

- Preparation: 200 to 250 specification statements per hour or four to five pages per hour
- Inspection: 200 to 250 specification statements per hour or four to five pages per hour

8.12.6 Participants and roles

Functional roles required for a high-level design inspection are as follows:

- Moderator who is a lead technical staff member with design and/or architecture experience
- Author of the high-level design
- Reader
- Recorder (this role may be performed by the moderator)

It is effective for the materials being inspected to be looked at from various viewpoints. For a high-level design the following viewpoints are recommended:

- Requirements author
- Detailed designer
- Validator (unit, integration, and system)
- Maintenance staff member
- User documentation author

It is acceptable for a single inspector to take more than one viewpoint. When possible these roles should be filled by the people who are actually responsible for the effort.

Be sure that the inspection team has at least one peer who has been responsible for high-level design, i.e., someone other than the author.

8.12.7 Inspection procedures

The high-level design should be examined against the requirements. Emphasis should be placed on detecting missing or incorrect specifications, logic, interfaces, and infrastructure (that is, the technical elements not apparent to the user, but necessary in a system, in order to implement the requirements, e.g., backup, recovery, checkpoints, sorts, spoolers, etc.).

Be sure that the high-level design is not so detailed that the detailed designer and coder are restricted to a single implementation. Be sure that there is enough detail for the detail designer to work without consulting the author of the high-level design.

Ensure that all modification requests have been addressed.

8.12.8 Exit criteria

- All defects found have been corrected or placed under modification request control.

8.12.9 Checklist

The following checklist should be used to verify that all relevant areas of the high-level design document have been examined.

1. Have all materials required for a high-level design inspection been received?
2. Are all materials in the proper physical format?
3. Have all high-level design standards been followed?
4. Is the high-level design complete, i.e., does it implement all of the requirements?
5. Does the human interface follow project standards?
6. Are all interfaces clear and well defined?
7. Is minimum data passed at each interface?
8. Is minimum global system data added or impacted by the design?
9. Are data structures clearly partitioned?
10. Has all the data been properly defined?
11. Has all the infrastructure been specified? That is, backup, recovery, checkpoints, etc.?
12. Has the design been adequately decomposed?
13. Are the error messages unique and meaningful?
14. Are unusual situations handled reasonably and nondestructively?
15. Have all reliability and performance requirements been designed?
16. Have all security considerations been designed?
17. Does the high-level design consider all existing constraints?
18. Does the high-level design contain unnecessary redundancy that is already implemented in another system component?
19. Does the high-level design provide an adequate base for the detail design?
20. Have maintainability issues been addressed?
21. Is the high-level design complete, correct, and unambiguous?
22. Is the high-level design feasible?
23. Is the high-level design verifiable? Is there a finite cost-effective process by which a person or machine can check that the software product meets the design?

8.12.10 Defect types

See the consolidated listing of defect types (Section 8.21).

8.13 Inspections of Detailed Design

8.13.1 Purpose

1. To ensure that the detailed design conforms to the high-level design
2. To ensure that all interface and procedural logic is complete and correct

8.13.2 Materials to be distributed

Distribute the following materials 5 working days prior to the inspection:

- Detailed design
- High-level design document
- File layouts (if applicable)
- Detailed design checklist
- All applicable modification requests

8.13.3 Entrance criteria

- The detailed design document is line-numbered.
- The detailed design document has been run through a spelling checker.
- The document conforms to the standard detailed design document format.
- The document contains all information types required by project standards (e.g., input, output, performance requirements, etc.).
- The high-level design has been inspected and has met the exit criteria.

8.13.4 Reference materials

- Design standards
- Hardware and software configuration
- Requirements document
- Architecture document

8.13.5 Coverage rates

- Preparation: 150 specification statements per hour or three to four pages per hour
- Inspection: 150 specification statements per hour or three to four pages per hour

8.13.6 Participants and roles

Functional roles required for a detailed design inspection are as follows:

- Moderator who is a lead technical staff member with design experience
- Author of the detailed design
- Reader
- Recorder (this role may be performed by the moderator)

It is effective for the materials being inspected to be looked at from various viewpoints. For a detailed design the following viewpoints are recommended:

- High-level designer
- Coder
- Validator (unit, integration, and system)
- Maintenance staff member

It is acceptable for a single inspector to take more than one viewpoint. When possible these roles should be filled by the people who are actually responsible for the effort.

Be sure that the inspection team has at least one peer who has been responsible for detailed design, i.e., someone other than the author.

8.13.7 Inspection procedures

The detailed design should be examined against the high-level design. Emphasis should be placed on detecting missing or incorrect logic as well as internal and external interfaces. Be sure that the detailed design is not so constrained that the coder has only one implementation alternative. Be sure that the detailed design has enough material so that the coder can implement the design without consultation with the detailed designer.

Ensure that all modification requests have been addressed.

8.13.8 Exit criteria

■ All defects found have been corrected or placed under modification request control.

8.13.9 Checklist

The following checklist should be used to verify that all relevant areas of the detailed design document have been examined:

1. Have all materials required for a detailed design inspection been received?
2. Are all materials in the proper physical format?
3. Have all detailed design standards been followed?
4. Is the detailed design complete, i.e., does it completely implement the high-level design?
5. Is the pseudocode (or other representation format) consistent in its level of detail?
6. For scattered changes to existing code, does the detailed design show what code needs to be changed and how it is to be changed?
7. Are the functions clearly specified?
8. Are the functions logically independent?
9. Does the calling protocol follow project standards?
10. Are error conditions handled in a nondestructive manner?
11. Has all the data been properly defined and initialized?
12. Is all defined data utilized?
13. Are unusual situations handled reasonably and nondestructively?
14. Have maintainability issues been addressed?
15. Is the detailed design verifiable? Is there a finite cost-effective process by means of which a person or machine can check that the software product meets the design?
16. Is the logic correct, clear, and complete?

8.13.10 Defect types

See the consolidated listing of defect types (Section 8.21).

8.14 Inspections of Code

8.14.1 Purpose

1. To ensure that the code implementation agrees with the detailed design
2. To ensure that the code is complete and correct

8.14.2 Materials to be distributed

Distribute the following materials 3 working days prior to the inspection:

- The clean compiled listing of the code and all other compiler reports
- All applicable modification requests
- Detailed design document

8.14.3 Entrance criteria

- The code is cleanly complied.
- The code is run through the syntax editor.
- The code is line-numbered.
- The detailed design has been inspected and has met the exit criteria.

8.14.4 Reference materials

- High-level design

8.14.5 Coverage rates

- Preparation: 150 lines of code per hour
- Inspection: 150 lines of code per hour

8.14.6 Participants and roles

Functional roles required for a code inspection are as follows:

- Moderator who is a lead technical staff member
- Author of the code
- Reader
- Recorder (this role may be performed by the moderator)

It is effective for the materials being inspected to be looked at from various viewpoints. For code the following viewpoints are recommended:

- Detailed designer
- Validator (unit, integration, and system)
- Maintenance staff member

It is acceptable for a single inspector to take more than one viewpoint. When possible these roles should be filled by the people who are actually responsible for the effort.

Be sure that the inspection team has at least one peer who has had experience writing in the language being inspected, i.e., someone other than the author.

8.14.7 Inspection procedures

Examine the code for conformance to the detailed design, conformance to the coding standards, and correctness. Focus on control logic, linkage parameters, internal and external interfaces, and data definitions and usage. Look for performance, structuring, and storage problems.

8.14.8 Exit criteria

- All defects found have been corrected or placed under modification request control.

8.14.9 Checklist

The following checklist should be used to verify that all relevant areas of the code have been examined.

8.14.9.1 Data reference defects

1. Is there a referenced variable whose value is unset or uninitialized?
2. For all array references, is each subscript value within the defined bounds of the corresponding dimensions?
3. For all array references, does each subscript have an integer value? This may not be a defect, but it is a dangerous practice.
4. For all references through pointer variables, is the referenced storage currently allocated?
5. Does a storage area have alias names with different pointer variables? This is not a defect, but it is a dangerous practice.
6. Does the value of a variable have a type or attribute other than that expected? This is a common problem for storage referenced through pointers.
7. Are there any explicit or implicit addressing problems? Examples are (a) the physical storage is smaller than the storage addressed in the program, and (b) the address is defined as byte address but used as bit address.
8. Does the index of a string exceed its boundary?
9. Are there any off-by-one defects in indexing operations or in subscript references to arrays?

8.14.9.2 Data declaration defects

1. Have all variables been explicitly declared? If a variable is not declared, is it understood that the variable is a global variable?
2. If a variable is initialized in the declarative statement, is it properly initialized?
3. Is each variable assigned the correct length, type, and storage class?
4. Are there any variables that have similar names (e.g., VOLT and VOLTS)? This is not a defect, but it is a sign of confusion.

8.14.9.3 Computation defects

1. Are there any computations using variables having inconsistent data types (e.g., a Boolean variable in an arithmetic expression)?
2. Are there any mixed-mode (such as integer and floating-point) computations?
3. Are there any computations using variables having the same type but different length?
4. Is an overflow or underflow exception possible during the computation of an expression?
5. Is it possible for the denominator in a division operation to be zero?
6. Is it possible that a variable goes outside its meaningful range?
7. For expressions with more than one operator, is the order of computation and precedence of operators correct?
8. Are there any invalid uses of integer arithmetic, particularly divisions? Note that $[2 \times (I/2)]$ may not be equal to I.
9. Are there any computations on nonarithmetic variables?

8.14.9.4 Comparison defects

1. Are there any comparisons between variables having incompatible data types?

2. Are there any mixed-mode comparisons or comparisons between variables of different length?

3. Are the comparison operators correct?

4. Does the Boolean expression state what it is supposed to state? Programmers often make mistakes when writing Boolean expressions involving and/or.

5. Is the precedence or evaluation order of the Boolean expressions correct?

6. Do the operands of a Boolean expression have logical values (0 or 1)?

7. Are there any comparisons of equality between two floating-point numbers? Note that $[10.0 \times 0.1]$ is seldom equal to 1.0.

8.14.9.5 Control flow defects

1. Does every loop eventually terminate? Devise an informal proof or arguments showing that each loop will terminate.

2. Does the program have any goto statements? If yes, can you eliminate them?

3. Is it possible that a loop will never be executed because the entry condition is false?

4. Are there any off-by-one defects (i.e., more than one or fewer than one iteration)?

5. For each switch statement, does it have a default branch?

6. Are there any nonexhaustive decisions? An example of a nonexhaustive decision is:

Error-prone code	**Recommended code**
if (condition A)	if (condition A)
execute routine A	execute routine A
else if (condition B)	else if (condition B)
execute routine B	execute routine B
else /* condition C must be true */	else if (condition C)
execute routine C	execute routine C
	else
	print error message

8.14.9.6 Interface defects

1. Is the number of formal parameters (in a called routine) equal to the number of actual parameters (in the calling routine)? Are their orders correct?

2. Do the attributes (e.g., type and length) of each formal parameter match the attributes of the corresponding actual parameters?

3. Does the unit system of each formal parameter match that of the corresponding actual parameters?

4. Does a function modify the value of a parameter which is intended to be an input value?

5. Do global variables have the same definitions and attributes in all functions referencing them?

8.14.9.7 Input/output defects

1. Have all files been opened before use?

2. Are end-of-file (EOF) conditions detected and handled correctly?

3. Are end-of-line conditions detected and handled correctly?

4. Do the format specifications match the information in the input/output (I/O) statements? For example, does the program expect an integer while the input is a character?

5. Are there spelling or grammatical errors in the printed or displayed output?

6. Does the program check the validity of its input?

8.14.9.8 Missing code

- The last and most common and serious defect in the program is missing code, i.e., when programs do not check a certain condition(s) or do not implement a certain function(s).

8.14.10 Defect types

See the consolidated listing of defect types (Section 8.21).

8.15 Inspections of Unit Test Plans

8.15.1 Purpose

1. To ensure that the scope, strategy, resources, and schedule of the unit testing process have been completely and accurately specified

2. To ensure that all items to be tested and all required tasks to be performed have been defined

3. To ensure that all personnel necessary to perform the testing have been identified

8.15.2 Materials to be distributed

Distribute the following materials 5 working days prior to the inspection:

- Unit test plan
- Requirements document
- High-level design document
- Detailed design document
- Unit test plan checklist

8.15.3 Entrance criteria

- The unit test plan document is line-numbered.
- The unit test plan document has been run through a spelling checker.
- The document conforms to the standard unit test plan document format.
- The document contains all information types required by project standards (e.g., items to be tested, items not to be tested, pass/fail criteria, etc.).
- The detailed design has been inspected and has met the exit criteria.

8.15.4 Reference materials

- Unit test standards
- Test bed or baseline environment

8.15.5 Coverage rates

- Preparation: four to five pages per hour
- Inspection: four to five pages per hour

8.15.6 Participants and roles

Functional roles required for a unit test plan inspection team are as follows:

- Moderator who is a lead technical staff member with unit test experience
- Author of the unit test plan
- Reader
- Recorder (this role may be performed by the moderator)

It is effective for the materials being inspected to be looked at from various viewpoints. For a test plan the following viewpoints are recommended:

- High-level designer
- Detailed designer
- Validator (integration and system)
- Maintenance staff member

It is acceptable for a single inspector to take more than one viewpoint. When possible these roles should be filled by the people who are actually responsible for the effort.

Be sure that the inspection team has at least one peer who has been responsible for unit testing, i.e., someone other than the author.

8.15.7 Inspection procedures

Verify that the unit test plan is complete and feasible, and that the plan fits the project schedule. Be sure that all human and automated resources have been identified and that the objective of the plan is to uncover deviations from the requirements, high-level design, and detailed design.

8.15.8 Exit criteria

- All defects have been corrected or have been placed under modification request control.

8.15.9 Checklist

The following checklist should be used to verify that all relevant areas of the unit test plan document have been examined:

1. Have all materials required for a unit test plan inspection been received?
2. Are all materials in the proper physical format?
3. Have all unit test plan standards been followed?
4. Has the testing environment been completely specified?
5. Have all resources been considered, both human and hardware/software?
6. Have all testing dependencies been addressed (driver function, hardware, etc.)?
7. Is the unit test plan complete, i.e., does it verify all of the requirements, and does it test all functional and structural variations from the high-level and detailed design?

8. Is each script detailed and specific enough to provide the basis for unit test case generation?

9. Are all test entrance and exit criteria sufficient and realistic?

10. Are invalid as well as valid input conditions tested?

11. Have all pass/fail criteria been defined?

12. Does the unit test plan outline the levels of acceptability for pass/fail and exit criteria (e.g., defect tolerance)?

13. Have all suspension criteria and resumption requirements been identified?

14. Are all items excluded from testing documented as such?

15. Have all test deliverables been defined?

16. Will software development changes invalidate the plan?

17. Is the intent of the unit test plan to show the presence of failures and not merely the absence of failures?

18. Is the unit test plan complete, correct, and unambiguous?

19. Are there holes in the plan; is there overlap in the plan?

20. Does the unit test plan offer a measure of test completeness and test reliability to be sought?

21. Are the test strategy and philosophy feasible?

8.15.10 Defect types

See the consolidated listing of defect types (Section 8.21).

8.16 Inspections of Unit Test Cases

8.16.1 Purpose

1. To ensure that the unit test plan has been followed accurately

2. To ensure that the set of unit test cases for the unit is complete

3. To ensure that all unit test cases are correct

8.16.2 Materials to be distributed

Distribute the following materials 5 working days prior to the inspection:

- Unit test cases
- Unit test plan
- Test programs (any automated tool, other than the code being tested, required to implement the unit test plan)
- Requirements
- High-level design
- Detailed design
- Unit test case checklist

8.16.3 Reference materials

- Unit test standards
- Test bed or baseline environment

8.16.4 Coverage rates

- Preparation: three to four pages per hour
- Inspection: three to four pages per hour

8.16.5 Participants and roles

Functional roles required for a unit test case inspection team are as follows:

- Moderator who is a lead technical staff member with unit test experience
- Author of the unit test case
- Reader
- Recorder (this role may be performed by the moderator)

It is effective for the materials being inspected to be looked at from various viewpoints. For a unit test case the following viewpoints are recommended:

- High-level designer
- Detailed designer
- Validator (integration and system)
- Maintenance staff member

It is acceptable for a single inspector to take more than one viewpoint. When possible these roles should be filled by the people who are actually responsible for the effort.

Be sure that the inspection team has at least one peer who has been responsible for unit testing, i.e., someone other than the author.

8.16.6 Inspection procedures

Verify that the unit test plan has been followed completely and accurately, and ensure that each case is tested once and only once.

8.16.7 Entrance criteria

- The unit test case document is line-numbered.
- The document conforms to the project's standard unit test case document format.
- The document contains all information types required by project standards (e.g., test items, input specifications, output specifications, intercase dependencies).
- The unit test plan has been inspected and has met the exit criteria.

8.16.8 Exit criteria

- All defects have been corrected or have been placed under modification request control.

8.16.9 Checklist

The following checklist should be used to verify that all relevant areas of the unit test case document have been examined.

1. Have all materials required for a unit test case inspection been received?
2. Are all materials in the proper physical format?
3. Have all unit test case standards been followed?

4. Are the functional variations exercised by each unit test case required by the unit test plan?

5. Are the functional variations exercised by each unit test case clearly documented in the unit test case description?

6. Does each unit test case include a complete description of the expected input, and output or result?

7. Have all testing execution procedures been defined and documented?

8. Have all testing dependencies been addressed (driver function, hardware, etc.)?

9. Do the unit test cases accurately implement the unit test plan?

10. Are all data set definitions and setup requirements complete and accurate?

11. Are operator instructions and status indicators complete, accurate, and simple?

12. Have all intercase dependencies been identified and described?

13. Is each condition tested once and only once?

14. Have all test entrance and exit criteria been observed?

15. Are the unit test cases designed to show the presence of failure and not merely the absence of failure?

16. Are the unit test cases designed to show omissions and extensions?

17. Are the unit test cases complete, correct, and unambiguous?

18. Are the unit test cases realistic?

19. Are the unit test cases documented so as to be 100 percent reproducible?

20. Has the entire testing environment been documented?

21. Has configuration management been setup, directories established, and have case data and tools been loaded?

8.16.10   Defect types

See the consolidated listing of defect types (Section 8.21).

8.17   Inspections of Integration Test Plans

8.17.1   Purpose

1. To ensure that the scope, strategy, resources, and schedule of the integration testing process have been completely and accurately specified

2. To ensure that all items to be tested and all required tasks to be performed have been defined

3. To ensure that all personnel necessary to perform the testing has been identified

8.17.2   Materials to be distributed

Distribute the following materials 5 working days prior to the inspection:

- Test plan
- Requirements document
- Architecture document
- High-level design document
- Integration test plan checklist

8.17.3 Entrance criteria

- The integration test plan document is line-numbered.
- The integration test plan document has been run through a spelling checker.
- The document conforms to the standard integration test plan document format.
- The document contains all information types required by project standards (e.g., items to be tested, items not to be tested, pass/fail criteria, etc.).
- The architecture and high-level design have been inspected and have met the exit criteria.

8.17.4 Reference materials

- Unit test plan
- Integration test standards
- Test bed or baseline environment

8.17.5 Coverage rates

- Preparation: five to seven pages per hour
- Inspection: five to seven pages per hour

8.17.6 Participants and roles

Functional roles required for an integration test plan inspection team are as follows:

- Moderator who is a lead technical staff member with integration test experience
- Author of the integration test plan
- Reader
- Recorder (this role may be performed by the moderator)

It is effective for the materials being inspected to be looked at from various viewpoints. For a test plan the following viewpoints are recommended:

- Requirements author
- Appropriate developers
- Architect
- High-level designer
- Validator (system)
- Maintenance staff member

It is acceptable for a single inspector to take more than one viewpoint. When possible these roles should be filled by the people who are actually responsible for the effort.

Be sure that the inspection team has at least one peer who has been responsible for integration testing, i.e., someone other than the author.

8.17.7 Inspection procedures

Verify that the integration test plan is complete and feasible, and that the plan fits the project schedule. Be sure that all human and automated resources have been identified and that the objective of the plan is to uncover deviations from the requirements, architecture, and high-level design, focusing on interfaces.

8.17.8 Exit criteria

■ All defects have been corrected or have been placed under modification request control.

8.17.9 Checklist

The following checklist should be used to verify that all relevant areas of the integration test plan document have been examined:

1. Have all materials required for an integration test plan inspection been received?
2. Are all materials in the proper physical format?
3. Have all integration test plan standards been followed?
4. Has the testing environment been completely specified?
5. Have all resources been considered, both human and hardware/software?
6. Have all testing dependencies been addressed (driver function, hardware, etc.)?
7. Is the integration test plan complete, i.e., does it verify all interfaces defined in the architecture and high-level designs?
8. Is each script detailed and specific enough to provide the basis for integration test case generation?
9. Are all test entrance and exit criteria sufficient and realistic?
10. Are invalid as well as valid input conditions tested?
11. Have all pass/fail criteria been defined?
12. Does the integration test plan outline the levels of acceptability for pass/fail and exit criteria (e.g., defect tolerance)?
13. Have all suspension criteria and resumption requirements been identified?
14. Are all items excluded from testing documented as such?
15. Have all test deliverables been defined?
16. Will software development changes invalidate the plan?
17. Is the intent of the integration test plan to show the presence of failures and not merely the absence of failures?
18. Is the integration test plan complete, correct, and unambiguous?
19. Are there holes in the plan; is there overlap in the plan?
20. Does the integration test plan offer a measure of test completeness and test reliability to be sought?
21. Are the test strategy and philosophy feasible?

8.17.10 Defect types

See the consolidated listing of defect types (Section 8.21).

8.18 Inspections of Integration Test Cases

8.18.1 Purpose

1. To ensure that the integration test plan has been followed accurately
2. To ensure that the set of integration test cases is complete
3. To ensure that all integration test cases are correct

8.18.2. Materials to be distributed

Distribute the following materials 5 working days prior to the inspection:

- Integration test cases
- Integration test plan
- Test programs (any automated tool, other than the code being tested, required to implement the integration test plan)
- Requirements
- Architecture
- High-level design
- Integration test case checklist

8.18.3. Entrance criteria

- The integration test case document is line-numbered.
- The document conforms to the project's standard integration test case document format.
- The document contains all information types required by project standards (e.g., test items, input specifications, output specifications, intercase dependencies).
- The integration test plan has been inspected and has met the exit criteria.

8.18.4. Reference materials

- Integration test standards
- Unit test cases
- Test bed or baseline environment

8.18.5. Coverage rates

- Preparation: three to four pages per hour
- Inspection: three to four pages per hour

8.18.6. Participants and roles

Functional roles required for an integration test case inspection team are as follows:

- Moderator who is a lead technical staff member with integration test experience
- Author of the integration test case
- Reader
- Recorder (this role may be performed by the moderator)

It is effective for the materials being inspected to be looked at from various viewpoints. For an integration test case the following viewpoints are recommended:

- Appropriate developers
- Architect
- High-level designer
- Validator (system)
- Maintenance staff member

It is acceptable for a single inspector to take more than one viewpoint. When possible these roles should be filled by the people who are actually responsible for the effort.

Be sure that the inspection team has at least one peer who has been responsible for integration testing, i.e., someone other than the author.

8.18.7 Inspection procedures

Verify that the integration test plan has been followed completely and accurately, and ensure that each case is tested once and only once.

8.18.8 Exit criteria

- All defects have been corrected or have been placed under modification request control.

8.18.9 Checklist

The following checklist should be used to verify that all relevant areas of the integration test cases have been examined:

1. Have all materials required for an integration test case inspection been received?
2. Are all materials in the proper physical format?
3. Have all integration test case standards been followed?
4. Are all interfaces tested as specified in the integration test plan?
5. Does each integration test case include a complete description of the expected input, and output or result?
6. Have all testing execution procedures been defined and documented?
7. Have all testing dependencies been addressed (driver function, hardware, etc.)?
8. Do the integration test cases accurately implement the integration test plan?
9. Are all data set definitions and setup requirements complete and accurate?
10. Are operator instructions and status indicators complete, accurate, and simple?
11. Have all intercase dependencies been identified and described?
12. Is each condition tested once and only once?
13. Are all entrance and exit criteria observed?
14. Are the integration test cases designed to show the presence of failure and not merely the absence of failure?
15. Are the integration test cases designed to show omissions and extensions?
16. Are the integration test cases complete, correct, and unambiguous?
17. Are the integration test cases realistic?
18. Are the integration test cases documented so as to be 100 percent reproducible?
19. Has the entire testing environment been documented?
20. Has configuration management been setup, directories established, and case data and tools loaded?

8.18.10 Defect types

See the consolidated listing of defect types (Section 8.21).

8.19 Inspections of System Test Plans

8.19.1 Purpose

1. To ensure that the scope, strategy, resources, and schedule of the system testing process have been completely and accurately specified

2. To ensure that all items to be tested and all required tasks to be performed have been defined

3. To ensure that all personnel necessary to perform the testing have been identified

8.19.2 Materials to be distributed

Distribute the following materials 5 working days prior to the inspection:

- Test plan
- Requirements document

8.19.3 Reference materials

- System test standards
- Test bed or baseline environment

8.19.4 Coverage rates

- Preparation: five to seven pages per hour
- Inspection: five to seven pages per hour

8.19.5 Participants and roles

Functional roles required for a system test plan inspection team are as follows:

- Moderator who is a lead technical staff member with system test experience
- Author of the system test plan
- Reader
- Recorder (this role may be performed by the moderator)

It is effective for the materials being inspected to be looked at from various viewpoints. For a test plan the following viewpoints are recommended:

- Requirements author
- Customer
- User documentation author
- Field support representative

It is acceptable for a single inspector to take more than one viewpoint. When possible these roles should be filled by the people who are actually responsible for the effort.

Be sure that the inspection team has at least one peer who has been responsible for system testing, i.e., someone other than the author.

8.19.6 Inspection procedures

Verify that the system test plan is complete and feasible, and that the plan fits the project schedule. Be sure that all human and automated resources have been identified and that the objective of the plan is to uncover deviations from the requirements.

8.19.7 Entrance criteria

- The system test plan document is line-numbered.
- The system test plan document has been run through a spelling checker.
- The document conforms to the standard system test plan document format.
- The document contains all information types required by project standards (e.g., items to be tested, items not to be tested, pass/fail criteria, etc.).

8.19.8 Exit criteria

- All defects have been corrected or have been placed under modification request control.

8.19.9 Checklist

The following checklist should be used to verify that all relevant areas of the system test plan document have been examined:

1. Have all materials required for a system test plan inspection been received?
2. Are all materials in the proper physical format?
3. Have all system test plan standards been followed?
4. Has the testing environment been completely specified?
5. Have all resources been considered, both human and hardware/software?
6. Have all testing dependencies been addressed (driver function, hardware, etc.)?
7. Is the system test plan complete, i.e., does it verify all requirements?
8. Is each script detailed and specific enough to provide the basis for system test case generation?
9. Are all test entrance and exit criteria sufficient and realistic?
10. Are invalid as well as valid input conditions tested?
11. Have all pass/fail criteria been defined?
12. Does the system test plan outline the levels of acceptability for pass/fail and exit criteria (e.g., defect tolerance)?
13. Have all suspension criteria and resumption requirements been identified?
14. Are all items excluded from testing documented as such?
15. Have all test deliverables been defined?
16. Is the intent of the system test plan to show the presence of failures and not merely the absence of failures?
17. Is the system test plan complete, correct, and unambiguous?
18. Are there holes in the plan; is there overlap in the plan?
19. Does the system test plan offer a measure of test completeness and test reliability to be sought?
20. Are the test strategy and philosophy feasible?

8.19.10 Defect types

See the consolidated listing of defect types (Section 8.21).

8.20   Inspections of System Test Cases

8.20.1   Purpose

1. To ensure that the system test plan has been followed accurately
2. To ensure that the set of system test cases is complete
3. To ensure that all system test cases are correct

8.20.2   Materials to be distributed

Distribute the following materials 5 working days prior to the inspection:

- System test cases
- System test plan
- Test programs (any automated tool, other than the code being tested, required to implement the system test plan)
- Requirements
- System test case checklist

8.20.3   Entrance criteria

- The system test case document is line-numbered.
- The document conforms to the project's standard system test case document format.
- The document contains all information types required by project standards (e.g., test items, input specifications, output specifications, intercase dependencies).
- The system test plan has been inspected and has met the exit criteria.

8.20.4   Reference materials

- System test standards
- Test bed or baseline environment

8.20.5   Coverage rates

- Preparation: three to four pages per hour
- Inspection: three to four pages per hour

8.20.6   Participants and roles

Functional roles required for a system test case inspection team are as follows:

- Moderator who is a lead technical staff member with system test experience
- Author of the system test cases
- Reader
- Recorder (this role may be performed by the moderator)

It is effective for the materials being inspected to be looked at from various viewpoints. For a system test case the following viewpoints are recommended:

- Requirements author
- Validator (system)
- Maintenance staff member

It is acceptable for a single inspector to take more than one viewpoint. When possible these roles should be filled by the people who are actually responsible for the effort.

Be sure that the inspection team has at least one peer who has been responsible for system testing, i.e., someone other than the author.

8.20.7 Inspection procedures

Verify that the system test plan has been followed completely and accurately, and ensure that each case is tested once and only once.

8.20.8 Exit criteria

■ All defects have been corrected or have been placed under modification request control.

8.20.9 Checklist

The following checklist should be used to verify that all relevant areas of the system test case document have been examined:

1. Have all materials required for a system test case inspection been received?
2. Are all materials in the proper physical format?
3. Have all system test case standards been followed?
4. Are all requirements tested as specified in the system test plan?
5. Does each system test case include a complete description of the expected input, and output or result?
6. Have all testing execution procedures been defined and documented?
7. Have all testing dependencies been addressed (driver function, hardware, etc.)?
8. Do the system test cases accurately implement the system test plan?
9. Are all data set definitions and setup requirements complete and accurate?
10. Are operator instructions and status indicators complete, accurate, and simple?
11. Have all intercase dependencies been identified and described?
12. Is each condition tested once and only once?
13. Are all entrance and exit criteria observed?
14. Are the system test cases designed to show the presence of failure and not merely the absence of failure?
15. Are the system test cases designed to show omissions and extensions?
16. Are the system test cases complete, correct, and unambiguous?
17. Are the system test cases realistic?
18. Are the system test cases documented so as to be 100 percent reproducible?
19. Has the entire testing environment been documented?
20. Has configuration management been setup, directories established, and case data and tools loaded?

8.20.10 Defect types

See the consolidated listing of defect types (Section 8.21).

8.21 Defect Types

DA—data	Defects in data specification; improper declaration, initialization, or description of data; incorrect data usage, conversion of data types, or array boundaries
DC—documentation	Inadequate or incorrect component descriptions (e.g., missing, incomplete, incorrect comments)
FN—functionality	Defects in the specification of the functions of a component
HF—human factors	Incorrect or improper operating procedures; no specification of what operating procedure to use; unnecessary operator involvement
IF—interface	Defects in the communication between software components (e.g., incorrect module invocation, incorrect passing of data), excluding defects in device or human interfaces
IO—input/output	Defects in communication with or specification of external data or devices
LO—logic	Defects in procedures or in sequence, selection, iteration of operations (e.g., incorrect boundary condition on a loop, incorrect comparison); incorrect algorithms or mathematical computation
MN—maintainability	An expectation that the work product is difficult to maintain (e.g., it is not understandable or has undesired side effects), excluding defects in documentation
PF—performance	An expectation of not meeting the required efficiency of execution (e.g., execution speed is too slow, too much memory is used)
SN—syntax	Defects in grammar, punctuation, spelling, and specification language usage
ST—standards	A deviation from procedural or representational standards
TC—test case	Incomplete or inaccurate specifications of a test condition, or a deviation from the test plan
TE—test environment	Defects in the definition or specification of the test hardware or software environment, level of security, or proprietary components
TP—test plan	Defects in the definition or specification of test scope, strategy (including test completeness and defect tolerance levels), personnel, tasks, items, or features
OT—other	An undefined or ambiguous defect condition

8.22 Inspection Meeting Notice

Inspection Meeting Notice

Meeting Date: _____

Project: _____   Release: _____
Activity: _____   Document: _____
Component: _____   Moderator: _____

Phone: _____ Location: _____

Meeting Type: ☐ Overview (O)   ☐ Inspection (I)   ☐ Re-Inspection (R)

Inspection Type: ☐ Requirements (RE)   ☐ Code (CD)   ☐ Integration Test Case (ITC)
                 ☐ Architecture (AR)   ☐ Unit Test Plan (UTP)   ☐ System Test Plan (STP)
                 ☐ High Level Design (HD) ☐ Unit Test Case (UTC)   ☐ System Test Case (STC)
                 ☐ Detail Design (DD)   ☐ Integration Test Plan (UTP)

This meeting has been scheduled for:

Date: _____
Time: _____
Location: _____
Duration: _____

Size of the materials is: _____   Expected preparation time is: _____

The following persons are scheduled to attend:

Name	Location	Role

8.23 Inspection Defect List

Inspection Defect List

Meeting Date: _____

Project: _____   Release: _____

Activity: _____   Document: _____

Component: _____   Moderator: _____

Meeting Type: ☐ Inspection (I)   ☐ Re-Inspection (R)   ☐ Maintenance (M)

Inspection Type: ☐ Requirements (RE)   ☐ Code (CD)   ☐ Integration Test Case (ITC)

☐ Architecture (AR)   ☐ Unit Test Plan (UTP)   ☐ System Test Plan (STP)

☐ High Level Design (HD)   ☐ Unit Test Case (UTC)   ☐ System Test Case (STC)

☐ Detail Design (DD)   ☐ Integration Test Plan (UTP)

Disposition: ☐ Accept (A)   ☐ Conditional (C)   ☐ Re-Inspect (R)

Location	Defect Description	Type	Class	Severity
_____	_____	____	____	____
_____	_____	____	____	____
_____	_____	____	____	____
_____	_____	____	____	____
_____	_____	____	____	____
_____	_____	____	____	____
_____	_____	____	____	____
_____	_____	____	____	____
_____	_____	____	____	____
_____	_____	____	____	____
_____	_____	____	____	____
_____	_____	____	____	____
_____	_____	____	____	____
_____	_____	____	____	____
_____	_____	____	____	____
_____	_____	____	____	____
_____	_____	____	____	____
_____	_____	____	____	____
_____	_____	____	____	____

Defect Type: DA=Data, DC=Documentation,   FN=Functionality, HF=Human Factors , IF=Interface,
IO=Input/Output, LO=Logic, MN=Maintainability, PF=Performance, SN=Syntax, ST=Standards,
TC=Test Case, TE=Test Environment, TP=Test Plan, OT=Other
Defect Class: M=Missing, W=Wrong , E=Extra
Defect Severity: J=Major, N=Minor

8.24   Inspection Defect Summary

Inspection Defect Summary

	Meeting Date: _____
Project: _____	Release: _____
Activity: _____	Document: _____
Component: _____	Moderator: _____

Meeting Type: ☐ Inspection (I)   ☐ Re-Inspection (R)   ☐ Maintenance (M)

Inspection Type: ☐ Requirements (RE)   ☐ Code (CD)   ☐ Integration Test Case (ITC)

☐ Architecture (AR)   ☐ Unit Test Plan (UTP)   ☐ System Test Plan (STP)

☐ High Level Design (HD)   ☐ Unit Test Case (UTC)   ☐ System Test Case (STC)

☐ Detail Design (DD)   ☐ Integration Test Plan (UTP)

Disposition: ☐ Accept (A)   ☐ Conditional (C)   ☐ Re-Inspect (R)

Defect	MINOR DEFECTS				MAJOR DEFECTS			
	M	W	E	Total	M	W	E	Total
DA: Data								
DC: Documentation								
FN: Functionality								
HF: Human Factors								
IF: Interface								
IO: Input/Output								
LO: Logic								
MN: Maintainability								
PF: Performance								
SN: Syntax								
ST: Standards								
TC: Test Case								
TE: Test Environment								
TP: Test Plan								
OT: Other								
Total								

8.25 Inspection Report

Inspection Report

Meeting Date: _____

Project: _____   Release: _____

Activity: _____   Document: _____

Component: _____   Moderator: _____

Meeting Type: ☐ Inspection (I)   ☐ Re-Inspection (R)   ☐ Maintenance (M)

Inspection Type: ☐ Requirements (RE)   ☐ Code (CD)   ☐ Integration Test Case (ITC)

☐ Architecture (AR)   ☐ Unit Test Plan (UTP)   ☐ System Test Plan (STP)

☐ High Level Design (HD)   ☐ Unit Test Case (UTC)   ☐ System Test Case (STC)

☐ Detail Design (DD)   ☐ Integration Test Plan (UTP)

Disposition: ☐ Accept (A)   ☐ Conditional (C)   ☐ Re-Inspect (R)

Inspection Duration: _____(hours)   Number of Inspectors: _____(all)

Overview Duration: _____(hours)   Total Preparation Time: _____(hours)

Size of Materials: _____(lines)   Number of Inspection Meetings: _____

Rework to be completed by: _____   Estimated Rework Effort: _____(hours)

Re-Inspection scheduled for: _____   Actual Rework Effort: _____(hours)

Inspectors:

_____   _____
_____   _____
_____   _____
_____   _____
_____   _____

Moderator Certification: _____

Completion Date: _____

Additional Comments:

_____
_____
_____
_____
_____
_____
_____

Inspections in Other Development Processes

The previous chapter contains a sample software inspection procedures manual. Because in-process inspections are most frequently used within software development, there is a tendency to think of them as only a software development quality control tool. In-process inspections actually have much wider applicability. To extend the range of our consideration, this chapter describes the application of in-process inspections to

- Documentation
- Hardware
- Course development

These examples do not exhaust the possible uses of inspections. Rather, in their diversity they demonstrate the basic principle that if there is a documented intermediate work product that can be understood by other peer developers, it can be verified by in-process inspection.

An in-process inspection procedures manual, regardless of the product being inspected, contains the same type of summary material that was included in the first nine sections of the sample in Chapter 8. Therefore, these sections are not repeated in this chapter. They would, of course, be modified for any procedures specific to the project. A project involving a combination of software, documentation, hardware, courses, and/or any other type of inspections would probably require the preparation of a single project inspection procedures manual combining these various types.

Applying Inspections to Documentation

The documentation development process is similar to software development, consisting of planning, design, implementation, and testing. As for other development processes, each of these stages produces work products that can be reviewed, inspected, or tested. A document development model is shown in Fig. 9.1 below for this example.

The documentation planning stage coincides with product planning, and produces three work products: documentation requirements, documentation plan, and documentation test plan. Each of these work products may be separate or may be included as subsections of the corresponding project planning document.

Documentation requirements take into account both what the customer needs to know to use and administer the product, and what the project team needs to know to maintain and update the product.

Based on the documentation requirements, the documentation plan identifies the documents to be developed. For each document it describes the intended audience, responsible documenter(s), document inspection dates, document delivery dates (to system test and to customer), required staff hours, and the document development environment.

The documentation test plan is written during the planning stage but is based partly on the document outlines. This part of the planning stage overlaps the document design stage. The document test plan describes how each document will be tested. For procedural documents, testing may involve using the document to perform the indicated procedure; for descriptive documents, testing may include a comparison with

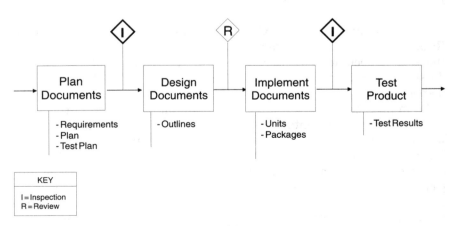

Figure 9.1 Documentation development model.

the hardware or software the document describes. Readers are used to test documents for comprehension.

Documentation design consists of producing a set of annotated document outlines for each document identified in the documentation plan. Implementation then consists of producing document units based on the document outlines.

During document implementation, a document unit consists either of a complete document or subsection (chapter) of a document. Short documents are presented as a single work product; long documents tend to be divided into chapters that cover a given topic. Document units include text and any graphical information. Document units are then compiled into a documentation package which is a complete set of inspected documents for end-users, product administrators, development, support, etc.

Documentation examination procedures include reviews, inspections, and document testing. (See Chapter 10 for a description of the relationship between reviews and inspections.) Document outlines are reviewed, not inspected. Outlines are used to determine not only what information is included in a document, but how it is organized, and the form of presentation used (text, graphical, tabular, etc.). There are many correct ways to organize and present material. The review determines the best way for the intended audience. Since the intended audience for the project documentation includes customers, developers, administrators, maintainers, and possibly others, representatives from each of these groups are included in the review.

The work products that are inspected and their inspection types are

- Documentation requirements (DR)
- Documentation plan (DP)
- Documentation test plan (DT)
- Document unit (DU)

Documentation packages consist entirely of materials that have already been inspected. Although a documentation package could be inspected against the documentation plan for completeness, this step is included in the documentation testing process, and so is unnecessary.

9.1 Inspection of Documentation Requirements

9.1.1 Purpose

1. To ensure requirements meet customer needs
2. To ensure that the product can be documented in line with the requirements
3. To detect omissions, defects, or extraneous requirements

9.1.2 Materials to be distributed

Distribute the following materials 5 working days prior to the inspection:

- Documentation requirements
- Project requirements
- Documentation requirements checklist
- All applicable modification requests (MRs)

9.1.3 Entrance criteria

- Documentation requirements document is line-numbered.
- Documentation requirements document has been run through a spelling checker.
- Documentation requirements document is formatted.
- Documentation requirements document conforms to standard for requirements documents.

9.1.4 Coverage rates

- Preparation: five to seven pages per hour
- Inspection: five to seven pages per hour

9.1.5 Participants and roles

Functional roles required for a documentation requirements inspection are:

- Moderator with experience writing requirements documents
- Author of the documentation requirements
- Reader
- Recorder

Other recommended participants are representatives from

- Documentation
- Development
- Customer
- Testing

9.1.6 Inspection procedures

Inspect against known customer needs, including customer request for proposal, if it exists. Inspect against development requirements to ensure consistency. Inspect against any outstanding MRs.

9.1.7 Exit criteria

- All defects found are corrected or placed under MR control.

9.1.8 Checklist

1. Have all requirements materials been provided?
2. Are all materials in correct format?

3. Do materials conform to standards?
4. Do document requirements cover all known customer needs?
5. Are requirements complete, correct, and unambiguous?
6. Are document requirements consistent with product requirements?

9.1.9 Defect types

CS—consistency	Inconsistent specification either within the document or with other requirements documents
CT—content	Inadequate, incorrect, or unnecessary information
DN—definition	Missing, wrong, or extra definition of terminology
HF—human factors	Poor or lacking regard to human factors
OR—organization	Awkward or noncohesive presentation of information
RD—readability	Difficult to understand; inappropriate language, syntax, word use, or notation
ST—standards	Failure to meet requirements or documentation standards
OT—other	Defect that does not fit any of the above types

9.2 Inspection of Documentation Plans

9.2.1 Purpose

1. To verify that the plan is consistent with itself and with documentation requirements
2. To ensure that the plan meets its objectives
3. To ensure that the plan is consistent with other project plan documents

9.2.2 Materials to be distributed

Distribute the following materials 5 working days prior to the inspection:

- Documentation plan
- Documentation requirements
- Documentation plan checklist
- Applicable project plan documents

9.2.3 Entrance criteria

- Documentation plan is line-numbered.
- Documentation plan has been run through a spelling checker.
- Documentation plan is formatted.
- Documentation plan conforms to standard for project plans.

9.2.4 Coverage rates

- Preparation: five to seven pages per hour
- Inspection: five to seven pages per hour

9.2.5 Participants and roles

Functional roles required for a documentation plan inspection are

- Moderator with experience writing project plans
- Author of the documentation plan
- Reader
- Recorder

Other recommended participants are representatives from

- Documentation
- Development
- Customer
- Testing

9.2.6 Inspection procedures

Inspect against the documentation requirements to ensure that all requirements are satisfied, and against development requirements to ensure consistency. Emphasis should be placed on detecting missing or incorrect plan elements. Also verify that the plan does not contradict itself or any other project plan.

9.2.7 Exit criteria

- All defects found are corrected or placed under MR control.

9.2.8 Checklist

1. Have all materials been provided?
2. Are all materials in correct format?
3. Do materials conform to standards?
4. Does documentation plan cover all requirements?
5. Is plan complete, correct, and unambiguous?
6. Is plan consistent with itself and with other project plans?

9.2.9 Defect types

CS—consistency	Inconsistent specification either within the document or with other planning documents
CT—content	Inadequate, incorrect, or unnecessary information
DN—definition	Missing, wrong, or extra definition of terminology
HF—human factors	Poor or lacking regard to human factors
OR—organization	Awkward or noncohesive presentation of information
RD—readability	Difficult to understand; inappropriate language, syntax, word use, or notation
ST—standards	Failure to meet requirements or documentation standards
OT—other	Defect that does not fit any of the above types

9.3 Inspection of Documentation Test Plans

9.3.1 Purpose

1. To verify that the plan is consistent with itself, the documentation plan, documentation requirements, and other applicable test plans
2. To ensure that the plan meets its objectives
3. To ensure that the plan is consistent with other project plan documents
4. To ensure that all elements of the proposed documents are covered by the test plan

9.3.2 Materials to be distributed

Distribute the following materials 5 working days prior to the inspection:

- Documentation test plan
- Documentation plan
- Documentation requirements
- Documentation outlines
- Documentation test plan checklist
- Applicable project test plan documents

9.3.3 Entrance criteria

- Documentation test plan is line-numbered.
- Documentation test plan has been run through a spelling checker.
- Documentation test plan is formatted.
- Documentation test plan conforms to standard for project test plans.

9.3.4 Coverage rates

- Preparation: five to seven pages per hour
- Inspection: five to seven pages per hour

9.3.5 Participants and roles

Functional roles required for a documentation test plan inspection are

- Moderator with experience writing project test plans
- Author of the documentation test plan
- Reader
- Recorder

Other recommended participants are representatives from

- Documentation
- Development
- Customer
- Testing

9.3.6 Inspection procedures

Inspect against the documentation and development requirements, to ensure that all requirements are satisfied. Emphasis should be placed on detecting missing or incorrect test plan elements, and ensuring that the test plan provides mechanisms for achieving its objectives. Inspect against the document outlines, to ensure that all elements of the documents are covered by the test plan. Also verify that the test plan does not contradict itself or any other project test plan.

9.3.7 Exit criteria

- All defects found are corrected or placed under MR control.

9.3.8 Checklist

1. Have all materials been provided?
2. Are all materials in correct format?
3. Do materials conform to standards?
4. Does documentation test plan cover all requirements?
5. Is test plan complete, correct, and unambiguous?
6. Is test plan consistent with itself and with other project test plans?
7. Does test plan provide for testing all document elements?

9.3.9 Defect types

CS—consistency	Inconsistent specification either within the document or with other test plans
CT—content	Inadequate, incorrect, or unnecessary information
DN—definition	Missing, wrong, or extra definition of terminology
HF—human factors	Poor or lacking regard to human factors
OR—organization	Awkward or noncohesive presentation of information
RD—readability	Difficult to understand; inappropriate language, syntax, word use, or notation
ST—standards	Failure to meet requirements or documentation standards
OT—other	Defect that does not fit any of the above types

9.4 Inspection of Document Units

9.4.1 Purpose

1. To ensure that completed units are consistent with documentation requirements and with document outlines
2. To ensure that units are complete, correct, and targeted to the appropriate audience
3. To ensure that documentation units contribute to customer understanding of the product
4. To verify that completed units conform to documentation standards

9.4.2 Materials to be distributed

Distribute the following materials 5 working days prior to the inspection:

- Document unit(s), including any preceding units needed for an understanding of the unit
- Documentation requirements
- Document outline
- Document units checklist

9.4.3 Entrance criteria
- Document unit is line-numbered.
- Document unit has been run through a spelling checker.
- Document unit is formatted.
- Document unit conforms to documentation standards.

9.4.4 Coverage rates
- Preparation: five to seven pages per hour
- Inspection: five to seven pages per hour

9.4.5 Participants and roles
Functional roles required for a document unit inspection are

- Moderator with documentation or product experience
- Author of the document unit
- Reader
- Recorder

Other recommended participants are representatives from

- Documentation
- Development
- Customer
- Testing

9.4.6 Inspection procedures
Inspect against the documentation and development requirements, to ensure all requirements are satisfied. Inspect against the document outlines, to ensure that all elements of the document exist and are correctly organized.

9.4.7 Exit criteria
- All defects found are corrected or placed under MR control.

9.4.8 Checklist
1. Have all materials been provided?
2. Are all materials in correct format?
3. Do materials conform to standards?
4. Does document unit satisfy all requirements?

5. Is document unit complete, correct, and unambiguous?

6. Is document unit free from any extraneous information?

9.4.9 Defect types

CS—consistency	Inconsistent specification either within the document or with other document units
CT—content	Inadequate, incorrect, or unnecessary information
DN—definition	Missing, wrong, or extra definition of terminology
HF—human factors	Poor or lacking regard to human factors
OR—organization	Awkward or noncohesive presentation of information
RD—readability	Difficult to understand; inappropriate language, syntax, word use, or notation
ST—standards	Failure to meet requirements or documentation standards
OT—other	Defect that does not fit any of the above types

Applying Inspections to Hardware Development

In this section we outline inspection procedures that have been tailored to the needs of a project developing electronic products. The scope of the inspection procedures ranges from project planning to circuit and test design activities. The reasons for the project using inspections are those that we have considered before, increased product quality and reduced development cost, plus one that is unique to this environment—reduction of the number of cycles needed to develop the final product.

The inspection types for this example are listed below.

- Project plan (PR)
- Feature specification (FS)
- Functional architecture (FA)
- Module specification (MS)
- Module interface specification (MI)
- Circuit features (CF)
- Circuit electrical design (ED)
- System test plan (TP)
- System test specification (TS)

The inspection types reflect the hardware development stages shown in the model in Fig. 9.2.

For simplicity, planning has been shown as a single stage at the start of the project. In reality, some of the plans are generated early in the project, such as the feature specifications and functional architecture, which are prerequisites to later steps. Others, such as the system test plans, are generated in parallel with the rest of the development process. Some examples of inspectable project plans are

Project plan: Describes the organization, procedures, tasks, schedules, and responsibilities of the project. This document is required for all subsequent project activities.

Functional architecture: Descriptions of the organization of features, modules, intermodule interfaces, and external interfaces; an overview of the software; a list of various equipages for different applications; and a discussion of evolutionary capabilities.

System test plan: Describes the test procedures to be used to validate the correct operation of the system.

The next phase, specification, documents what the modules are supposed to do and how they do it. Each module is logically described by the module specification which includes a high-level block diagram and associated descriptions, input/output (I/O) signal list, a provisioning summary, and a data list.

An intermodule interface specification is also prepared, which speci-

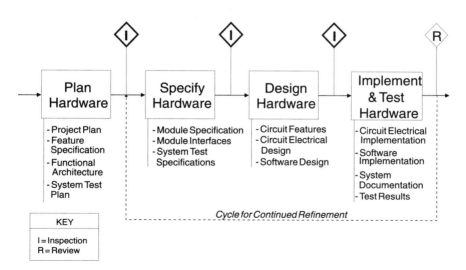

Figure 9.2 Hardware development model.

fies the signal paths flowing between modules, down to the signal name and timing. The functional architecture is the basic driving force behind these specifications.

Next, during the electrical design phase, a logic-level design of the module is performed. Additional activities include functional partitioning, software interfaces, and testability, among others. A whole spectrum of documentation results, including schematics, signal timing diagrams, presumptive equipment placements, parts lists, circuit descriptions, and others.

During the testing phase, the test plans and specifications are executed to verify the correct operation of the product. Their results are analyzed, and the project either enters another cycle of development for continued refinement, or the completed product is implemented.

Inspection types for each of these phases are described in the sections that follow. The format in which they are presented differs slightly from the format used by the sample software inspection procedures. The format is adjustable, and you should select a format that best suits your project needs.

Note also that while the sample software inspection procedures made use of a composite list of defect types, the sample hardware inspection procedures supply a separate defect list for each inspection type. Moreover, although many of the same defect types appear in several lists, the definitions of the defect types vary somewhat from list to list. This variation recognizes that the same general defect type may have different meanings within the context of different types of inspections. Inspectors also apply defect types better when they are separated into different defect lists for each type of inspection.

9.5   Inspection of Project Plans

9.5.1   Purpose

1. To verify that the plan is consistent with itself and with project requirements

2. To ensure that the plan meets its objectives

3. To ensure that the plan does not violate any other project plan documents

9.5.2   Materials to be distributed

Distribute the following materials 5 working days prior to the inspection:

- Project plan
- Project plan objectives
- Project plan checklist

9.5.3   Entrance criteria

- Objective list is numbered and procedure-oriented.
- The project plan is line-numbered.

- The project plan has been run through a spelling checker.
- The project plan conforms to document format standards.

9.5.4 Coverage rates

- Preparation: five to seven pages per hour
- Inspection: five to seven pages per hour

9.5.5 Participants and roles

Functional roles required for a project plan inspection are

- Moderator who is a lead engineer with systems engineering experience
- Author of the project plan
- Reader
- Recorder

Other recommended participants are representatives from

- Hardware development
- Software development
- Systems development
- Physical design

The total number of inspectors should be limited to 10 people.

9.5.6 Inspection procedures

The plan is examined against the objective list, by looking at each objective and the implied procedure for achieving it. Emphasis should be placed on detecting missing or incorrect project plan elements, and on ensuring that the plan provides mechanisms for reaching the stated objectives. Also verify that the plan does not contradict itself or other project plan documents or violate project requirements.

9.5.7 Exit criteria

- The plan meets all its objectives.
- The plan is consistent with other project plans.
- The plan is consistent with itself.
- The plan does not violate any project requirements.
- All found defects have been corrected or resolved.

9.5.8 Checklist

Given the individual nature of each project planning specification, a set of checklist items particular to the plan being examined should be prepared.

9.5.9 Defect types

DC—documentation	Inadequate, incorrect, inconsistent, or vague description
FN—functional	The function does not satisfy requirements
IF—interface	Project plan interface does not meet required capability

RE—requirements	The function is correct but is inconsistent
SN—syntax	Defect in grammar, punctuation, spelling, or language
ST—standards	Failure to meet standards
OT—other	Defect that does not fit any of the above types

9.6   Inspection of Feature Specification

9.6.1   Purpose

1. To verify that the document is consistent with itself
2. To ensure that the document meets customer and system engineering requirements, and conforms to developer input
3. To ensure that the document specifies the design requirement in sufficient detail

9.6.2   Materials to be distributed

Distribute the following materials 5 working days prior to the inspection:

- Project feature document
- Any pertinent system engineering documents
- Any documents describing interfacing equipment requirements
- Any relevant customer documents
- Project feature document checklist

9.6.3   Entrance criteria

- The project feature document is line-numbered.
- The project feature document has been run through a spelling checker.
- The project feature document conforms to documentation standards.

9.6.4   Coverage rates

- Preparation: five to seven pages per hour
- Inspection: five to seven pages per hour

9.6.5   Participants and roles

Functional roles required for a project feature document inspection are

- Moderator who is a lead engineer with systems engineering experience
- Author of the project feature document
- Reader
- Recorder

Other recommended participants are representatives from

- Hardware development
- Software development
- Systems development

- Physical design
- System engineering
- System planning and test

The total number of inspectors should be limited to 12 people.

9.6.6 Inspection procedures

The project feature document is examined against customer, engineering, and development requirements. Place emphasis on detecting missing or incorrect feature definitions and requirements. Also verify that the feature document does not contradict itself or other relevant documentation.

9.6.7 Exit criteria

- All items in the checklist are covered.
- The project feature document is consistent with all documents included in the materials distributed.
- The project feature document is consistent with itself.
- The project feature document does not violate any customer, system engineering, or development requirements.
- All defects found have been corrected or resolved.

9.6.8 Checklist

Does the project feature document contain explicit guidelines (or explicit don't cares) for the following items:

1. Cost
2. Physical dimensions
3. Power requirements (voltage ranges, dissipation, etc.)
4. Density (channels per shelf, per bay)
5. User interface requirements (physical, electrical, software)
6. Equipment interface requirements (physical, electrical, protocols, message sets)
7. Schedule
8. Short- and long-term reliability
9. Details of functions performed
10. Alarm and maintenance information [type of testing, built-in self-test (BIST), performance data base]
11. Standards/requirements that must be met [e.g., International Consultive Committee of Telephone and Telegraphy (CCITT), network equipment building system (NEBS), Energy Information Administration (EIA)]

9.6.9 Defect types

DC—documentation	Inadequate, incorrect, inconsistent, or vague description
FN—functional	The function does not satisfy requirements
IF—interface	The interface does not meet requirements

RE—requirements	The function is correct but is inconsistent with higher-level requirements
SN—syntax	Defect in grammar, punctuation, spelling, or language
ST—standards	Failure to meet standards
OT—other	Defect that does not fit any of the above types

9.7   Inspection of Functional Architecture

9.7.1   Purpose

1. To verify that the architecture design meets the project feature document requirements
2. To ensure that the design is clear and completely documented

9.7.2   Materials to be distributed

- Architecture design
- Feature specification
- Architecture design checklist

9.7.3   Entrance criteria

- A block diagram of the system
- A line-numbered functional description of each block in the block diagram
- Definition of major signals including timing diagrams, if appropriate
- Functional description has been run through a spelling checker
- Architecture design conforms to design document standards

9.7.4   Coverage rates

- Preparation: five to seven pages per hour
- Inspection: five to seven pages per hour

9.7.5   Participants and roles

Functional roles required for an architecture design inspection are

- Moderator who is a senior engineer
- Author of the architecture design
- Reader
- Recorder

Other recommended participants are representatives from

- Hardware development
- Software development
- System planning and test
- Very large-scale integration (VLSI) development
- Author of the project feature document

The total number of inspectors should be limited to 10 people.

9.7.6 Inspection procedures

The architecture design is examined against the project feature document. Emphasis should be placed on verifying the correctness of the functional partitioning. Also verify that any required custom VLSI can be implemented in a timely fashion.

9.7.7 Exit criteria

The architecture design meets the objectives set in the project feature specification.

- The implementation is feasible.
- All circuit packs, software, and VLSI are specified to sufficient detail.
- All found defects have been corrected or resolved.

9.7.8 Checklist

1. Can all functions described in the project feature specification be implemented?
2. Does the architecture design meet the project feature specifications' density, power, and cost requirements?
3. Is the functional description of each block detailed enough to define new circuit packs, and to define any software and/or new VLSI on those circuit packs sufficiently?

9.7.9 Defect types

DC—documentation	Inadequate, incorrect, inconsistent, or vague block functional description. Inadequate detail in block diagram
FE—feasibility	Implementation of a block as described is not technically feasible
FN—functional	The function does not conform with the project feature document
IF—interface	The interface does not meet required capability
RE—requirements	The function is correct but is inconsistent with a higher-level requirement
SN—syntax	Defect in grammar, punctuation, spelling, or language
OT—other	Defect that does not fit any of the above types

9.8 Inspection of Module Specifications

9.8.1 Purpose

The module specification inspection is recommended when two or more circuit packs are being developed that have a common functional role, and need to be considered as a single, higher-order entity called a "module."

- To verify that the functions of the module are properly specified and technically feasible
- To verify that specified requirements are consistent with the functional architecture and that module I/O is consistent with corresponding interface specifications.

9.8.2 Materials to be distributed

- Module specification
- Feature specification
- Module specification checklist

9.8.3 Entrance criteria

- The module specification is appropriately line-numbered and labeled.
- The text of the module specification has been run through a spelling checker.
- The module specification conforms to standards for a module specification document.

9.8.4 Coverage rates

- Preparation: five to seven pages per hour
- Inspection: five to seven pages per hour

9.8.5 Participants and roles

Functional roles required for a module specification inspection are

- Moderator who is a hardware designer not connected with the design of the module
- Author of the module specification document
- Reader
- Recorder

Other recommended participants are representatives from

- Hardware development
- Software development
- Systems development
- Physical design
- Hardware engineers involved in aspects of the given module
- Hardware engineers involved in specification of adjacent interfaces

The number of inspectors should be limited to eight people.

9.8.6 Inspection procedures

Module specifications are examined against interface specifications, requirements, and the functional architecture:

- Verify that the context diagram and primary I/O signal list are consistent with the corresponding interface specifications and are complete with respect to the requirements and functional architecture.
- Examine the data flow diagram (DFD) level by level to determine consistency and completeness with respect to the functional architecture and requirements.
- Verify that the list of provisionable items, performance measurements, and externally stimulated defect conditions are consistent with the functional architecture and requirements.

- Verify that the high-level block diagram and associated description is capable of implementing the requirements and is technically feasible.
- Verify that the maintenance and diagnostic plan is necessary and sufficient for the high-level implementation plan and that it is consistent with the overall project maintenance plan.
- Verify that the implementation lists are necessary and sufficient and are consistent with requirements.

9.8.7 Exit criteria

- The functions of the module are specified and are clear and precise.
- The specified functions are consistent with the functional architecture and external and internal requirements and are sufficient.
- Supporting requirements lists, such as I/O, provisioning, performance, and externally stimulated maintenance alarms are consistent.
- The high-level implementation plan is consistent with and sufficiently covers required functions, and is technically feasible.
- The maintenance and diagnostic plan is consistent with the overall project maintenance plan.
- Implementation-derived supporting lists are consistent with the implementation plan.
- All defects found have been corrected or resolved.

9.8.8 Checklist

1. Are all adjacent modules shown in boxes on the context diagram?
2. Are all interface signals mentioned in the primary I/O list and present as an individual data flow or part of a group data flow?
3. Are the inputs and outputs compatible to the next lower level's design decomposition.
4. Is each store and data-flow either self-evident or defined in the data dictionary?
5. Is the module maintainable in real time?
6. Can the module be diagnosed while in the frame but out-of-service?

9.8.9 Defect types

DC—documentation	The organization or presentation of the module specification document is incorrect
FN—functional	Function is not consistent with or does not satisfy architecture or requirements
IF—interface	I/O signal does not agree with corresponding interface specification
MT—maintenance	The ability to provide real-time maintenance or out-of-service diagnostics is impaired
RE—requirements	The function is correct but is inconsistent
SN—syntax	Defect in grammar, punctuation, spelling, or language in the specifications
ST—standards	Failure to conform to project standards
OT—other	A defect that does not fit into any of the above types

9.9   Inspection of Module Interface Specifications

9.9.1   Purpose

Module interface inspection is recommended when two or more circuit packs are being developed that have a common functional role, and need to be considered as a single, higher-order entity called a "module."

1. To verify that the specified interface meets its description and capabilities as described in the architecture design document
2. To verify that the interface is not unnecessarily complex
3. To ensure that the interface specification is clearly and completely written

9.9.2   Materials to be distributed

- Intermodule interface specification
- Functional architecture
- Module specification
- Intermodule interface specification checklist

9.9.3   Entrance criteria

- Interface specification is line-numbered or labeled, as appropriate.
- Interface specification has been run through a spelling checker.
- Interface specification contains the following sections as required by project standards:
  —A description of the interface
  —A list of modules connected via this interface
  —The general format of interface signal groups
  —Name and definition of each interface signal
- Timing and other supporting diagrams for each signal.

9.9.4   Coverage rates

- Preparation: five to seven pages per hour
- Inspection: five to seven pages per hour

9.9.5   Participants and roles

Functional roles required for an intermodule interface specification are

- Moderator who is a module circuit designer of a module not using the interface
- Author of the interface specification
- Reader
- Recorder

Other recommended participants are representatives from

- Hardware development
- Software development
- Systems development
- Physical design

- Architecture committee
- Engineers with responsibility for modules using the interface

The number of participants should be limited to eight people.

9.9.6 Inspection procedures

The interface specification should be inspected against the functional architecture to

- Verify that the description of the interface is consistent with that given in the functional architecture.
- Verify that the list of modules using the interface is consistent with the functional architecture specification.
- Verify that the general format, naming, and timing of each signal are consistent with each other and with the functional architecture specification.
- Verify that the signal names and timing meet project standards.
- Verify that the specification is clear and complete.

9.9.7 Exit criteria

The interface specification is inspected against the functional architecture. Verify that

- The specification is consistent with the interface description of the functional architecture specification.
- The modules using the interface are the same as those stated in the functional architecture specification.
- The interface is not unnecessarily complex.
- The interface specification is clearly written and can stand alone as a precise description for use by module designers.
- All defects found have been corrected and resolved.

9.9.8 Checklist

1. Does the interface meet basic design principles?
2. How reliable is the interface?
3. What kinds of clocks are required to use the interface? Are they expected to exist?
4. How noise-sensitive is the interface? What kind and level of noise emissions can be expected?
5. Is there a standard method in using the interface, such as a custom VLSI device?
6. Is the interface fast enough to meet minimum speed requirements of the system?
7. Are various parameters slow enough so as not to place a great burden on adjacent modules?
8. Are there any other interface designs which are obviously simpler?

9.9.9 Defect types

CM—complexity	The interface is unnecessarily complex
DC—documentation	A defect in the format of the interface specification

FN—functional   The interface does not match its description in the functional architecture document or does not meet external or internal requirements

RE—requirements   The function is correct but is inconsistent

SG—signal   Incorrect timing, definition, or naming of a specific signal

SN—syntax   Defect in grammar, punctuation, spelling, or language in the specifications

ST—standards   A failure to conform to project standards

OT—other   Defect that does not fit any of the above types

9.10 Inspection of Circuit Features

9.10.1 Purpose

1. To verify that the functions of the circuit are properly specified, and are consistent with the architecture design and system feature document.

2. To ensure that the high-level implementation plan follows the project terminal circuit design guidelines.

3. To verify that the implementation is technically feasible.

9.10.2 Materials to be distributed

- Circuit feature document
- Feature specification
- Functional architecture
- Circuit feature document checklist

9.10.3 Entrance criteria

- Circuit feature document is line-numbered.
- Circuit feature document has been run through a spelling checker.
- Circuit feature document contains the following sections as required by project standards:

—Description of the circuit, and the functions it performs

—High-level block diagram and brief description of the implementation strategy

—High-level maintenance and diagnostic plan for the circuit explaining the basic maintenance strategy

—List of provisionable parameters and general method describing how the provisioning is performed (e.g., via the intrashelf data and address bus)

—Description of any functions performed by software and a description of the hardware-software interface

—Description of all clocks and major external signals the circuit requires

9.10.4 Coverage rates

- Preparation: five to seven pages per hour
- Inspection: five to seven pages per hour

9.10.5 Participants and roles

Functional roles required for a circuit feature document inspection are

- Moderator who is a hardware designer
- Author of the circuit feature document
- Reader
- Recorder

Other recommended participants are representatives from

- Hardware development
- Software development
- Systems development
- Physical design
- Software engineers who develop code for the circuit
- Hardware engineers who design circuit packs that interface with this circuit

The total number of inspectors should be limited to eight people.

9.10.6 Inspection procedures

The circuit feature document is inspected against the architecture design and the system feature document. Verify that

- All functions described or implied by the architecture design, and the system feature document are incorporated.
- The list of provisionable items, and performance measurements are consistent with the architecture design and system feature document.
- The high-level block diagram and associated description are capable of implementing the functions described, and are technically feasible.
- The maintenance and diagnostic plan is sufficient.

9.10.7 Exit criteria

- The specified functions are consistent with the architecture design and system feature document.
- Supporting requirements lists, such as I/O, provisioning, performance, and externally stimulated maintenance alarms, are consistent with the architecture design and system feature document.
- The maintenance and diagnostic plan is consistent with the design guidelines.
- All defects found have been corrected or resolved.

9.10.8 Checklist

1. Have all terminal circuit design guidelines been met?
2. Is the software/hardware interface specified sufficiently?
3. Is the circuit maintainable in real time?

9.10.9 Defect types

DC—documentation	The organization or presentation of the circuit feature document is incorrect
FN—functional	Function is not consistent with or does not satisfy architecture design or system feature document

IF—interface	I/O signal does not agree with architecture design
MT—maintenance	The ability to provide real-time maintenance or out-of-service diagnostics is impaired
RE—requirements	The function is correct but is inconsistent with a higher-level requirement
SN—syntax	Defect in grammar, punctuation, spelling, or language in the specifications
ST—standards	Failure to conform to project standards
OT—other	A defect that does not fit any of the above types

9.11 Inspection of Circuit Electrical Designs

9.11.1 Purpose

1. To verify that the circuit conforms to its circuit feature document and/or module specifications
2. To verify the correctness of the circuit's logic design, power dissipation, testability, component selection, and software interface

9.11.2 Materials to be distributed

- Circuit features specification
- Circuit electrical design
- Circuit electrical design checklist
- Materials from the overview meeting (see below)

9.11.3 Entrance criteria

An overview is required before the inspection meeting is held. All participants in the inspection meeting attend the overview. The objective of the overview is to introduce the circuit to the inspection team. The designer should bring to the overview the following:

- The circuit feature document and/or module specifications.
- A complete functional block diagram of the circuit.
- A detailed description of the circuit. The description should be at the gate level, but should also describe all features and functions performed.
- Timing diagrams, figures, etc. that support the circuit description.
- Complete circuit schematic drawings as produced by SysCAD (UNIX System V computer-aided design).
- Programming information for all programmable logic devices and nonprogram store PROMs (programmable read-only memory). A flow-chart of the intended program is adequate for program-store PROMs. If such a program has real-time constraints, calculations showing that the constraints have been met by the flowchart may also be required.
- If a microprocessor resides on the circuit, the memory map is required.
- Procedures for exercising and diagnosing the circuit.
- Device specifications of any custom, unusual, or complex components.
- Circuit power estimate.
- Voltage requirements along with current draw.

9.11.4 Coverage rates

(Note: In this case, the preparation and inspection rates are different. It is expected that some of the materials require greater preparation, but can be examined by the inspection team more quickly after individual study of the underlying details.)

- Preparation: five pages per hour
- Inspection: 10 pages per hour

9.11.5 Participants and roles

Functional roles required for a circuit electrical design inspection are:

- Moderator who is a circuit engineer
- Author of the circuit electrical design
- Reader
- Recorder

Other recommended participants are representatives from

- Circuit software development, if software resides on the board
- VLSI development for each concurrently developed VLSI component used
- Additional circuit designers, preferably designers of circuit packs that interface the one being inspected
- Production engineering
- Test engineering

The total number of inspectors should be limited to six people.

9.11.6 Inspection procedures

Because of the complexity of most circuit packs, each inspector is not responsible for the entire circuit; instead the moderator assigns different tasks (e.g., points below) to each of the inspectors at the overview. Between the time the overview is held and the inspection meeting, each inspector performs his or her assigned task. The following tasks will be performed:

- Verify that all specifications in the circuit feature document are met.
- Verify that the logic design, including programmable logic devices and PROMs, is consistent with the circuit description, and functional block diagram.
- Make sure the software interface is consistent with the logic design, is clear and precise, and implies a relatively simple software driver.
- Verify that the memory map corresponds to the software needs [in particular, the amount of random access memory (RAM) and erasable programmable read-only memory (EPROM) used is reasonable and if possible flexible].
- Make sure that the circuit power estimation meets project specifications.
- Make sure all components are approved.
- Verify that the signal timing specifications are complete and correct.
- Verify that the circuit can be manufactured.
- Verify that all circuit interconnections are complete and correct.
- Verify that each circuit is testable with automatic test equipment.
- Verify that the design meets the terminal circuit design guidelines.

9.11.7 Exit criteria

The circuit electrical design is inspected against the circuit feature document and module specifications. Verify that

- The circuit electrical design meets the requirements in the circuit feature document.
- All external interfaces are complete and conform to signal, voltage, and timing requirements.
- All custom VLSI is used correctly.
- Real-time fault coverage meets requirements.
- The circuit can be manufactured.
- Each circuit is factory testable.
- Power dissipation allocation for each circuit meets requirements.
- Software requirements are properly specified and implementable.
- All documentation meets project, design engineering specifications (DES), and company standards.
- All items in checklist are covered.
- All found defects are corrected or resolved.

9.11.8 Checklist

1. Are unusual, complex, or custom components used correctly?
2. Are as many faults as possible covered by at least one maintenance technique? Are all defect detectors exercisable?
3. Are there any constants or operating modes that should be provisionable or appear on the backplane?
4. Is the circuit self-recovering, i.e., does the circuit recover to normal operation from occasional glitches without processor intervention?
5. Are all timing margins adequate for worst-case conditions?
6. What clocks are needed?
7. How easy is the logic to debug? Should additional circuitry or test points be added to aid debugging?
8. Are there any special speed requirements on any component, such as random access memory (RAM) access time?
9. Can the circuit be manufactured?

9.11.9 Defect types

CO—component	An inappropriate choice or use of a component
DC—documentation	An inconsistency between elements of the documentary material
FN—function	An algorithm or feature is inconsistent with circuit pack requirements
IF—interface	The circuit pack's interface signals violate requirements
LO—logic	The circuit pack logic is incorrect or violates requirements
MN—manufacture	The component or interface has manufacturing problems
MT—maintainability	The ability to provide in-service maintenance is impaired

RE—requirements	The function is correct but is inconsistent with a higher-level requirement
SN—syntax	Defect in grammar, spelling, or punctuation within the documentary materials
ST—standards	The documentation does not meet project, DES, or company standards
SW—software interface	The ability to provide software support is impaired
TI—timing	Race conditions exist or worst-case specifications are violated
TS—testability	The ability to automatically test the circuit pack is impaired
OT—other	Defect does not fit any of the above types

9.12   Inspection of System Test Plans

9.12.1   Purpose

1. To confirm that the system test plan validates that all requirements set in the project feature document are met
2. To verify that the plan is consistent with itself
3. To ensure that the plan provides sufficient information for the system test specification to be written

9.12.2   Materials to be distributed

- System test plan
- System test plan checklist
- Feature specification
- Project schedule
- Other relevant documents

9.12.3   Entrance criteria

- The system test plan should include test equipment and schedules.
- The plan should be line-numbered.

9.12.4   Coverage rates

- Preparation: five to seven pages per hour
- Inspection: five to seven pages per hour

9.12.5   Participants and roles

Functional roles required for a system test plan inspection are

- Moderator who is a lead engineer
- Author of the system test plan

- Reader
- Recorder

Other recommended participants are representatives from

- Hardware manufacturing
- Software development
- System test

The total number of inspectors should be limited to eight people.

9.12.6 Inspection procedures

The system test plan is inspected against the feature specification. Verify that

- The system test plan correctly states the test requirements for complete confirmation of all functions described in the feature specification.
- The system test plan does not contradict itself or any other relevant documents.

9.12.7 Exit criteria

- The system test plan represents a plan that verifies that all requirements set in the feature specification are met.
- All items in the checklist are covered.
- The system test plan is consistent with all documents included in the materials distributed.
- The system test plan is consistent with itself.
- All defects found have been corrected or resolved.

9.12.8 Checklist

1. Are all requirements set in the feature specification discussed in the system test plan?
2. Is the test equipment list sufficient?
3. Is the test schedule correct?
4. Is sufficient information provided for the system test specification to be written?

9.12.9 Defect types

DC—documentation	The documentation style of a particular topic obscures the function, either through inconsistency or vagueness
FN—functional	The function to be tested does not agree with the project feature document's requirements
RE—requirements	The function is correct but is inconsistent with a higher-level requirement
SN—syntax	Defect in grammar, punctuation, spelling, or language in the specifications
ST—standards	A failure to meet the checklist above
TS—testability	The ability to test the system is impaired
OT—other	Defect that does not fit any of the above types

9.13   Inspection of System Test Specifications

9.13.1   Purpose

To verify that the system test specification describes a correct and sufficiently detailed test procedure in accordance with the system test plan

9.13.2   Materials to be distributed

- System test specification
- System test specification checklist
- System test plan
- Other relevant documents

9.13.3   Entrance criteria

- The system test specification is line-numbered.

9.13.4   Coverage rates

- Preparation: five to seven pages per hour
- Inspection: five to seven pages per hour

9.13.5   Participants and roles

Functional roles required for a system test specification inspection are

- Moderator who is a lead engineer
- Author of the system test specification
- Reader
- Recorder

  Other recommended participants are representatives from
- System test
- Hardware manufacturing
- Software development

  The total number of inspectors should be limited to eight people.

9.13.6   Inspection procedures

The system test specification is inspected against the system test plan. Verify that:

- The system test specification correctly specifies, in sufficient detail, all tests required by the system test plan.
- The system test specification does not contradict the system test plan, itself, or any other relevant documents.

9.13.7   Exit criteria

- All tests required by the system test plan are correctly specified.
- All items in the checklist are covered.

- The system test specification is consistent with itself and all relevant documents.
- All defects found have been corrected or resolved.

9.13.8 Checklist

1. Does the plan describe a test for all the items mentioned in the system test plan?
2. For each test, is the test equipment configuration as well as the system configuration described in sufficient detail?
3. Is test result documentation described, and is the proposed documentation adequate?
4. Is an estimation of the completeness of each test given?
5. Is the test equipment list sufficient?

9.13.9 Defect types

DC—documentation	The documentation style of a particular topic obscures the function, either through inconsistency or vagueness
FN—function	The function is incorrect, missing, or not required
RE—requirements	The item is correct but is inconsistent with a higher-level requirement
SN—syntax	Defect in grammar, punctuation, spelling, or language in the specifications
ST—standards	A failure to meet test standards
TS—testability	The test specification cannot be performed
OT—other	Defect does not fit any of the above types

Applying Inspections to Training Development

Our model for training development, shown in Fig. 9.3, is from the instructional quality planning and methods (IQPM) model developed at American Telephone and Telegraph (AT&T) Bell Laboratories. It consists of the following stages: planning, design, course development, course documentation, and course trial.[1] Each of these stages produces one or more work products that are either reviewed or inspected.

As with documentation, training requires resolving issues of alternatives first. Therefore, to address this objective best, the work product of the assessment and analysis development stages are reviewed and only the work of the following development and preparation stages are inspected:

- Training unit activities (UA)
- Completed training units (TU)

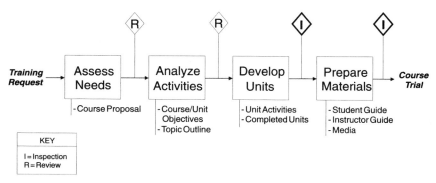

Figure 9.3 Training development model.

- Student guide (SG)
- Instructor's guide (IG)
- Training media (TM)

For these work products, a determination of correctness is possible. For example, unit activities and completed units are inspected to see if they correspond with the unit objectives and the topic outline. If these components do not match the corresponding objectives and outline topics, they are wrong, i.e., a defect exists. Issues and alternatives are not part of the inspection meeting, since they have to be resolved before unit development begins.

The planning stage is initiated by a customer request for training. As a result of this request a needs assessment is performed to determine training requirements. If the needs assessment determines that training is the proper solution, these results are synthesized in a training requirements document. The appropriate training solutions to implement the requirements are documented in the training plan. These training solutions in turn result in a course proposal(s).

In the design stage, a task analysis turns course proposals into statements of skills and knowledge needed. These are translated into course and unit objectives and a topic outline. Objectives state the major outcomes of the training and indicate how to measure the expected performance. The topic outline is a detailed list of the course contents.

The topic outline defines the course units for the development stage. Within each unit, objectives are used to determine specific content and devise unit activities. Unit activities consist of exercises, laboratories, practice sessions, and other similar activities used to reinforce instruction. Completed course units are self-contained instructional segments that focus on a single topic or a related set of topics. Course units typically contain the following components:

- *Unit overview:* Sets the stage for the unit topic(s)
- *Unit objectives:* Describe what the unit plans to accomplish and how the student will demonstrate achievement of the accomplishment(s)
- *Student notes:* Explain the contents of course visuals
- *Visuals:* Copies of transparencies used for the course
- *Activities:* Procedures used to involve students in the learning process and/or to assess their progress
- *Solutions to activities:* Answers to course activities
- *Unit summary:* Review of major points of the unit

Note that this list assumes a course that is instructor-led and uses transparencies as the standard course presentation medium. For courses that are self-paced or use instructional videotapes and/or cassettes, or other media, the list differs.

The course units are compiled into a student guide, which also contains overall course objectives and a course summary. The student guide often also includes course prerequisites, a glossary of terms, and a list of any acronyms used.

The instructor's guide contains all the student guide materials plus notes to the instructor about classroom setup, any special procedures to follow (e.g., the use of two overhead projectors for sections of the course), points to be made, instructions to students for activities, examples, anticipated instructional difficulties, reference materials, etc. It is not intended as a script for the instructor to follow.

The media for the course may be a package of visuals, a videotape, a series of cassettes, a self-instruction workbook, a procedures manual for computer-aided instruction, some combination of these, or some other medium. Whatever the medium is, it should be well suited to the particular learning task, within the time and budget constraints of the training plan.

9.14   Inspection of Unit Activities

9.14.1   Purpose

1. To verify that the unit activities are consistent with unit objectives
2. To ensure that activities and their solutions are correct
3. To confirm that activities are used appropriately and that they contribute to learning

9.14.2   Materials to be distributed

Distribute the following materials 5 working days prior to the inspection:

- Unit activities
- Solutions to activities

- Unit objectives
- Unit activity checklist

9.14.3   Entrance criteria

- Text for unit activities is line-numbered.
- Text has been run through a spelling checker.
- Solutions are provided.

9.14.4   Coverage rates

- Preparation: five to seven pages per hour
- Inspection: five to seven pages per hour

9.14.5   Participants and roles

Functional roles required for a unit activities inspection are

- Moderator, preferably with course development experience
- Author
- Reader
- Recorder

Required viewpoint representation includes

- Subject matter expert
- Training strategist

Recommended viewpoint representation, as indicated, includes

- Instructor
- Technical editor
- Technical writer

9.14.6   Inspection procedures

Activities are examined against the unit objectives. Do activities help to accomplish the stated objectives? Emphasis should be placed on assuring that activities add to the learning process and on identifying any additional activities that would be advisable. Activities are also checked for clarity and appropriateness to the student population, and for the correctness of the solutions. Exercises should be narrowly focused, testing or practicing a single skill or concept. Laboratories are more comprehensive, applying a group of skills or concepts to achieve a given result.

9.14.7   Exit criteria

- All defects have been corrected.

9.14.8   Checklist

1. Are the exercises and laboratories used correctly?
2. Are activities consistent with the learning level of unit objectives (recall, application, synthesis)?

3. Do activities match the expected task level of the unit objectives (single or multiple concept or procedure)?

4. Are major unit objectives exercised?

5. Are there unnecessary activities?

6. Are activities correct and accurate?

7. Are instructions clear and complete?

8. Do activities address student ability level? Are they challenging without being beyond student abilities? Are they balanced between direct and more complex?

9. Are there a sufficient number of activities?

10. Are the activities such that they can be completed within the time restraints of the course?

9.14.9 Defect types

CS—consistency	Failure to match objectives with activities or instructional strategy
CT—content	Inadequate, incorrect, inconsistent, or vague information
HF—human factors	Failure to accommodate perceptual, sensory, or physical learning considerations
ID—instructional design	Incorrectly stated objectives or learning hierarchy
PF—performance	Failure of activity to produce a correct response
RD—readability	Difficult to understand; inappropriate grammar, syntax, word use, or notation
ST—standards	Failure to meet training standards
SY—synthesis	Teaching topics poorly grouped, fail to produce transferable concept
OT—other	Defect that does not fit any of the above types

9.15 Inspection of Completed Training Units

9.15.1 Purpose

1. To verify that completed units are consistent with unit objectives and the topic outline

2. To ensure that units are complete, correct, and targeted to the appropriate audience

3. To ensure that completed units contribute to student learning

4. To verify that completed units conform to courseware standards

9.15.2 Materials to be distributed

Distribute the following materials 5 working days prior to the inspection:

- Completed unit(s)
- Unit objectives
- Unit checklist

9.15.3 Entrance criteria

- Text for completed unit(s) is line-numbered.
- Text has been run through a spelling checker.

9.15.4 Coverage rates

- Preparation: five to seven pages per hour
- Inspection: five to seven pages per hour

9.15.5 Participants and roles

Functional roles required for the completed unit(s) inspection are

- Moderator, preferably with course development experience
- Author
- Reader
- Recorder

Required viewpoint representation includes

- Subject matter expert
- Training strategist

Recommended viewpoint representation, as indicated, includes

- Instructor
- Technical editor
- Technical writer
- Media specialist
- Graphic artist
- Customer

9.15.6 Inspection procedures

Completed units are examined against the unit objectives. Does the unit accomplish the stated objectives? The information presented should be clear, succinct, correct, well organized, and appropriate to the intended student population. There should be sufficient examples, illustrations, diagrams, etc. to assist in the students' understanding of the material, but no extraneous or unhelpful material. The material should adhere to established courseware standards.

9.15.7 Exit criteria

- All defects have been corrected.

9.15.8 Checklist

1. Does each unit contain an overview and a summary?
2. Are all learning concepts implied by the objectives adequately covered?
3. Are any extraneous learning concepts included?
4. Are the course materials correct and up-to-date?

5. Does textual material reflect key items contained on visuals or other course media?
6. Are there enough examples, illustrations, diagrams, etc. to amplify key concepts?
7. Are there any unnecessary or incomplete examples, illustrations, diagrams, etc.?
8. Are examples, diagrams, illustrations, etc. clearly and completely labeled?
9. Are all materials legible, uncluttered, and easy to follow?
10. Are materials presented in the appropriate order?
11. Are materials at the appropriate level for the students?

9.15.9 Defect types

CS—consistency	Failure to match objectives with activities or instructional strategy
CT—content	Inadequate, incorrect, inconsistent, or vague information
HF—human factors	Failure to accommodate perceptual, sensory, or physical learning considerations
ID—instructional design	Incorrectly stated objectives or learning hierarchy
PF—performance	Failure of activity to produce a correct response
RD—readability	Difficult to understand; inappropriate grammar, syntax, word use, or notation
ST—standards	Failure to meet training standards
SY—synthesis	Teaching topics poorly grouped, fail to produce transferable concept
OT—other	Defect that does not fit any of the above types

9.16   Inspection of Student Guide

9.16.1 Purpose

To verify that the student guide is complete and conforms with established standards

9.16.2 Materials to be distributed

Distribute the following materials 5 working days prior to the inspection:

- Student guide
- Student guide checklist

9.16.3 Entrance criteria

- All sections are included and appropriately labeled.
- All text not previously inspected is line-numbered.
- Text has been run through a spelling checker.

9.16.4 Coverage rates

- Preparation: five to seven pages per hour
- Inspection: five to seven pages per hour

9.16.5 Participants and roles

Functional roles required for a student guide inspection are

- Moderator, preferably with course development experience
- Author
- Reader
- Recorder

Required viewpoint representation includes

- Training strategist

Recommended viewpoint representation, as indicated, includes

- Instructor
- Technical editor
- Technical writer
- Media specialist
- Graphic artist
- Customer

9.16.6 Inspection procedures

The student guide is inspected against the established standards for a student guide and the student guide checklist. The guide must contain all required components packaged in the prescribed order. In addition, materials that were not included in earlier inspections (such as the index, glossary, etc.) must be inspected for completeness and accuracy. The content of the completed units and unit activities will have already been inspected, and is not inspected again at this time.

9.16.7 Exit criteria

- All defects have been corrected.

9.16.8 Checklist

1. Does the guide contain all of the following components:
   —Course cover page
   —Contents page
   —Introduction to the course
   —Completed units, including activities and solutions
   —Glossary
   —References/bibliography (optional)
   —Appendices (optional)
   —Index
2. Are the components presented in the order listed?
3. Are the components complete and accurate?
4. Are there any extraneous components?

5. Do materials conform to established standards (especially important for audio, visual, or computerized materials)?

6. Are headings, labels, notations, type styles, etc. used consistently throughout?

9.16.9 Defect types

CS—consistency	Failure to match objectives with activities or instructional strategy
CT—content	Inadequate, incorrect, inconsistent or vague information
HF—human factors	Failure to accommodate perceptual, sensory, or physical learning considerations
ID—instructional design	Incorrectly stated objectives or learning hierarchy
PF—performance	Failure of activity to produce a correct response
RD—readability	Difficult to understand; inappropriate grammar, syntax, word use, or notation
ST—standards	Failure to meet training standards
SY—synthesis	Teaching topics poorly grouped, fail to produce transferable concept
OT—other	Defect that does not fit any of the above types

9.17 Inspection of Instructor's Guide

9.17.1 Purpose

To verify that the instructor's guide is complete and consistent with established standards

9.17.2 Materials to be distributed

Distribute the following materials 5 working days prior to the inspection:

- Instructor's guide
- Instructor's guide checklist

9.17.3 Entrance criteria

- All sections are included and appropriately labeled.
- All text not previously inspected is line-numbered.
- Text has been run through a spelling checker.

9.17.4 Coverage rates

- Preparation: five to seven pages per hour
- Inspection: five to seven pages per hour

9.17.5 Participants and roles

Functional roles required for a unit activities inspection are

- Moderator, preferably with course development experience
- Author

- Reader
- Recorder

Required viewpoint representation includes

- Training strategist

Recommended viewpoint representation, as indicated, includes

- Technical editor
- Technical writer
- Media specialist
- Graphic artist
- Customer

9.17.6 Inspection procedures

The instructor's guide is inspected against the established standards for an instructor's guide and the instructor's guide checklist. The guide must contain all required components packaged in the prescribed order. In addition, materials that were not included in earlier inspections (such as the instructor notes, index, glossary, etc.) must be inspected for completeness and accuracy. The content of the completed units and unit activities will have already been inspected, and is not inspected again at this time.

9.17.7 Exit criteria

- All defects have been corrected.

9.17.8 Checklist

1. Does the guide contain all of the following components?
   —Course cover page
   —Contents page
   —Course information
   —Introduction to the course
   —Course catalog entry
   —Intended student population
   —Administrative information
   —Course preparation information
   —Course outline
   —Instructor qualifications
   —Instructor preparation
   —Course materials
   —Course preparation checklist
   —Course delivery information
   —Course schedule
   —Course presentation
   —Student guide materials
   —Completed units, including activities and solutions

—Glossary

—References/bibliography (optional)

—Appendices (optional)

—Index

—Additional reference material (optional)

2. Are the components presented in the order listed?

3. Are the components complete and accurate?

4. Are there any extraneous components?

5. Do materials conform to established standards?

6. Are headings, labels, notations, type styles, etc. used consistently throughout?

9.17.9 Defect types

CS—consistency	Failure to match objectives with activities or instructional strategy
CT—content	Inadequate, incorrect, inconsistent, or vague information
HF—human factors	Failure to accommodate perceptual, sensory, or physical learning considerations
ID—instructional design	Incorrectly stated objectives or learning hierarchy
PF—performance	Failure of activity to produce a correct response
RD—readability	Difficult to understand; inappropriate grammar, syntax, word use, or notation
ST—standards	Failure to meet training standards
SY—synthesis	Teaching topics poorly grouped, fail to produce transferable concept
OT—other	Defect that does not fit any of the above types

9.18 Inspection of Training Media

9.18.1 Purpose

1. To verify that media are correct and consistent with unit objectives

2. To confirm that media are appropriately used and that they contribute to learning

9.18.2 Materials to be distributed

Distribute the following materials 5 working days prior to the inspection:

- Course media
- Unit objectives
- Course media checklist

9.18.3 Entrance criteria

Media has been "test run"; i.e., tapes, slides, visuals, etc. have been screened for visibility and audibility.

9.18.4   Coverage rates

- Preparation: 10 to 15 visuals/slides pages per hour; 1/2 hour of tape time per hour
- Inspection: 10 to 15 visuals/slides per hour; 1/2 hour of tape time per hour

9.18.5   Participants and roles

Functional roles required for a unit activities inspection are

- Moderator, preferably with course development experience
- Author
- Reader
- Recorder

  Required viewpoint representation includes

- Subject matter expert
- Training strategist

  Recommended viewpoint representation, as indicated, includes

- Instructor
- Technical editor
- Technical writer
- Media specialist
- Graphic artist
- Customer

9.18.6   Inspection procedures

Media are examined against the course objectives and established media standards. Do media help to accomplish the stated objectives? Emphasis should be placed on ensuring that media add to the learning process and are appropriately and effectively used. Media are also checked for clarity and appropriateness to the student population.

9.18.7   Exit criteria

- All defects have been corrected.

9.18.8   Checklist

Because of the variability of the different types of media, a general media checklist is not provided.

9.18.9   Defect types

CS—consistency	Failure to match objectives with activities or instructional strategy
CT—content	Inadequate, incorrect, inconsistent, or vague information
HF—human factors	Failure to accommodate perceptual, sensory, or physical learning considerations
ID—instructional design	Incorrectly stated objectives or learning hierarchy

PF—performance	Failure of activity to produce a correct response
RD—readability	Difficult to understand; inappropriate grammar, syntax, word use, or notation
ST—standards	Failure to meet training standards
SY—synthesis	Teaching topics poorly grouped, fail to produce transferable concept
OT—other	Defect that does not fit any of the above types

9.19   References

1. Cheu, J. M. Y., and N. F. Maccarelli, *Instructional Quality Planning and Methods,* AT&T Bell Laboratories, November 1984.

Chapter

10

The Role of Reviews

Reviews of all types are widely used by developers to improve the "quality" of their work. They are a procedure for the interactive group examination of a work product or development process, like inspections, but in general reviews are thought of as being more informal or flexible. A close look at reviews reveals that there is a family of review procedures that have diverse uses, methods, and attendees. This "structure" is dependent on the use of the review, not on the development phase or the product it is used for.

In this chapter we describe reviews as a specific type of quality management procedure, their relationship with inspections, and their apparent structure. We describe four types of reviews, their similarities and differences, and identify what each type of review is used for and suggest objectives and procedures. Our intent is to formally define reviews so that they may be used with the same consistency and control as inspections.

10.1 What Reviews Are

Quality can mean many things, and as we have pointed out in Chapter 2, its definition varies over time during the development of the product. In the education, evaluation, verification, validation, and assurance (EEVVA) model, shown in Table 10.1, reviews are defined as a procedure for meeting a specific quality objective—evaluation. An evaluation assesses the worth and usefulness of a product or procedure and determines possible alternatives. This goal contrasts with inspections, whose quality objective is verification, which ensures that the product conforms to its specifications and is correct. Although a review varies

TABLE 10.1   The EEVVA Model

Quality objective	Procedure
Education—communication of information	Tutorial
Evaluation—assessment of value, worth, alternatives	Review
Verification—conformance to specifications	Inspection
Validation—proof of performance	Test
Assurance—compliance with practices and procedures	Audit

somewhat with its use, there are some characteristics that are common to all formal reviews.

1. Reviews are part of the defined project methodology.

2. The objective of the review is oriented to some form of evaluation of the product, procedure, or development process.

3. Identifying and resolving issues, not defects, is emphasized.

4. Resource data is available for the reviews, which can be used to estimate project resource requirements and to assess how well these resources were used.

In addition, review procedures can frequently be based on those of the in-process inspection, which are well defined and understood.

10.1.1   Types of reviews

We have identified five types of reviews (inspections are included for comparison) that appear to have widespread use in many different projects. They are

1. *Overviews:* Provide information about the product and the development process that was used, both within an inspection process and more broadly.

2. *Technical reviews:* Assess available alternatives and ensure that the developing product is acceptable.

3. *Inspections:* Ensure that the product conforms to its specifications, is correct, and complies with all necessary procedures.

4. *Management reviews:* Form decisions for further project actions based on present and past project performance.

5. *Informal reviews:* Oriented to the developer's purposes; may assume various forms.

Overviews, technical reviews, and management reviews can be required for specific development processes, can have predetermined quality objectives, and their results can be reported. Therefore, like inspections, overviews, technical reviews, and management reviews can be an integral part of the project's defined in-process quality management procedures.

Informal reviews though, are not standardized, required, or reported. And although each informal review may have a specific objective, as a class they have no predetermined quality objectives. Therefore, their role in organizational quality management is largely indeterminate. However, this does not gainsay their benefit for the individual developer.

10.1.2   Reviews and the EEVVA model

Table 10.2 shows our estimate of how reviews address the quality objectives outlined by the EEVVA model. The quality objective called "decision" is a combination of validation and assurance, which have been introduced in Chapter 2. This is because decisions primarily consider validation and assurance of the development process. This objective is emphasized for management reviews, and to a far lesser extent for the other review types.

The number of Xs indicates our assessment of the relative contribution of each review type to the quality objectives. The inspection process is included for comparison. Note that since informal reviews have no predetermined quality objective, they are assigned equal, but minor weight for all the quality objectives.

10.2   Reviews and the Work Unit

Reviews as a whole, and specifically technical reviews, have their major impact when the product is not yet well defined, often in the early

TABLE 10.2   Quality Objectives of Review and Inspections

	Examination quality objectives			
Examination type	Education	Evaluation	Verification	"Decision"
Overview	XXXX	XX	X	—
Technical review	X	XXXX	XX	X
Inspection	X	XX	XXXX	X
Management review	X	XX	—	XXXX
Informal review	X	X	X	X

stages of development. At this stage questions of alternative development approaches predominate, questions that reviews are designed to address. The assumption that these issues have already been resolved allows the inspection process to concentrate on verifying the correctness of the work product.

In Chapter 2, we introduced the concept of the work unit and showed how the inspection process fits in. It is useful here to show how reviews fit into the work unit also. Figure 10.1 illustrates this relationship.

Overviews are not illustrated in Fig. 10.1 as they are frequently used within inspections or technical reviews, as an implicit step within the procedures. When explicitly employed, they are fully defined and may be used at various points within the work unit to contribute to the general understanding of the developers' work and of how the work product fits into the overall project picture.

Technical reviews are shown as part of the formal work unit procedures. The relationship between inspections and technical reviews is somewhat variable, and needs to be defined by the project's development plan. Technical reviews and inspections are sometimes both recommended for assessing the quality of a work product. When used together they have dependent, although different, quality objectives. It is logical to complete the technical review first, since inspections assume that review issues have been resolved. The completion of the technical review is frequently an entry criterion for the subsequent inspection of that work product.

Management reviews are outside the work unit, and depend on the technical reviews and inspections within each work unit. This allows management reviews to concentrate on issues of project direction, resources, and progress. They are compatible with both technical reviews

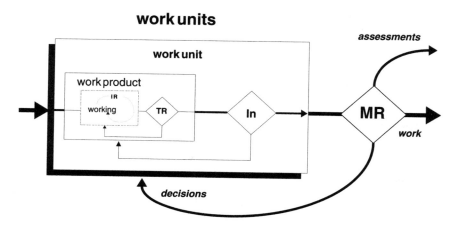

Figure 10.1 Relationship of reviews in the work unit.

and inspections at any stage of development. The results of prior technical reviews or inspections are frequently entry criteria for subsequent management reviews. Management reviews also play a further role on completion of product development, when they track project progress and provide an overall assessment of the project, helping to guide future management decisions.

Informal reviews are shown within the developers' work cycle as a device developers may use to gain feedback about their work. The informal reviews also help to establish development conventions and to define interfaces to other work products. Informal reviews are not part of the formal project development procedures, although their use is highly recommended.

All of these review procedures are cyclic. The output from each layer of review or inspection feeds into the next layer. Moreover, each layer provides feedback to improve procedures. Information gained from the assessment of prior development form the basis for the procedures used for subsequent development. Management reviews may in fact feed forward into a totally new project.

If you envision a chain of work units each feeding into the next one, then the forging of that chain is the final product. And that final product is likely to be no stronger than its weakest link. But if each of those links is strong, they provide the foundation for future products, each one stronger and better than those that came before. That is the goal of an integrated review process.

10.3   The Structure of Reviews

In Chapter 4, we identified seven parameters for defining inspections. These parameters can also be used for defining review procedures, and for providing insight into the differences and similarities among the various types of reviews.

The seven defining parameters are

1. *Purpose:* What the review accomplishes
2. *Entry criteria:* What the review looks at, the necessary materials, their condition, project standards and procedures
3. *Reporting categories:* How we name and classify the review findings
4. *Checklists:* What the review is looking for and the extent of our search, with examples
5. *Exit criteria:* When we are through; the conditions our materials must meet when we are finished with the review
6. *Participants:* Who performs the review
7. *Procedures:* How the review is performed

In this section, we discuss overviews, technical reviews, and managerial reviews in terms of these parameters. Informal reviews are not included because they are by their nature not definable. For a discussion of inspections in terms of these parameters, see Chapter 4.

10.3.1 Overviews

Overviews are infrequently used as stand-alone examination procedures. Most often they are used within other in-process examinations, such as inspections, but they can be formally defined and used explicitly. Overviews can be considered for development procedures as well as products.

10.3.1.1 Purpose of overviews. The primary purpose of an overview is education—to communicate information about the work product. Questions of intent and procedure can also be properly addressed at this time. Therefore, the purpose of an overview can be any or some mix of the following:

1. Inform the attendees about the work product

2. Establish that the intentions of the work product are within project guidelines

3. Determine that the procedures used for the development of the work product are appropriate

10.3.1.2 Entry criteria. There are none when overviews are used as an independent review procedure. However, when overviews are used within another review, they must meet the entry criteria for that procedure.

10.3.1.3 Reporting categories. Record the duration of the overview, the number of participants, and the general topic covered. Any major discrepancies that are found in the work product or in the development procedures should be reported. Reporting overview activities and findings ensures a complete project record that is useful in later analysis of the effectiveness of the overviews.

10.3.1.4 Checklists. Usually not provided.

10.3.1.5 Exit criteria. None.

10.3.1.6 Participants. Those persons who have an interest in the work product or can make a contribution to its understanding are invited. All members of a subsequent review should attend.

10.3.1.7   Procedures.   Usually the author is the presenter and another person, who is objective, moderates, although special circumstances may dictate otherwise. There are no other recommended procedures. When overviews are required by other review procedures, they are defined by those procedure.

10.3.2   Technical reviews

Technical reviews are widely used by all types of development projects. They may be used alone or in combination with inspections or other quality control procedures. A typical use of technical reviews is for identifying and resolving the issues that often arise during the design and specification of work products.

10.3.2.1   Purpose of technical reviews

1. Assess the value of technical concepts and alternatives in the project environment
2. Establish consistency in the use and representation of technical concepts
3. Ensure that technical concepts are used correctly
4. Inform participants of the technical content of the work product

10.3.2.2   Entry criteria.   Completed documentation of a work product, to standards, with prior work, specifications, and references.

10.3.2.3   Reporting categories.   Issues, not defects, are reported and classified, typically as

- Type
  - —Content: Relating to the subject of the material
  - —Format: Relating to the representation of the material
- Status
  - —Open: Issue to be resolved (by the author unless otherwise noted)
  - —Closed: Issue resolved at the review meeting
- Responsibility (applicable to open issues only)
  - —None (blank): The author is responsible
  - —Other: Person or agency responsible (other than the author)

Figures 10.2 and 10.3 are examples of a technical review issue list and a technical review report, respectively. Compare these with the inspection defect list and inspection report forms in Chapter 4.

Technical Review Issues List

Meeting Date: _____   Page: _____

Project: _____   Release: _____

Activity: _____   Document: _____

Component: _____   Moderator: _____

Meeting Type: ☐ Review (R)   ☐ Re-Review (RR)

Review Type: ☐ Requirements (RQR)   ☐ External Design (EDR)   ☐ Internal Design (IDR)

Location	Issue Description	Type	Issue Status	Responsible
_____	_____	____	____	____
_____	_____	____	____	____
_____	_____	____	____	____
_____	_____	____	____	____
_____	_____	____	____	____
_____	_____	____	____	____
_____	_____	____	____	____
_____	_____	____	____	____
_____	_____	____	____	____
_____	_____	____	____	____
_____	_____	____	____	____
_____	_____	____	____	____
_____	_____	____	____	____
_____	_____	____	____	____
_____	_____	____	____	____
_____	_____	____	____	____
_____	_____	____	____	____
_____	_____	____	____	____
_____	_____	____	____	____
_____	_____	____	____	____
_____	_____	____	____	____
_____	_____	____	____	____
_____	_____	____	____	____

Issue Type: CONTENT = C; FORMAT = F

Issue Status: OPEN = O; CLOSED = C

Responsible: blank for Author; initials of party or area responsible for resolution of Issue if other than Author

Figure 10.2 Technical review issues list.

Technical Review Report

Meeting Date: _____

Project: _____   Release: _____

Activity: _____   Document: _____

Component: _____   Moderator: _____

Meeting Type: ☐ Review (R)   ☐ Re-Review (RR)

Review Type: ☐ Requirements (RQR)   ☐ External Design (EDR)   ☐ Internal Design (IDR)

Disposition: ☐ Accept (A)   ☐ Conditional (C)   ☐ Re-Review (R)

Review Duration: _____(hours)   Number of Reviewers: _____(all)

Size of Materials: _____(lines)   Total Preparation Time: _____(hours)

Overview Duration: _____   Estimated Rework Effort: _____(hours)

Re-Review scheduled for: _____   Actual Rework Effort: _____(hours)

Other Reviewers:

_____   _____

_____   _____

_____   _____

_____   _____

Moderator Certification: _____   Completion Date: _____

Issues:

TYPE	STATUS		(the number of each category)	
	Open	Closed	TOTAL	Others Responsibile
Content				
Format				
TOTAL				

Additional Comments:

_____

_____

_____

Figure 10.3 Technical review report.

10.3.2.4 Checklists. Usually provided, checklists are created from project experience, professional knowledge and corporate standards for the type of product and its representation. They provide guidance to the reviewers to help ensure that the product is examined completely.

10.3.2.5 Exit criteria. Specify the content and form of the work product required for the next stage of development. The review is not considered closed until all the issues raised at the review meeting are resolved.

10.3.2.6 Participants. Select technical peers who can make a detailed contribution to the technical review. On occasion, management may participate, especially if resource or policy issues need to be addressed. Technical review roles should be established, similar to those for inspections, with a moderator, reader, and recorder, none of whom is the author.

10.3.2.7 Procedures. Specify guidelines for conducting the technical review, typically preparation and examination rates, and the method to be used for examining the material. Depending on the type of work product and project, the technical review may be the only examination used, or, alternatively, the work product may first be reviewed and then inspected. In each case the review procedures should take into consideration the requirements of the next activity.

10.3.3 Management reviews

Management reviews are used extensively to provide the project with control and assurance. They focus on issues that impact the product, the development process, and the project; they deal with the characteristics of what is being built, how it is built, and with the resources used to build it.

But management reviews make use of a limited and expensive project resource—management attention and time. Since there are few or no guidelines available for management reviews, we have made an attempt to define them so that the management resource may be used as effectively as possible, and further, so that a base definition can be developed from which to improve.

10.3.3.1 Purpose of management reviews

1. To decide on project direction and resolve procedural issues

2. To evaluate product strategy and technical alternatives for the product and the project

3. To monitor the progress of the development process

4. To ensure conformance to project practices, standards, and procedures

5. To focus on "special" issues

10.3.3.2 Entry criteria. Project dependent and variable over time; they usually can not be predetermined and change with each management review. Many management reviews address either a specific work product or the status of a series of work products. In these cases, the verified work product(s) or their status reports would be required for entry into the management review.

10.3.3.3 Reporting categories. Actions and action items are recorded. Since the emphasis of the review is on arriving at decisions or initiating actions, a record of these actions is essential. It is recommended that action items include

1. Issue addressed

2. Action proposed

3. Responsibility

4. Due date

Action items can then be tracked and closed on completion. It is also useful to record the duration of the management review, number of participants, preparation time, and number of issues addressed. This information is useful in assessing the effectiveness of the reviews.

10.3.3.4 Checklists. A guideline of the review procedures and an agenda are recommended. In addition, the outstanding action item list may be summarized and updated for each review.

10.3.3.5 Exit criteria. It is recommended that an appropriately completed and/or updated action list be required for meeting closure.

10.3.3.6 Participants. This includes managers responsible for the project and invited technical personnel with a contribution to make to a specific issue. A moderator (usually the senior manager) and a recorder are recommended. No single reader is recommended because a variety of issues are addressed, which may be raised by several participants. The number of participants is project-dependent and may vary by review.

10.3.3.7 Procedures. Variable, depending on project guidelines, issues addressed, decisions to be reached, and materials presented. As general guidelines, project procedures should

1. Limit the duration of the meeting.
2. Limit the agenda and prioritize issues to be addressed.
3. Determine a priori the types of issues to be considered.

10.3.4   Reviews versus inspections

Like inspections, reviews have their place in quality management procedures. Each organization has a range of quality objectives it must meet, and no one quality control procedure can do the entire job. At one time, testing was considered to be the only necessary product validation method. However, experience has shown that there is a large payoff for managing quality throughout the development cycle, and inspections and reviews are among the quality control procedures that are available prior to testing.

A distinct advantage of the inspection process is that it is a well-defined and understood procedure. It can be supported, taught, and its results compared within a project and across projects. It includes standardized parameters for defining, evaluating, and tuning itself and the development process it supports.

Reviews are less well defined and understood. Only technical reviews are starting to be defined with some precision, and to be measured. Technical review procedures are beginning to be taught and documented for some projects. But management reviews, which tend to be the most prevalent type, have not received the technical attention required to closely define their procedures and expected results. We hope that these guidelines provide a start.

10.4   Conclusion

Reviews offer one more opportunity to achieve a common set of examination procedures that can span a project's quality needs throughout development, using the EEVVA model as a consistent guide. But for reviews to fulfill this role, those in charge of projects need to determine how and where reviews are used, define and document their procedures, and develop a set of measurements for evaluating review results.

In view of this, it may seem that reviews are going to become more like inspections, and procedurally this may be the case. But the focus of reviews is always on identifying and resolving issues, a focus well outside the scope of the inspection process. Such a focus is highly desirable and is essential to the widespread use of reviews.

LIDS, the Lotus Inspection Data System

A Personal Computer System for the Management of Inspection Data

The Lotus Inspection Data System (LIDS) collects and analyzes inspection data. The analysis of inspection data contributes to and augments the effectiveness of inspection by measuring the effort required to find defects, and assaying the defect types and numbers found. Also, defect trends can be tracked, and potentially defect-prone or poorly inspected components identified. These analyses are dependent on the availability of an inspection data base and analysis tool that can provide a responsive means for storing and evaluating the inspection data.

There are three reasons for providing this description of LIDS: first, it acquaints you with an existent product that is available to perform this evaluation quickly, with little effort needed for tool development; second, it describes an architectural model that can be used with different evaluation techniques; and, third, it shows a number of types of inspection analyses which can be performed.[*]

A.1 Introduction

The Lotus Inspection Data System (LIDS) provides facilities for the entry, storage, analysis, reporting, and maintenance of data from project inspections. LIDS consists of a formatted Lotus 1-2-3 spreadsheet for Microsoft Disk Operating System (MS-DOS) personal computers and uses standard Lotus 1-2-3 features. It operates under any 2.n version of Lotus 1-2-3. The inspection data may also be extracted from LIDS for more extensive analysis by other systems.

LIDS menus guide you through the selection of functions. These menus are hierarchical and operate similarly to those of Lotus 1-2-3.

---

[*]For more information about LIDS, contact RGE Software Methodologies at 30 Main Street, Port Washington, NY 11050, telephone (516) 944-8058.

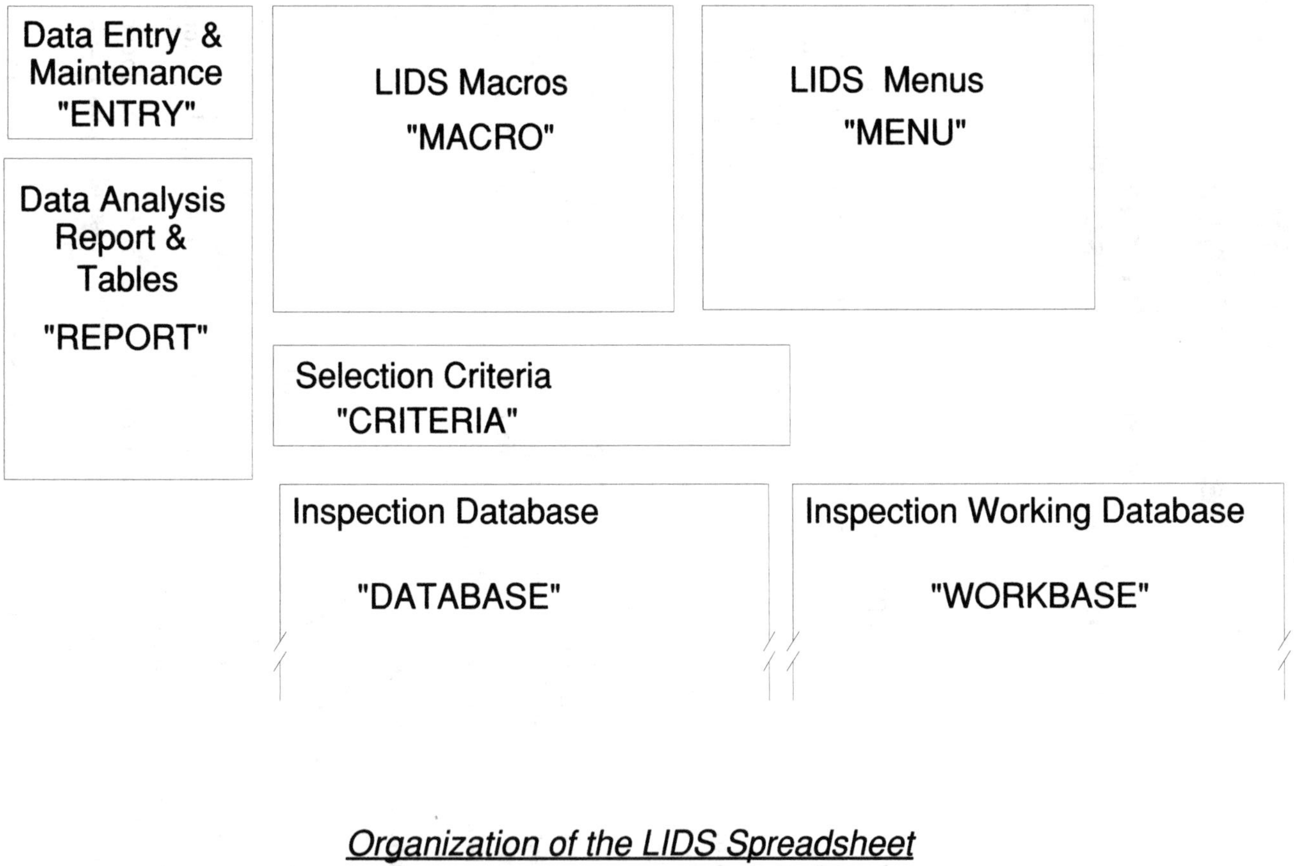

Figure A.1 LIDS architecture.

Organization of the LIDS Spreadsheet

Data Entry & Maintenance
"ENTRY"

Data Analysis Report & Tables
"REPORT"

LIDS Macros
"MACRO"

LIDS Menus
"MENU"

Selection Criteria
"CRITERIA"

Inspection Database
"DATABASE"

Inspection Working Database
"WORKBASE"

For example, to analyze inspection data you would select ANALYSIS from the top LIDS menu. The inspection data is copied from the data base to the workbase (a work area within the LIDS spreadsheet, identified in Figure A.1). Using subsequent menus to specify various selection criteria, a portion of the data base is selected for analysis and the unwanted inspection records are deleted from the workbase. The selected inspections can then be analyzed further using successive menu choices.

LIDS provides functions for reviewing the results and preparing tabular and graphical reports of the analysis. Although familiarity with Lotus 1-2-3 is recommended to operate LIDS, few native Lotus commands are normally used except to initialize Lotus 1-2-3, load the LIDS spreadsheet, and quit Lotus 1-2-3. All LIDS functions, including the inspection data base, are packaged within a single spreadsheet.

The architecture of the LIDS spreadsheet is shown in Figure A.1. There are four major components, or areas, of the spreadsheet which you will interact with when using LIDS. First, there is a data entry area (ENTRY), which looks like a project's inspection summary report that is used to enter the identification, performance, and defect data for each inspection. Second, there is a data base area (DATABASE), which is used to store the inspection records. Third is a working data base area (WORKBASE) that is used for the selection of inspection records during data analysis. Fourth are the data analysis tables (REPORT), where results of analysis are placed for display and reporting. Each of these spreadsheet areas are visible at one time or another during LIDS operations.

There are three other components of the spreadsheet that are normally not visible, but which make possible all LIDS functions. They are the LIDS menu (MENU), macros (MACRO), and selection criteria (CRITERIA). The menus call on the macros and the selection criteria to perform the various LIDS functions for entering data, storing it in the data base, analyzing the accumulated inspection records, and, if necessary, making changes to the inspection records. These three components drive LIDS and are not intended to be modified during normal use.

When working with the LIDS spreadsheet, it is important to note that inspection data has a different appearance in the data entry and data analysis areas from the data base. Inspection data is entered, maintained, and displayed following analysis as tables, reports, and graphs. It is stored and displayed in the data base though, as a linear record of fields containing the inspection identification, performance, and summary defect data. When you wish to examine, change, or review an inspection record, LIDS compresses the fields back to the entry format for ease of use. The linear inspection record is used for selection, analysis, and some maintenance. It also makes it straightforward to extract the data base for use in other spreadsheet or data management systems.

A.2   Requirements

A.2.1   Hardware

- An MS-DOS-compatible personal computer (PC)
- Hard disk storage for Lotus 1-2-3, the LIDS worksheets, and report and graphics files that will be produced
- Graphics display.

A.2.2   Software

- MS-DOS Version 2 or higher
- Lotus 1-2-3 Version 2.n
- LIDS master spreadsheet.

A.2.3   Personnel Qualifications

- Ability to operate an MS-DOS PC
- Completion of Lotus 1-2-3 on-line tutorial, or equivalent operating experience
- Knowledge of project inspection data entry, analysis, and reporting requirements.

A.2.4   Restrictions

The major restriction of LIDS is that it does not produce any printed reports or graphs directly, but rather prepares Lotus 1-2-3 American Standard Code for Information Interchange (ASCII) and graphic files. These files can then be used by a wide variety of word processing, desktop publishing, and graphics programs to produce reports.

Further, the LIDS inspection data base is limited to 8000 records. This is a maximum and may be further restricted by hardware and operational considerations. The LIDS spreadsheet is 200 kilobytes (Kbytes), and each inspection record requires an additional 1200 bytes. Also, each LIDS operation, such as sorting or selecting records, requires additional computer time as the number of inspection records increase. Depending on the capacity and speed of the computer that is used, you may want to limit a typical LIDS data base to hundreds rather than thousands of inspections.

Larger projects will probably want to segment their inspection data bases along functional, representational, organizational, or some other boundaries anyway. Smaller projects would typically segment their inspection data base by function and release. For those cases when a broader study is required, the data bases can be extracted and merged for further analysis by LIDS or another system.

A.3   Operating LIDS

Before using LIDS for either the first time or for a new inspection data base, copy the LIDS master spreadsheet and identify the copy with an appropriate file name for the project's inspections. This copy will be the working LIDS data base, and should be backed up after making any additions or changes. Retain the original copy of LIDS as the master spreadsheet. LIDS is now ready for you to add data, with the most recently entered inspection record placed progressively at the end of the data base. Note: Do not perform any analysis until at least two inspection records have been entered into the data base.

To start LIDS, load the Lotus 1-2-3 program. When Lotus initialization is completed, retrieve the working copy of the LIDS data base using the Lotus open or file retrieval commands. The LIDS menu is automatically initiated when the spreadsheet containing the data base is loaded and ready.

Selection of any LIDS menu option is performed by placing the cursor over the option name and depressing the Enter key. Alternatively, the first character of the option name may be entered to select the option (each menu's options have unique first characters for this reason). A QUIT option is provided on each menu to enable you to return to the previous level of the LIDS menu hierarchy (or to the Lotus READY mode from the initial LIDS menu). QUIT should always be used to exit a LIDS menu rather than using the ESCape key. The use of ESCape will cause a return to the Lotus READY mode rather than backing up to the preceding LIDS menu.

If you exit LIDS, LIDS may be restarted at any time from the Lotus READY mode by depressing the ALT and the M keys together, called ALT-M. This will restart LIDS from the Lotus READY mode at the top menu. Alternatively, ALT-X can be used. This facility (depressing the ALT and the X keys together) will restart LIDS from the ANALYSIS/RESULTS menu. This feature may save a number of steps if you inadvertently fall out of LIDS following a lengthy selection process. The selected records in WORKBASE will remain as they were before you left LIDS.

The LIDS spreadsheet must be saved before ending a work session to preserve any additions or changes that have been made to the data base (analysis does not change the data base). Use either the LIDS SAVE function or the native Lotus file save commands. It is important to remember that all of the work you have done with LIDS will only be permanently recorded on disk if you explicitly save the spreadsheet.

To end a LIDS working session, first save the active LIDS spreadsheet if you have made any changes that you wish to retain. Then exit from the LIDS menu by entering the QUIT option on the first, or top level, LIDS menu. This will place you in Lotus READY mode. Use the Lotus quit command to exit, and the session will be over.

A few guidelines for applying LIDS are

- Make a hard copy of each entered inspection and keep it with the original inspection records.

- Overall statistics, such as the number of inspections performed or total inspection effort, are useful and can be obtained from the inspection report. The defect charts for type, class, and severity may also be useful for the entire data base, as well as for selected sets.

- Analyze the inspections further in small groups. Select a current range of inspection dates. Then select on other criteria, such as type of inspection or product, to refine the set. In this way the results are timely and in-process, and are relevant to product development.

- The inspection performance and evaluation graphs will become cluttered if a large number of inspections (more than about 50) are used. Practical reasons of timeliness and utility will probably dictate that smaller rather than larger groups of inspections be evaluated together.

- Continually evaluate the inspection data. Develop a regular reporting program that tracks both current inspections and trends.

- Where any changes or additions are involved, remember—save, save, save the LIDS spreadsheet.

- Finally, LIDS can also be used to track inspection schedules. Make an initial entry for each forthcoming inspection with a unique designation, such as a special disposition. These scheduled inspections can then be followed and reported. Update this record when the inspection is performed.

A.4 Using LIDS Menus

LIDS functions are accessed through the LIDS menus (Figures A.2 to A.5). The menus are hierarchically organized into three major service areas: ENTRY, ANALYSIS, and MAINTenance. Inspection data may also be accessed through "native" Lotus commands if you have the necessary experience and knowledge using Lotus 1-2-3. The LIDS data base may also be extracted to other spreadsheets, or other systems, for more extensive analysis. You should always exercise caution to assure that the LIDS spreadsheet with the most current inspection data is saved before using any native Lotus functions.

The initial or top-level LIDS menu presents the following choices:

ENTRY ANALYSIS MAINT SAVE QUIT

- ENTRY is used to add new inspection records to the data base.

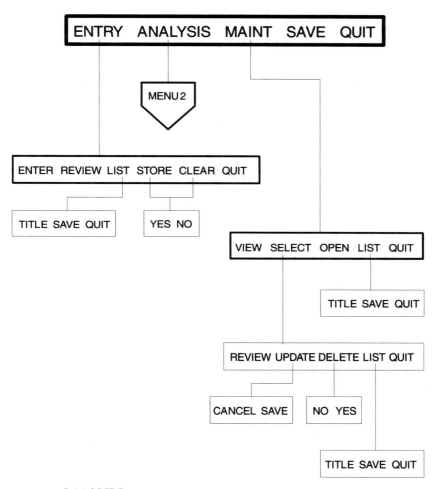

Figure A.2 Initial LIDS menu.

- ANALYSIS pro.ides reports and graphs of inspection data for all or a selected part of the data base.
- MAINT allows you to view and print the data base, to change information in the data base, and to select a record to be printed, updated, or deleted from the data base.
- SAVE writes the LIDS spreadsheet back to disk to preserve any additions, deletions, or changes that were made to the inspection data.
- QUIT returns control to native Lotus mode for ending the session.

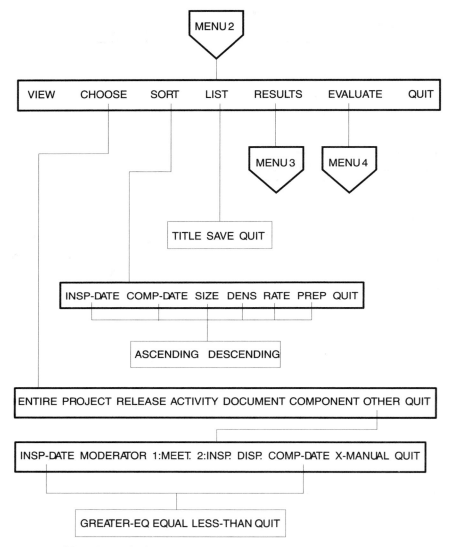

Figure A.3 Menu 2—analysis.

When SAVE is selected to rewrite the LIDS spreadsheet, reply with Enter to verify the file when requested by Lotus, and then with "R" when permission to rewrite is requested. Depress the Enter key to restore the LIDS menu.

QUIT exits LIDS and returns to the Lotus READY mode where any native Lotus 1-2-3 commands may be used. This is the normal path for

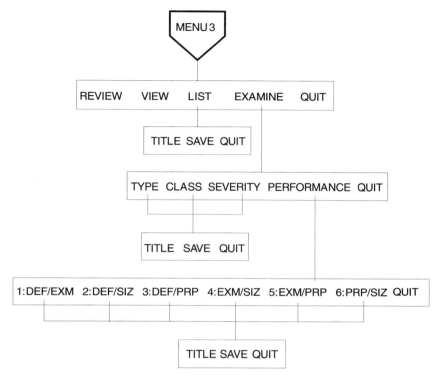

Figure A.4 Menu 3—results.

terminating LIDS and Lotus. At lower-level menus, QUIT returns to the previous menu.

A.4.1   ENTRY

The ENTRY menu offers the following options:

ENTER REVIEW LIST STORE CLEAR QUIT

A.4.1.1   ENTER.   When selected, the ENTER option positions the cursor at the first location of the inspection data entry area of the LIDS spreadsheet. Cursor movement is restricted to data entry cells only, skipping over calculation and formatted fields. The cursor may be positioned with any of the cursor movement keys, and data may be entered or changed in any cell, in any sequence, and at any time while the ENTER option is active. To remove unwanted data, replace the data in the cell with blanks.

  To complete data entry and to return to the ENTRY menu, enter no-

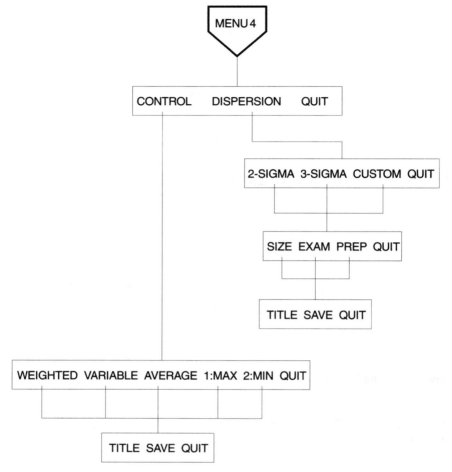

Figure A.5 Menu 4—evaluation.

data, i.e., depress the Enter key without any other entries. Be sure to verify the data and make any necessary corrections before leaving the ENTER option. There will be a delay when exiting ENTER while LIDS recalculates the new data. ENTER may be reselected to make changes at any time prior to selecting the STORE or CLEAR options. Refer to Section A.5 for the format of the input data.

A.4.1.2 REVIEW. REVIEW allows you to move about the data entry area using any of the cursor movement keys, including page-up, page-down, tab, home, and end. Use REVIEW to check your work before storing the inspection record in the data base. Be careful not to enter any data while in REVIEW mode. Exit REVIEW by depressing the Enter key with no-data.

A.4.1.3 LIST. The LIST option will write a file of the inspection data entry report. See Figure A.6 for a sample. The report files are ASCII, and Lotus always appends a .PRN file name extension. It is recommended that the entered data be listed, and printed later for documentation. All occurrences of LIST options in any of the menus behave similarly, and when LIST is selected, the following options are presented:

TITLE SAVE QUIT

You may optionally prepare a report title by selecting the TITLE option. Type a meaningful report title and then press the Enter key to record the title and to return to this menu. After entering the report title, or not, choose the SAVE option to write the report to disk. SAVE will request a report file name of eight or less characters (do not enter an extension). If the file name is unique, the report will be written and you will be presented with a Lotus menu. Reply with Enter and you will be returned to the previous menu.

If the file name is already present you have the option of canceling the write operation or rewriting the file. Enter R, and the file will be rewritten. Enter C and the operation will be canceled and you will be returned to Lotus ready mode. Alt-M or Alt-X returns you to LIDS at the initial or the RESULTS menu respectively.

QUIT returns you immediately to the ENTRY menu.

A.4.1.4 STORE. The STORE option adds the entered inspection data to the data base. It will be reformatted and added as the last record of the inspection data base. Permission is requested before the STORE operation is performed. Selecting YES stores the data and NO returns you to the ENTRY menu.

On completion, STORE offers the option of clearing the entry area. Again, either YES or NO will clear or leave the data intact. STORE returns you to the ENTRY menu either directly or after the entry area is cleared.

A.4.1.5 CLEAR. The CLEAR option resets the inspection data entry area to null and zero values. Confirmation, YES or NO, is requested before the CLEAR option is executed. On completion, CLEAR returns you to the ENTRY menu. If the entry area is cleared, some calculated fields will be reinitialized to an "ERR" value. This is normal, and is the result of the calculation dividing by zero in the initialized state.

A.4.1.6 QUIT. QUIT returns you to the initial LIDS menu.

A.4.2 ANALYSIS

Analysis is the central function of LIDS and, given its large variety of selection, reporting, and evaluation options, the most complicated. Though this set of options may be complex, they are the most valuable part of the system. Some practice with the options is helpful when first learning LIDS. Remember, nothing is changed on the disk resident data base unless you choose to SAVE the results of your work. If you exit LIDS in the middle of an analysis, ALT-X brings you back to the RESULTS options menu where you can resume your work. ALT-M allows you to restart from the beginning.

Selecting ANALYSIS will first copy all of the inspection records from the data base to the workbase. The time required for the initialization of workbase depends on the size of the data base and the speed of your computer. After the initialization is completed, ANALYSIS will present the following menu options:

VIEW CHOOSE SORT LIST RESULTS EVALUATE QUIT

As you can see from the diagrams of the menus (Figures A.2 to A.5), the majority of LIDS functions are for the analysis of the inspection data. A brief summary of the analysis functions follows.

- VIEW allows you to look at the selected inspection records currently in workbase.

- CHOOSE selects the inspection records for subsequent analysis based on various criteria.

- SORT sequences the chosen inspection records.

- LIST writes an ASCII file of the identification and performance data for the chosen inspection records. Defect data is not listed.

- RESULTS provides tabular and graphical reports of the defects and performance of the chosen inspections.

- EVALUATE provides a variety of statistical quality control and dispersion graphs of the chosen inspections.

- QUIT returns control to the initial LIDS menu.

Analysis of the inspection data always begins with choosing the inspection records to be analyzed. Either all of the data base records may be chosen, or only those meeting specified criteria for key fields. When the inspection records have been chosen, they may be sorted and listed. The analysis is now ready for both tabular and graphical reporting of the results and statistical evaluation. Tabular reports and graphs are displayed for review. They may be titled and then saved on a user-named disk file for later printing using a variety of word processing and graphics programs. The Lotus PrintGraph utility may also be used to print a copy of the graphs. Instructions for using PrintGraph are in the "Graph" section of the Lotus manual.

A.4.2.1 VIEW. VIEW provides a general facility to scan the selected inspection data base records. When ANALYSIS is first chosen the entire data base is copied into a work area called workbase, and VIEW enables you to review these records prior to making any further selections. The field names appear as a fixed upper margin, and the first field of the inspection records, which is an inspection number inserted into workbase by ANALYSIS, appears as a fixed left margin. The cursor control keys, including paging, may be used to display any inspection record and field, but the cursor will not enter either the upper or left margins. Data cannot be changed when VIEW is active. To exit VIEW and return to the ANALYSIS menu, depress the Enter key with no-data.

A.4.2.2 CHOOSE. The CHOOSE option displays the following menu:

ENTIRE PROJECT RELEASE ACTIVITY DOCUMENT COMPONENT
OTHER QUIT

- ENTIRE selects all the data base records (this is the default when ANALYSIS is first entered and the entire contents of the data base will be in workbase). ENTIRE can also be selected to reinitialize a series of new choices.

- QUIT always returns you to the ANALYSIS menu.

- OTHER presents additional menu options to choose from:

INSP-DATE MODERATOR 1:MEET. 2:INSP. DISP. COMP-DATE
X-MANUAL QUIT

A.4.2.2.1 CHOOSE options. Each of the options on these two menus requests the entry of a criteria value before proceeding. Inspection records are selected by performing a logical comparison between the criteria value and the specified field value for each record currently in workbase. Only records matching the criteria are chosen from workbase. The others are deleted. A separate copy of the data base in workbase is used so that the original inspection records are not altered by any actions of ANALYSIS. On completion, VIEW may be used for further examination of the chosen records. Use these options to choose the inspection records by the indicated criteria. X-MANUAL allows you to manually choose the inspection records from workbase.

When specifying selection criteria, keep in mind that a logical comparison is performed and is sensitive to the presence of leading or trailing blanks, and they should not be included either in the inspection data or in the criteria. Selection criteria may include the " * " and " ? " wildcard characters, as well as the " ~ " negative selection character (*not* the specified value) to extend the flexibility of the selection criteria for use in other than date fields (INSP-DATE and COMP-DATE). Refer to the "Data Commands" section of the Lotus manual for instructions on their use.

Numeric dates of the form mm/dd/yy, with the slashes present, are used as a selection criteria for the INSP-DATE and COMP-DATE fields by LIDS. There is a subsequent menu selection for each of these two date options:

GREAT-EQ EQUAL LESS-THAN QUIT

- GREAT-EQ chooses records whose inspection or completion dates are greater than or equal to the criteria date.

- EQUAL chooses records whose inspection or completion dates are equal to the criteria data.

- LESS-THAN chooses records whose inspection or completion dates are less than the criteria date.

If a date is invalid, i.e., 9/31/87, a RE-SELECT menu is displayed. Dates may be repeatedly selected until the proper set of inspection records is obtained.

X-MANUAL is unique. This option is provided to allow you to manually choose the records you wish to analyze. When X-MANUAL is used, you may alter any of the selection fields in the working copy of the data base. Workbase is opened to you for input. You may enter a new value or use the Lotus edit function to place a unique character in one of the selection fields for each record that you wish to include in the analysis. All of the keyboard, cursor direction keys, function keys, and Enter key are available.

For example, if you choose the Project field for manual selection, either replace the current Project name with a " = " character, or by using the Lotus edit key (F2), place " = " as the first character in the field. When you have marked all of the records that you wish to choose, exit X-MANUAL by keying Enter with no-data.

X-MANUAL then returns you to the CHOOSE menu, where you may now use any of the other options and criteria that are appropriate for selecting the inspection records you have marked. In this example, you would select the PROJECT option and use " =* " as the selection criteria to choose every record with the Project field beginning with " = ".

You may perform CHOOSE multiple times against the workbase records before using any of the other ANALYSIS options, such as SORT or EVALUATE, resulting in a selected set of records that concurrently meet a number of different criteria for the same or different selection fields. When the records matching the selection criteria are chosen, you will be returned to the ANALYSIS menu.

A.4.2.3   SORT.   The SORT option arranges the chosen inspection records into ascending or descending order by a selected sort key field. This is a single-key sort, without a secondary key. SORT displays the key selection menu:

INSP-DATE COMP-DATE SIZE DENS RATE PREP QUIT

A.4.2.3.1   SORT options.   The SORT options specify the key fields, except QUIT, that are used for EVALUATION of the inspection records. Sorting has no effect on reporting the RESULTS of the inspections, only on their EVALUATION. These fields include the dates when the inspections were held or completed, and inspection performance factors:

- INSP-DATE orders the inspection records by the date the inspection meeting was held.

- COMP-DATE orders the inspection records by the date the inspection was completed, including all rework.

- SIZE orders the inspection records by the size (lines) of the inspected work product.

- DENS orders the inspection records by the major defect density (in defects per 1000 lines).

- RATE orders the inspection records by the rate the work product was examined (in lines per hour).

- PREP orders the inspection records by the rate at which the product was prepared (the size of the work product divided by the total preparation time; then divided by the total number of inspectors less the author).

When any of these menu options is selected, it is immediately followed by a menu requesting the choice of sorting in either ascending or descending sequence:

ASCENDING DESCENDING

You must choose one or the other. You will return to the ANALYSIS menu when sorting is completed.

A.4.2.4 LIST. The LIST option of the ANALYSIS menu will write an ASCII file containing the identification and performance fields of the selected (and possibly sorted) inspection records (Figure A.7). The options for LIST are

TITLE SAVE QUIT

LIST performs in the same manner as described in Section A.4.1.3. Use LIST to record the subset of inspection records that you have chosen.

A.4.2.5 RESULTS. The RESULTS option calculates the data analysis tables for the set of chosen inspection records and allows further examination of their detected defects and performance. RESULTS compiles these figures and presents the following menu of options:

REVIEW VIEW LIST EXAMINE QUIT

A.4.2.5.1 REVIEW. REVIEW allows you to examine the data analysis results, using the cursor control keys to move between the inspection performance report totals and averages, and the tables of defect totals, averages, percentages, and relative percentages.

Data may not be entered or changed while in REVIEW mode. To exit from REVIEW and to return to the RESULTS menu, depress the Enter key with no-data.

A.4.2.5.2 VIEW. VIEW allows you to scan the selected inspection records in workbase that have been analyzed. VIEW does not permit the entry or modification of data. To exit VIEW and to return to the RESULTS menu, depress the Enter key with no-data.

A.4.2.5.3 LIST. LIST writes an ASCII file of the results for the chosen set of inspections. It includes the inspection totals, averages, and defect tables. See Figure A.8 for an example. The options for LIST are

TITLE SAVE QUIT

LIST performs in the same manner as described in Section A.4.1.3.

A.4.2.5.4 EXAMINE options. The EXAMINE menu provides four options (other than QUIT). The first three prepare graphs of the percentage of defects by their type, class, and severity. The fourth option,

PERFORMANCE, analyzes the inspections with respect to their major defect density, examination rate, preparation rate, and size.

TYPE CLASS SEVERITY PERFORMANCE QUIT

- TYPE prepares a histogram of the percentage of defects by defect type for major defects, minor defects, and all defects.

- CLASS prepares a histogram of the percentage of defects by defect class (missing, wrong, and extra) for major defects, minor defects, and all defects.

- SEVERITY prepares a histogram of the percentage of defects by major and minor severity for total, missing, wrong, and extra defects.

- PERFORMANCE presents a menu of options to choose graphs of the inspection performance factors.

- QUIT returns to the previous menu.

A.4.2.5.4.1 Graph options.   When the TYPE, CLASS, or SEVERITY graph option is selected, the appropriate bar graph will be displayed on the monitor (Figures A.10 through A.12). Depressing any key erases the graph and, similar to LIST, the following options menu is presented:

TITLE SAVE QUIT

- TITLE allows you to specify the title line of the selected graph. On completion, TITLE will redisplay the graph on the monitor with the entered title as the second title line. Depressing any key returns the user to the graph options menu.

- SAVE requests that you name a save file (maximum of eight characters) for the graph for later printing (Figures A.10 through A.17). The graph is written to the named file with a .PIC extension. If the named file is not already present, the graph file will be SAVEd. A Lotus menu then appears. Key Enter with no-data and you return to LIDS at the previous menu.

  If the named file is present, Lotus will request confirmation in order to rewrite it. Reply with "R" and the new graph will be saved. Key Enter with no-data and you will return to LIDS at the previous menu. If you instead decide to cancel the write, key Enter or "C" and the write request for the graph file is canceled. You will then be returned to the Lotus READY mode. ALT-X or ALT-M return you to LIDS at the RESULTS or initial menu.

- QUIT returns you to the previous menu.

A.4.2.5.4.2 PERFORMANCE options.   The PERFORMANCE menu provides six choices for scatter plots of the major defect density, size, examination rate, and preparation rate of the chosen inspections, including a plot of the quadratic regression analysis of their relationships. When PERFORMANCE is selected, there will be an initial delay while the regression analysis is computed.

Note: PERFORMANCE does not operate for less than four inspection records, and an error message indicating the condition and asking for RE-SELECT is displayed.

The PERFORMANCE menu is

1:DEF/EXM 2:DEF/SIZ 3:DEF/PRP 4:EXM/SIZ 5:EXM/PRP 6:PRP/SIZ QUIT

- 1:DEF/EXM graphs major defect density versus examination rate.
- 2:DEF/SIZ graphs major defect density versus work product size.
- 3:DEF/PRP graphs major defect density versus preparation rate.
- 4:EXM/SIZ graphs examination rate versus work product size.
- 5:EXM/PRP graphs examination rate versus preparation rate.
- 6:PRP/SIZ graphs preparation rate versus work product size.
- QUIT returns you to the preceding menu.

For each of these options, except QUIT, the graph is displayed on the monitor (Figure A.13). Depressing any key erases the graph and presents the following options menu:

TITLE SAVE QUIT

These graph options operate in the same way as described in Section A.4.2.5.4.1.

A.4.2.6 EVALUATE. The EVALUATE option of the ANALYSIS menu graphically compares the distribution of the major defect densities, sizes, examination rates, and preparation rates with statistical limits for the selected inspections. This differs from the RESULTS option, which compares these same inspection parameters with each other. EVALUATE is mostly used to assess the quality of the product, whereas RESULTS primarily looks at the performance of the inspection process. The EVALUATE menu is

CONTROL DISPERSION QUIT

QUIT, of course, returns you to the previous menu.

A.4.2.6.1 CONTROL. Performs a graphical comparison of the major defect density of the inspections with statistically determined control limits. These are the lower control limit (LCL) and the upper control limit (UCL) (see Chapter 6 in this book). They are derived by applying statistical process control theory to the inspection defect data, and are indicators of inspections with either excessive or deficient defects. These results are helpful for evaluating the quality of the work product and the inspections, particularly when used with the dispersions of the sizes and rates of the inspections.

When CONTROL is selected the next menu requests the mode for determining the control limits. The choice is based on how you want the work product size to be used to compute the LCL and UCL:

WEIGHTED VARIABLE AVERAGE 1:MAX 2:MIN QUIT

- WEIGHTED: the LCL is based on the maximum size of the set of inspections; the UCL on the average size of the set (this makes the LCL somewhat more stringent).

- VARIABLE: the LCL and UCL are based on the actual size of each work product in the set of inspections (if the work products are sorted into size order, the control limits will be either smoothly increasing or decreasing)

- AVERAGE: the LCL and UCL are based on the average size of the set of inspections

- 1:MAX: the LCL and UCL are based on the maximum size of the set of inspections

- 2:MIN: the LCL and UCL are based on the minimum size of the set of inspections

- QUIT returns to the previous menu
  (Note: The LCL is never taken as less than 0, and frequently is 0)

When any of these options is selected, a control graph with the major defect density of the inspections, the mean, the LCL, and the UCL is presented. After examining the graph, depressing any key erases it and the following options menu is presented:

TITLE SAVE QUIT

These graph options operate in the same way as described in Section A.4.2.5.4.1. QUIT returns you to the CONTROL menu.

Multiple choices of the control mode from the CONTROL menu allow you to determine the sensitivity of the control limits to the distribution of the work product sizes in the set. Using the maximum size of the set produces the most stringent limits, while the control limits for the minimum size are the loosest. One of these menu choices most likely provides appropriate control limits for the set to discriminate between acceptable inspections and those requiring more attention. A sample is shown in Figure A.14.

A.4.2.6.2 DISPERSION.   Performs a graphical comparison of the sizes, examination rates, and preparation rates of the selected set of inspections. The inspection parameter, the mean of the set and a reference dispersion, some number of standard deviations (sigma) from the mean, are displayed. Dispersion charts are used to detect those inspections that deviate from the norm in their size or rates. The user determines how large the reference dispersion is by selecting the number of standard deviations from the next, SIGMA, menu:

2-SIGMA 3-SIGMA CUSTOM QUIT

A.4.2.6.2.1 SIGMA options.   The choice of sigma depends on the degree of variability of the data. Sigma is selected so that only about 20 percent of the inspections exceed it. Two standard choices are provided, two or three times sigma, as well the facility for setting the dispersion to a custom value between 1 and 4. If the reference dispersion is near 1-sigma, the set of inspections are fairly uniform; if the reference is closer to 4-sigma, the inspections vary widely.

Correspondence between inspections that exceeded the UCL on the control graph and have fairly normal dispersions are defect-prone candidates. Those inspections that are near or less than the LCL on the control graph and exceed the reference dispersions are potentially poorly inspected work products.

QUIT returns the user to the previous menu. After choosing sigma the PARAMETER menu is displayed, offering one of the following inspection parameters as options:

SIZE EXAM PREP QUIT

A.4.2.6.2.1.1 PARAMETER options

- SIZE displays the dispersion of the sizes of the inspection work products, along with their mean and n-sigma reference.

- EXAM displays the dispersion of the examination rates of the inspection work products, along with their mean and n-sigma reference.

- PREP displays the dispersion of the preparation rates.

- QUIT returns to the previous menu.

When any of these options is selected, a graph with the inspection parameter, the mean, and the upper and lower (never less than 0) n-sigma reference dispersions will be presented. See Figures A.15

through A.17 for samples. After examining the graph, depressing any key erases it and the following options menu is presented:

TITLE SAVE QUIT

These graph options operate in the same way as described in Section A.4.2.5.4.1. QUIT returns you to the PARAMETER menu.

A.4.2.7 QUIT. The QUIT option on the first ANALYSIS menu returns you to the initial LIDS menu.

A.4.3 MAINT

LIDS inspection data maintenance is performed on either a record or on the data base. Record-oriented (SELECT) maintenance is available for changes to all inspection identification, performance, and defect data, and is the only method provided for deletion of an inspection record from the data base. Maintenance of the data base (OPEN) is most convenient for changes that affect more than one record, and which deal only with inspection identification fields, not performance or defect data.

The MAINTenance menu has the following options:

VIEW SELECT OPEN LIST QUIT

The usual sequence of these options is to first VIEW the inspection data base in order to identify the desired record or fields to be changed. Then choose the appropriate maintenance mode, SELECT or OPEN, to update the record or records, or the data base. Document the changes through LIST.

A.4.3.1 VIEW. VIEW provides a general facility for the LIDS user to scan the entire inspection data base. The data base field names appear as a fixed upper margin, and the inspection record names as a fixed left margin. The cursor control keys, including paging, may be used to display any inspection record and field, but the cursor will not enter either the upper or left margins. Data cannot be changed when VIEW is active.

The Lotus row numbers appear in the leftmost border of the display. The row number is used to identify an inspection record for subsequent maintenance. When the desired inspection record is found, the row number should be recorded for use with the SELECT option. An incorrect row number will select an unintended inspection record for maintenance. LIDS verifies that the SELECTed row number is within the valid data base range, and requests another SELECTion if the row number is invalid.

To exit VIEW and return to the MAINT menu, key Enter with no-data.

A.4.3.2 SELECT. When the SELECT option is chosen, you are requested to enter the row number for the desired inspection record. Do not use a row number lower than that for the first data base record. LIDS validates the record row number, and requests that you make another selection if it is lower than the allowed range. Just press Enter and reselect. If the row number exceeds the data base range, zeros appear in the entry area. QUIT and reselect. After the inspection record row number is entered, there is a delay while the data is copied into the entry area and recalculated.

SELECT then offers the following options:

REVIEW UPDATE DELETE LIST QUIT

A.4.3.2.1 REVIEW. REVIEW allows you to view the selected record. The cursor control keys are used to scan the data fields. No data should be entered while REVIEW is active. Enter no-data to exit and return to the SELECT menu.

A.4.3.2.2 UPDATE. UPDATE positions the cursor to the first data entry cell of the entry area and allows data to be entered. The cursor movement keys may be used to move to any data cells in any sequence. A data field may be cleared by replacing its contents with blank. When all of the intended changes have been made, depressing Enter with no-data recalculates the inspection record and exits UPDATE. LIDS then requests permission to save the updated record:

CANCEL SAVE

- CANCEL: permission is denied to save the updated record. LIDS returns to the SELECT options menu.
- SAVE: permission is given to save the updated record. The contents of the data entry area replace the record in the data base. LIDS then returns to the SELECT options menu.

A.4.3.2.3 DELETE. DELETE removes the selected record from the data base. Confirmation is requested before the record is deleted, thus

NO YES

If permission to delete is denied, no action is taken and LIDS returns to the SELECT options menu. On confirmation, the record is removed from the data base, the data entry area is cleared, and LIDS returns to the MAINT menu.

We suggest listing a record before either update or deletion. The listed copy may be the only convenient backup if an error is made updating data, or if the wrong record is deleted.

A.4.3.2.4 LIST. LIST writes an ASCII copy of the inspection record to disk in the data entry format (see sample report in Figure A.6). The LIST menu offers the following options:

TITLE SAVE QUIT

LIST operates the same way as described in Section A.4.1.3, and returns the user to the SELECT menu when completed.

A.4.3.2.5 QUIT. QUIT for the SELECT menu returns to the MAINT menu.

A.4.3.3 OPEN. In OPEN mode, the identification data of the records in the inspection data base is available for update. When OPEN is selected, the cursor is placed on the first field of the first data base record. The cursor may be moved throughout the identification section of the data base using the cursor directional keys. Updates are performed by placing the cursor over the desired field, keying the replacement data, and depressing the Enter key. Alternatively, the Lotus Edit mode (keying F2) may be used. See the Lotus manual for more details in the use of the Edit (F2) key. Data may be removed by replacing the field with a blank entry.

The reason that only identification data can be altered in OPEN mode is that a change to a numeric field that is used in computations (lines, for example, is used in both density and rate calculations) may leave the record out of balance until (or if) it is recalculated. Therefore, performance and the defect fields are not available in OPEN update mode. Also, note that all dates are stored in Lotus internal date format (although their display format in the data base is mm/dd/yy), and will appear as a numeric value in the Lotus update window, where January 1, 1900 is 1. Updates should be made in the Lotus internal date format (e.g., 11/24/90 is 33201).

After making your changes, using the Lotus Edit key (F2) if you wish, and depress the Enter key with no-date to complete OPEN update. LIDS will return to the MAINT menu.

A.4.3.4 LIST. The LIST option for the MAINTenance menu writes an ASCII file of the identification and performance data of the LIDS data base (Figure A.9). The LIST options menu appears as

TITLE SAVE QUIT

These options operate the same as described in Section A.4.1.3. LIST
returns to the MAINT menu when completed.

A.4.3.5 QUIT. QUIT returns to the initial LIDS menu.

A.5 Input Data Format

Three types of inspection data are entered into LIDS:

1. Inspection identification (Table A.1)

2. Inspection performance (Table A.2)

3. Inspection defects (Table A.3)

For ease of entry and recognition, all alphabetic entries should be
made in uppercase. Do not insert any leading or trailing blanks. The
format and content of input data is determined by the project.

Additionally, note that numeric-labels are numeric entries preceded
with " ' ", the apostrophe character. (During analysis, however, enter
the fully formatted date, with the slashes, for the requested inspection
or completion date criteria, e.g., 3/19/92.)

The inspection defect types (Table A.4) are described by a two-letter
code.

TABLE A.1   Inspection Identification Data

Name	Description	Format (content)
Insp. date	Date of inspection	Numeric-label ('dd/mm/yy)
Project	Development project	Alphanumeric
Release	Development release	Alphanumeric
Activity	Development activity	Alphanumeric
Document	Development document	Alphanumeric
Component	Component name	Alphanumeric
Moderator	Moderator's last name	Alpha (I, R, O)
Meeting type	Type of meeting	Alpha
Insp. type	Type of inspection	Alpha (e.g., RQ, HL, DD, CD, TP, TC, etc.)
Disposition	Inspection exit disposition: Must be present for meeting types I and R. Must *not* be present for meeting type O.	Alpha (A, C, R): A = accept C = conditional R = reinspect

TABLE A.2   Inspection Performance Data

Name	Description	Format (content)
Lines	Lines of inspected documents	Numeric
Duration	Time for inspection meeting	Numeric (HH.h)
Exam. rate	Examination rate	(Computed value)
Team size	Number of team members (including author and moderator)	Numeric
Total prep.	Sum of team preparation time	Numeric (HHH.h)
Defects/1000 lines	Total defect density	(Computed value)
Rework	Actual effort for rework	Numeric (HHH.h)
Effort	Total staff hours	(Computed value)
Maj./1000 lines	Major defect density	(Computed value)
Prep. rate	Average preparation rate (excluding the author)	(Computed value)
Comp. date	Completion date, including all rework	Numeric-label ('dd/mm/yy)

TABLE A.3   Inspection Defect Data

Name	Description	Format
Inspection defects	Count of defects per type/class/severity	Numeric

TABLE A.4   Defect Types

Type	Name
DA	Data
DC	Documentation
FN	Functionality
HF	Human factors
IF	Interface
LO	Logic
MN	Maintainability
PF	Performance
ST	Standards
OT	Other
—	(Expansion)

A.6   Output Data Format

LIDS output data consists of four types of reports:

1. Data entry/maintenance
2. Data analysis
3. Graphical analysis
4. Summary of data base and workbase records

All of these reports may be viewed on-line as well as written to an ASCII file.

A.6.1   Date Entry/Maintenance Report

This report is an image of the LIDS on-line data entry area. All of the field definitions described in Section A.5 apply to this report.

A.6.2   Data Analysis Report

The data analysis report is generated for the subset of the inspection records that were chosen. The number of records for inspection, reinspection, and overview meetings are reported as the count of I-records, R-records, and O-records, respectively. The data analysis report comprises three sections: (1) inspection record totals (Table A.5) (2) inspection record averages (Table A.6), and (3) data analysis tables.

A.6.2.1   Data Analysis Tables.
There are four data analysis tables: (1) total defects, (2) average defects, (3) percentage defects, and (4) relative percentage errors. Each analysis table uses the same format as the data entry table, and reports the inspection defects by type, class, and severity as well as by summary and grand totals for the selected records. The relative percentage table computes the percentage of each defect with respect to the minor error total and the major defect total, as appropriate to its category.

A.6.3   Summary of Inspection Records

The inspection record summary report (Table A.7) lists the identification and performance data for each record in the LIDS data base, or in the working data base, following your selection. The summaries are written to an ASCII file and are for reference in tracking the data base contents, and for attachment to the data analysis reports to identify the subset of inspection records that have been analyzed. The listing of the inspections in workbase have a record number as the first field to identify the inspections on the performance and evaluation reports.

TABLE A.5   Inspection Record Totals

Name	Description	Units
Records	Number of inspection records analyzed for this report	Integer
Total effort	Total staff effort for inspections. Computed as: (total duration * average team size) + total preparation	HHHH.(h)
Total lines	Total lines inspected	Integer
Total exam	Total of *all* members' examination time	HHHH.(h)
% Exam	% of total time for examination	%%
Effort/1000 lines	Effort per lines	HHHH.(h)
Total Prep.	Sum of inspection preparation time	HHHH.(h)
% Prep.	Preparation as a % of effort	%%
Def/1000 lines	Density of *all* defects	NNN.(n)
Total Rework	*All* rework effort	HHH.(h)
% Rework	% of total time for rework	%%
Maj./1000 lines	Density of major defects; computed as: (majors / lines) * 1000	NNN.(n)
Maj.	Number of major defects	Integer
% Maj.	% of major defects of total	%%
Rework/1000 lines	Rework per 1000 lines	HHH.(h)
Defects	Total of *all* defects reported	Integer
Rework/def.	Rework per total defects	HH.(h)
Rework/maj.	Rework per major defect	HH.(h)
I-records R-records O-records	Number of records of each type present in total of selected records	NNN

A.6.4   Graphical Analysis Reports

There are four types of graphs produced by LIDS:

1. Defect analysis
2. Inspection performance
3. Defect control
4. Parameter dispersion

Graphs that are produced by LIDS are saved as Lotus .PIC files and may be printed using the Lotus PrintGraph utility program or a variety of desktop publishing, graphics, or word processing programs.

TABLE A.6   Inspection Record Averages

Name	Description	Units
Duration	Average meeting time	HH.(h)
Effort	Average inspection effort	HHH.(h)
Lines	Average lines inspected	Integer
Team size	Average size of inspection team	NN.(n)
Defects	Average number of all defects found	NNN.(n)
Effort/defect	Effort per total errors	HH.(h)
Exam. rate	Average lines examined per hour. Computed as: avg. lines / avg. duration	NNNN.(n)
Maj.	Average number of major errors	NNN.(n)
Effort/major	Average effort per major defect	HH.(h)
Prep. rate	Average lines prepared per hour by each inspector. Computed as: (avg. lines * team size) / avg. preparation	NNN.n
Prep./person	Average preparation time per inspection team member. Computed as: tot. prep. / (no. insp * team size)	HHH.h
Effort/person	Average effort per person. Computed as: effort / team size	HHH.h
Rework	Average of rework time/insp.	HH.(h)

TABLE A.7 Data Base Fields

Field	Definition	Size
PROJ	Project name	9
REL	Release number	7
ACTIVITY	Product function	6
DOC	Document identification	9
COMPONENT	Component description	24
INSP-DATE	Date that the first meeting of the inspection was held (01/00/00 is an incomplete or false date)	10
MODERATOR	Name of the moderator	12
MEET	Type of meeting I = inspection R = reinspection O = overview	5
INSP	The type of inspection	5
DSP	The disposition decided for the verification of rework: A = accept C = conditional R = reinspect	4
LINES	The total number of lines inspected at all meetings	6
DUR	Total duration of all meetings	5
TEAM	The total number of members of the inspection team, including the moderator and author	5
PREP	The total preparation time of all members for all meetings	5
REWRK	The time required by the author to resolve all defects	6
EFFRT	Total effort for the inspection for all members and for all meetings, with the author's rework	6
EXAM. RATE	The number of lines inspected per hour	10
DEFECTS	The total number of defects reported, regardless of severity	7
MAJ	The total number of major defects reported	5
DENS	The total number of major defects per 1000 lines	6
PREP. RATE	The average number of lines prepared per hour—not including the author	10
COMP-DATE	The date that the moderator certifies completion of the inspection (01/00/00 means an incomplete or invalid date)	10

A.7 Sample Reports

A.7.1 Inspection Data Entry/Maintenance

This inspection record was written to an ASCII file using the LIST option on the ENTRY menu, and the file was then formatted with a word processor.

```
************************* INSPECTION REPORT *************************
**** Prototype Code - based on existing system
****                                                      04/20/91
****                                                      10:09 AM
********************** INSPECTION DATA ******************************
                         INSPECTION ID
                                           Insp. Date: 12/09/90
      Project:PBX200            Release:R2.14
      Activity:AP12            Document:INTLIST
   Component:PROG/DISP FUNCTION KEYS
   Moderator:CLYD          Meeting Type:I
   Insp. Type:C             Disposition:C

                    INSPECTION PERFORMANCE

      Lines:  414      Duration:    2       Exam. Rate:      207
  Team Size:    3     Total Prep:    5   Def/1000 Lines:    36.2
     Rework:    3   Total Effort: 14.0   Maj/1000 Lines:    33.8
                     Prep. Rate:  166
                     (excluding author)    Comp. Date: 12/10/90

                    INSPECTION DEFECTS

    |       MINOR            |       MAJOR          |
    |   M     W     E   | TOT |   M     W     E   | TOT | TOTALS
  -----------------------------------------------------------------
  DA |                  |   0 |   1     0         |   1 |      1
  DC |   0     1        |   1 |                   |   0 |      1
  FN |                  |   0 |                   |   0 |      0
  HF |                  |   0 |                   |   0 |      0
  IF |                  |   0 |   1               |   1 |      1
  LO |                  |   0 |   0    12         |  12 |     12
  MN |                  |   0 |                   |   0 |      0
  PF |                  |   0 |                   |   0 |      0
  ST |                  |   0 |                   |   0 |      0
  OT |                  |   0 |                   |   0 |      0
  -- |                  |     |                   |     |
  -- |                  |     |                   |     |
  -----------------------------------------------------------------
  TOT|   0     1     0  |   1 |   2    12     0   |  14 |     15
                  CATEGORY TOTALS:    2    13     0    ==========
```

Figure A.6 Inspection data entry report.

A.7.2   Selected Inspection Records

The criteria for choosing the analyzed set of inspections records was INSP = C (choosing all code inspections). The selected records were then sorted into ascending COMP-DATE order. An ASCII file was written using the LIST option of the ANALYSIS menu, and the file was then formatted with a word processor.

```
******************************** SELECTED INSPECTION RECORDS ********************************
******** All code inspections - ascending comp-date sequence          ******
********                                                     04/20/91  ******
********                                                     10:17 AM  ******
*******************************************************************************************
```

INSP #	PROJ	REL	ACT	DOC	COMPONENT	INSP-DATE	MODERATOR	MEET	INSP
1	PBX200	R2.14	AP12	INTLIST	PROG/DISP FUNCTION KEYS	12/09/90	CLYD	I	C
2	PBX200	R2.16	AP15	TRNLIST	TRANSLATION TYPE 2	12/15/90	MACH	I	C
3	PBX200	R2.110	AP12	INTLIST	LCD INDICATORS	01/09/91	PITC	I	C
4	PBX200	R2.111	AP08	INTLIST	OPS	01/10/91	CLYD	I	C
5	PBX200	R2.116	AP12	INTLIST	CALL ACTIVE DISPLAY	01/30/91	DARE	I	C
6	PBX200	R2.112	AP09	INTLIST	STATUS DMA	01/16/91	MACH	I	C
7	PBX200	R2.117	AP09	INTLIST	STATUS CHANNEL	02/12/91	MACH	I	C
8	PBX200	R2.123	AP12	INTLIST	KEY HANDLER	03/20/91	MACH	I	C
9	PBX200	R2.124	AP12	INTLIST	AUDIBLE ALERTING/CON	03/21/91	DARE	I	C
10	PBX200	R2.125	AP12	INTLIST	DO NOT DISTURB	03/27/91	MACH	I	C

INSP #	DSP	LINES	DUR	TEAM	PREP	REWRK	EFFRT	EXAM.RATE	DEFECTS	MAJ	DENS	PREP.RATE	COMP-DATE
1	C	414	2	3	5	3	14.0	207	15	14	33.8	166	12/10/90
2	C	1200	2.25	3	3.5	10	20.3	533	10	4	3.3	686	01/02/91
3	C	85	0.75	3	1.5	0.5	4.3	113	2	2	23.5	113	01/09/91
4	C	81	1	3	1	1	5.0	81	8	1	12.3	162	01/10/91
5	C	240	1	3	2	0.5	5.5	240	4	4	16.7	240	02/10/91
6	C	330	2.5	3	3	10	20.5	132	10	8	24.2	220	02/12/91
7	C	570	2.5	3	3.5	8	19.0	228	16	2	3.5	326	03/05/91
8	C	40	0.3	3	1	0.5	2.4	133	2	2	50.0	80	03/20/91
9	C	120	1	3	3	0.5	6.5	120	7	3	25.0	80	03/21/91
10	C	140	0.8	3	2	0.5	4.9	175	8	5	35.7	140	04/06/91

Figure A.7 Identification and performance fields of selected inspection records.

A.7.3 Inspection Data Analysis Report

This report was prepared for the set of "code" inspection records that were selected from the ANALYSIS menu. The LIST option of the RESULTS menu prepared an ASCII file, which was then formatted with a word processor.

```
********************* INSPECTION DATA ANALYSIS REPORT ***************
**** All code (type C) inspections
****                                                       04/20/91
****                                                       10:23 AM
********************************************************************
********************** INSPECTION RECORD TOTALS ********************

        Records:   10   Total Effort: 102      Total Lines:    3220
     Total Exam: 42.3       % Exam:    41%  Effort/1000 Lines:  31.8
     Total Prep: 25.5       % Prep:    25%     Def/1000 Lines:  25.5
     Total Rwrk: 34.5       % Rwrk:    34%     Maj/1000 Lines:  14.0
           Maj:   45        % Maj:    55%  Rework/1000 Lines:  10.7
        Defects:   82   Rework/Def:   0.4
                        Rework/Maj:   0.8


     I-Records:   10     R-Records:    0         O-Records:       0

********************* INSPECTION RECORD AVERAGES ******************

        Duration:  1.4        Effort: 10.2           Lines:      322
       Team Size:  3.0       Defects:  8.2    Effort/Defect:      1.2
      Exam. Rate:  228          Maj:   4.5       Effort/Maj:      2.3
      Prep. Rate:  253   Prep/Person:  1.3    Effort/Person:      3.4
                            Rework:  3.5

*********************** DEFECT ANALYSIS TABLES ********************
            ********** TOTAL INSPECTION DEFECTS **********
    |        MINOR              |        MAJOR              |
    |   M     W      E  |  TOT  |  M     W      E  |  TOT  | TOTALS
    ---------------------------------------------------------------
 DA |   0     0      0  |   0  |   1     0      0  |   1  |     1
 DC |  20     9      0  |  29  |   0     0      0  |   0  |    29
 FN |   0     0      0  |   0  |   0     0      0  |   0  |     0
 HF |   0     0      0  |   0  |   0     2      0  |   2  |     2
 IF |   0     0      0  |   0  |   4     4      0  |   8  |     8
 LO |   0     4      1  |   5  |   6    28      0  |  34  |    39
 MN |   1     0      0  |   1  |   0     0      0  |   0  |     1
 PF |   0     0      0  |   0  |   0     0      0  |   0  |     0
 ST |   0     0      0  |   0  |   0     0      0  |   0  |     0
 OT |   0     2      0  |   2  |   0     0      0  |   0  |     2
 -- |                   |      |                   |      |
 -- |                   |      |                   |      |
    ---------------------------------------------------------------
 TOT|  21    15      1  |  37  |  11    34      0  |  45  |    82
            CATEGORY TOTALS:   32    49      1         ==========
```

Figure A.8 Selected inspection data analysis records.

```
           ********** AVERAGE INSPECTION DEFECTS **********
      |       MINOR              |          MAJOR             |
      |  M      W      E  |  TOT  |  M      W      E  |  TOT  | TOTALS
------------------------------------------------------------------------
DA |  0.0    0.0    0.0 |  0.0  |  0.1    0.0    0.0 |  0.1  |   0.1
DC |  2.0    0.9    0.0 |  2.9  |  0.0    0.0    0.0 |  0.0  |   2.9
FN |  0.0    0.0    0.0 |  0.0  |  0.0    0.0    0.0 |  0.0  |   0.0
HF |  0.0    0.0    0.0 |  0.0  |  0.0    0.2    0.0 |  0.2  |   0.2
IF |  0.0    0.0    0.0 |  0.0  |  0.4    0.4    0.0 |  0.8  |   0.8
LO |  0.0    0.4    0.1 |  0.5  |  0.6    2.8    0.0 |  3.4  |   3.9
MN |  0.1    0.0    0.0 |  0.1  |  0.0    0.0    0.0 |  0.0  |   0.1
PF |  0.0    0.0    0.0 |  0.0  |  0.0    0.0    0.0 |  0.0  |   0.0
ST |  0.0    0.0    0.0 |  0.0  |  0.0    0.0    0.0 |  0.0  |   0.0
OT |  0.0    0.2    0.0 |  0.2  |  0.0    0.0    0.0 |  0.0  |   0.2
-- |                    |       |                    |       |
-- |                    |       |                    |       |
------------------------------------------------------------------------
TOT|  2.1    1.5    0.1 |  3.7  |  1.1    3.4    0.0 |  4.5  |   8.2
           CATEGORY TOTALS:  3.2    4.9    0.1               ==========


           ********** TOTAL PERCENTAGE DEFECTS **********
      |        MINOR             |          MAJOR             |
      |  M      W      E  |  TOT  |  M      W      E  |  TOT  | TOTALS
------------------------------------------------------------------------
DA |  0.0%   0.0%   0.0%|  0.0%|  1.2%   0.0%   0.0%|  1.2%|   1.2%
DC | 24.4%  11.0%   0.0%| 35.4%|  0.0%   0.0%   0.0%|  0.0%|  35.4%
FN |  0.0%   0.0%   0.0%|  0.0%|  0.0%   0.0%   0.0%|  0.0%|   0.0%
HF |  0.0%   0.0%   0.0%|  0.0%|  0.0%   2.4%   0.0%|  2.4%|   2.4%
IF |  0.0%   0.0%   0.0%|  0.0%|  4.9%   4.9%   0.0%|  9.8%|   9.8%
LO |  0.0%   4.9%   1.2%|  6.1%|  7.3%  34.1%   0.0%| 41.5%|  47.6%
MN |  1.2%   0.0%   0.0%|  1.2%|  0.0%   0.0%   0.0%|  0.0%|   1.2%
PF |  0.0%   0.0%   0.0%|  0.0%|  0.0%   0.0%   0.0%|  0.0%|   0.0%
ST |  0.0%   0.0%   0.0%|  0.0%|  0.0%   0.0%   0.0%|  0.0%|   0.0%
OT |  0.0%   2.4%   0.0%|  2.4%|  0.0%   0.0%   0.0%|  0.0%|   2.4%
-- |                    |      |                    |      |
-- |                    |      |                    |      |
------------------------------------------------------------------------
TOT| 25.6%  18.3%   1.2%| 45.1%| 13.4%  41.5%   0.0%| 54.9%| 100.0%
           CATEGORY TOTALS: 39.0%  59.8%   1.2%              ==========


          ********** RELATIVE PERCENTAGE DEFECTS **********
      |        MINOR             |           MAJOR            |
      |  M      W      E  |  TOT  |  M      W      E  |  TOT  |
------------------------------------------------------------------------
DA |  0.0%   0.0%   0.0%|  0.0%|  2.2%   0.0%   0.0%|  2.2%|
DC | 54.1%  24.3%   0.0%| 78.4%|  0.0%   0.0%   0.0%|  0.0%|
FN |  0.0%   0.0%   0.0%|  0.0%|  0.0%   0.0%   0.0%|  0.0%|
HF |  0.0%   0.0%   0.0%|  0.0%|  0.0%   4.4%   0.0%|  4.4%|
IF |  0.0%   0.0%   0.0%|  0.0%|  8.9%   8.9%   0.0%| 17.8%|
LO |  0.0%  10.8%   2.7%| 13.5%| 13.3%  62.2%   0.0%| 75.6%|
MN |  2.7%   0.0%   0.0%|  2.7%|  0.0%   0.0%   0.0%|  0.0%|
PF |  0.0%   0.0%   0.0%|  0.0%|  0.0%   0.0%   0.0%|  0.0%|
ST |  0.0%   0.0%   0.0%|  0.0%|  0.0%   0.0%   0.0%|  0.0%|
OT |  0.0%   5.4%   0.0%|  5.4%|  0.0%   0.0%   0.0%|  0.0%|
-- |                    |      |                    |      |
-- |                    |      |                    |      |
------------------------------------------------------------------------
TOT| 56.8%  40.5%   2.7%|100.0%| 24.4%  75.6%   0.0%|100.0%|
```

Figure A.8 (*Continued*)

328 Appendix

A.7.4 Inspection Data Base Records

All of the inspection records in the data base are listed. The listing was prepared from an ASCII file written by the LIST option of the MAINTenance menu. A record identification number has been added when the file was formatted with a word processor.

```
*********************************** INSPECTION DATABASE RECORDS ***********************************
********* All inspections in database.                                    ******
*********                                                       04/20/91   ******
*********                                                       10:31 AM   ******
*************************************************************************************************
```

(#)	PROJ	REL	ACT	DOC	COMPONENT	INSP-DATE	MODERATOR	MEET	INSP
1	PBX200	R2.11	AP12	OUTLIST	PROG/DISP FUNCTION KEYS	11/12/90	CLYD	I	D
2	PBX200	R2.12	AP15	TRNLIST	TRANSLATION TYPE 1	11/22/90	MACH	I	D
3	PBX200	R2.13	AP15	TRNLIST	TRANSLATION TYPE 3	11/29/90	MACH	R	D
4	PBX200	R2.14	AP12	INTLIST	PROG/DISP FUNCTION KEYS	12/09/90	CLYD	I	C
5	PBX200	R2.15	AP09	EXTLIST	STATUS PART 1	12/11/90	MACH	I	D
6	PBX200	R2.16	AP15	TRNLIST	TRANSLATION TYPE 2	12/15/90	MACH	I	C
7	PBX200	R2.17	AP08	OUTLIST	OPS	01/02/91	MACH	I	D
8	PBX200	R2.18	AP12	OUTLIST	LCD INDICATORS - SERVICE	01/07/91	PITC	I	D
9	PBX200	R2.19	AP09	EXTLIST	STATUS BUS	01/08/91	MACH	I	D
10	PBX200	R2.110	AP12	INTLIST	LCD INDICATORS	01/09/91	PITC	I	C
11	PBX200	R2.111	AP08	INTLIST	OPS	01/10/91	CLYD	I	C
12	PBX200	R2.112	AP09	INTLIST	STATUS DMA	01/16/91	MACH	I	C
13	PBX200	R2.113	AP09	OUTLIST	LCD INDICATORS - USER	01/17/91	DARE	I	D
14	PBX200	R2.114	AP09	EXTLIST	STATUS CHANNEL	01/21/91	MACH	R	D
15	PBX200	R2.115	AP12	OUTLIST	CALL WAITING DISPLAY	01/27/91	CLYD	I	D
16	PBX200	R2.116	AP12	INTLIST	CALL ACTIVE DISPLAY	01/30/91	DARE	I	C
17	PBX200	R2.117	AP09	INTLIST	STATUS CHANNEL	02/12/91	MACH	I	C
18	PBX200	R2.118	AP15	TRNLIST	TRANSLATION TYPE 4	02/20/91	MACH	I	D
19	PBX200	R2.119	AP12	OUTLIST	AUDIBLE ALERTING	03/11/91	CLYD	I	D
20	PBX200	R2.120	AP12	OUTLIST	KEY HANDLER AND DND	03/13/91	MACH	I	D
21	PBX200	R2.121	AP12	OUTLIST	DIAL_0 AND LDN	03/15/91	MACH	I	D
22	PBX200	R2.122	AP12	OUTLIST	DIRECTED RECALL/COS	03/19/91	DARE	I	D
23	PBX200	R2.123	AP12	INTLIST	KEY HANDLER	03/20/91	MACH	I	C
24	PBX200	R2.124	AP12	INTLIST	AUDIBLE ALERTING/CON	03/21/91	DARE	I	C
25	PBX200	R2.125	AP12	INTLIST	DO NOT DISTURB	03/27/91	MACH	I	C

Figure A.9 Listing of inspection data base records.

(#)	DSP	LINES	DUR	TEAM	PREP	REWRK	EFFRT	EXAM.RATE	DEFECTS	MAJ	DENS	PREP.RATE	COMP-DATE
1	C	280	1.25	3	3	1	7.8	224	9	3	10.7	187	11/13/90
2	R	280	2	3	2.5	30	38.5	140	14	4	14.3	224	11/27/90
3	C	280	1.5	3	1.5	2	8.0	187	5	2	7.1	373	12/02/90
4	C	414	2	3	5	3	14.0	207	15	14	33.8	166	12/10/90
5	C	520	2.25	3	3.5	7.5	17.8	231	17	10	19.2	297	01/06/91
6	C	1200	2.25	3	3.5	10	20.3	533	10	4	3.3	686	01/02/91
7	C	240	1.5	3	2	7.5	14.0	160	8	1	4.2	240	01/07/91
8	A	80	0.5	3	1.5	0	3.0	160	2	0	0.0	107	01/07/91
9	R	440	2	3	3	30	39.0	220	18	10	22.7	293	01/22/91
10	C	85	0.75	3	1.5	0.5	4.3	113	2	2	23.5	113	01/09/91
11	C	81	1	3	1	1	5.0	81	8	1	12.3	162	01/10/91
12	C	330	2.5	3	3	10	20.5	132	10	8	24.2	220	02/12/91
13	C	250	1	3	1.5	0.5	5.0	250	4	1	4.0	333	01/17/91
14	C	440	1	3	1.5	15	19.5	440	9	3	6.8	587	02/12/91
15	A	350	1.5	3	2	0	6.5	233	3	0	0.0	350	01/27/91
16	C	240	1	3	2	0.5	5.5	240	4	4	16.7	240	02/10/91
17	C	570	2.5	3	3.5	8	19.0	228	16	2	3.5	326	03/05/91
18	R	400	3	3	2.25	0	11.3	133	18	4	10.0	356	02/21/91
19	A	80	0.5	3	1.3	0	2.8	160	0	0	0.0	123	03/13/91
20	C	200	1.8	4	4.5	9	20.7	111	13	8	40.0	133	03/14/91
21	C	36	0.5	3	1.7	1	4.2	72	5	2	55.6	42	03/17/91
22	C	370	2	3	4	5	15.0	185	13	5	13.5	185	03/20/91
23	C	40	0.3	3	1	0.5	2.4	133	2	2	50.0	80	03/20/91
24	C	120	1	3	3	0.5	6.5	120	7	3	25.0	80	03/21/91
25	C	140	0.8	3	2	0.5	4.9	175	8	5	35.7	140	04/06/91

Figure A.9 (Continued)

A.7.5 Inspection Analysis Graphs

Eight analysis graphs will illustrate the results and the evaluation of the 10 inspections that were selected. These are

- Defect types
- Defect classes
- Defect severity
- Performance (major defects vs. examination rate, one of six options)
- Major defect control (WEIGHTED option)
- SIZE dispersion (CUSTOM (sigma = 1) option)
- EXAMination rate dispersion (CUSTOM (sigma = 1) option)
- PREParation rate dispersion (CUSTOM (sigma = 1) option)

Each graph was titled and written to a Lotus .PIC file, and was then formatted with a graphics program.

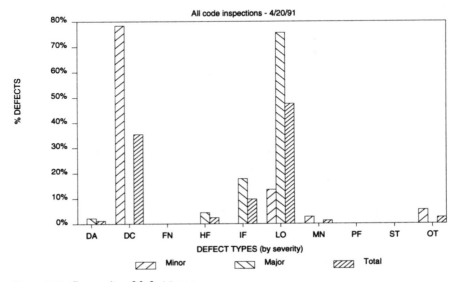

Figure A.10 Composite of defect types.

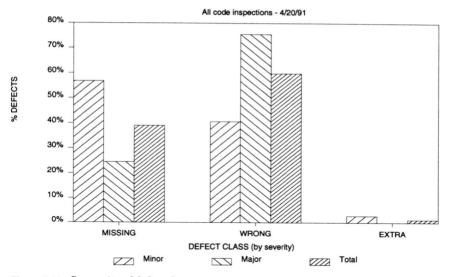

Figure A.11 Composite of defect class.

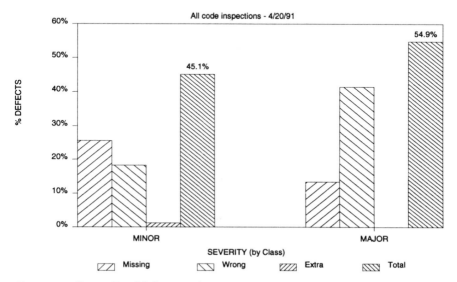

Figure A.12 Composite of defect severity.

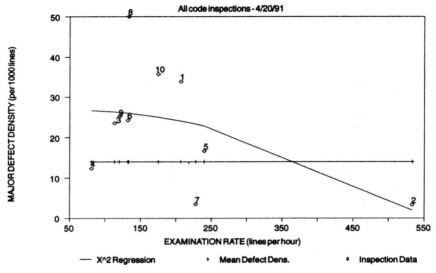

Figure A.13 Major defects versus examination rate.

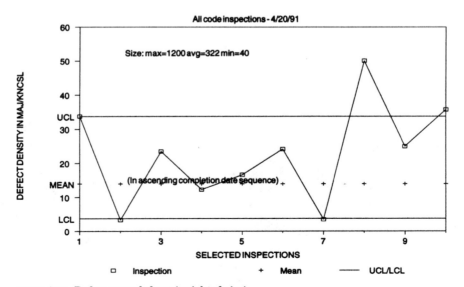

Figure A.14 Defect control chart (weighted size).

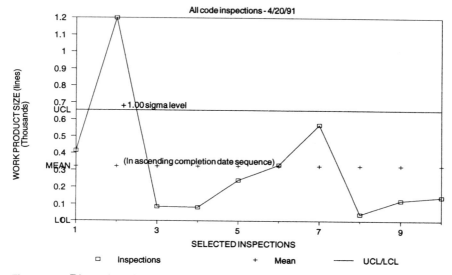

Figure A.15 Dispersion of work product size.

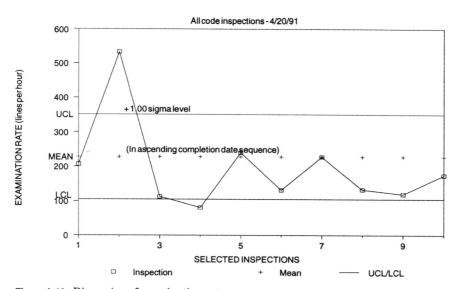

Figure A.16 Dispersion of examination rate.

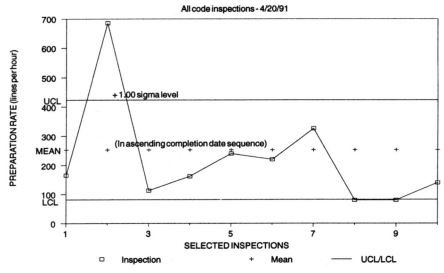

Figure A.17 Dispersion of preparation rate.

An Annotated Bibliography on Software Inspections*

Bill Brykczynski
David A. Wheeler

Institute for Defense Analyses
1801 N. Beauregard St.
Alexandria, VA 22311-1772

bryk@ida.org
703-845-6641

wheeler@ida.org
703-845-6662

The technique of formal software inspection has existed for over fifteen years. The productivity and quality benefits that result from an effective inspection process are impressive. However, software inspections are not yet practiced routinely in industry. There is a variety of information relating to software inspections available in the literature, but to our knowledge a comprehensive bibliography on the subject has not yet been published.

Below is the authors' bibliography of inspection-related references. Abstracts are provided verbatim for some of the references. The bibliography is separated into three parts. Part I contains references focusing on the subject of software inspection. Part II provides additional references relating to software reviews and walkthroughs. Part III identifies software engineering textbooks that have chapters discussing inspection techniques.

---

*Reprinted with permission of Bill Brykczynski and David Wheeler, who retain all rights to this material.

Software inspections are a detailed examination of a work product, such as requirements, design, code, and test cases. Inspections follow a defined process, involving steps such as work product overview, preparation, inspection, rework, and follow-up. The inspected work product is small, for example, four to five pages of code. The inspection meeting is attended by a small number (e.g., four to five) of coworkers and lasts less than two hours. A role (e.g., moderator, author, reader, tester) is assigned to each inspector, and the primary objective of the inspection is to detect defects. The work product author is responsible for defect removal, and corrections or suggested improvements are not allowed during the inspection meeting. The reader paraphrases the work product during the inspection meeting. Error-cause analysis is usually performed after an inspection to identify process improvements that would prevent future occurrences of the same type of defect.

If you want to quickly learn about inspections and their productivity and quality benefits, the authors recommend reading the following three papers: [Fagan 1986], [Kelly 1992], and [Russell 1991].

If references of particular significance have been omitted, the authors would appreciate hearing about them.

Part I—Inspection References

[Ackerman 1982]
Ackerman, A. Frank, Amy S. Ackerman, and Robert G. Ebenau. "A Software Inspections Training Program," COMPSAC '82: 1982 Computer Software and Applications Conference, Chicago, IL Nov. 8–12, pp. 443–444. IEEE Computer Society Press.

[Ackerman 1984]
Ackerman, A. Frank, Priscilla J. Fowler, and Robert G. Ebenau. 1984. "Software Inspections and the Industrial Production of Software," Software Validation, H. L. Hausen, ed., pp. 13–40, Elsevier, Amsterdam.

> Abstract: Software inspections were first defined by M. E. Fagan in 1976. Since that time they have been used within IBM and other organizations. This paper provides a description of software inspections as they are being utilized within Bell Laboratories and the technology transfer program that is being used for their effective implementation. It also describes the placement of software inspections within the overall development process, and discusses their use in conjunction with other verification and validation techniques.

[Ackerman 1989]
Ackerman, A. Frank, Lynne S. Buchwald, and Frank H. Lewski. "Software Inspections: An Effective Verification Process," IEEE Software, Vol. 6, No. 3, May 1989, pp. 31–36.

Abbreviated Introduction: This article is an attempt to clarify what software inspections are, to explain how you can use them to improve both your process and your product, and to summarize what is known about their effectiveness.

[Ascoly 1976]
Ascoly, Joseph, Michael J. Cafferty, Stephen J. Gruen, and O. Robert Kohli. "Code Inspection Specification," IBM Corp., Kingston, NY, Technical Report TR 21.630, 1976.

Abstract: Examination of computer programs by people other than the coder is recognized as a tangible method for improving quality in programming. This report is intended for use as a specification for conducting inspections of program code. Inspections are considered to be a more rigorous form of examination than walk-throughs. They stress participant preparation, error detection versus solution hunting and education, and accountability for resolution of problems detected. Inspections are applicable in both systems and application programming environments.

[Bisant 1989]
Bisant, David B. and James R. Lyle. "A Two-Person Inspection Method to Improve Programming Productivity," IEEE Transactions on Software Engineering, Vol. 15, No. 10, Oct. 1989, pp. 1294–1304.

Abstract: This paper reviews current research and investigates the effect of a two-person inspection method on programmer productivity. This method is similar to the current larger team method in stressing fault detection, but does not use a moderator.

The experiment used a Pretest-Posttest Control Group design. An experimental and control group of novices each completed two programming assignments. The amount of time taken to complete each program (Time1, Time2) was recorded for each subject. The subjects of the experimental group did either a design inspection, a code inspection, or both during the development of the second program. An analysis of variance was performed and the relationship between Time1 and Time2 was modeled for both groups. A comparison of the models revealed the experimental group improved significantly in programming speed as a result of using the two-person inspection. It also appeared as though this method was more effective at improving the performance of the slower programmers.

This two-person method could have its application in those environments where access to larger team resources is not available. If further research establishes consistency with this method then it might be useful as a transition to the larger team method.

[Blakely 1991]
Blakely, Frank W. and Mark E. Boles. "A Case Study of Code Inspections," Hewlett-Packard Journal, Vol. 42, No. 4, Oct. 1991, pp. 58–63.

Abstract: Code inspections have become an integral part of the software development life cycle in many organizations. Because it takes some project time and because engineers initially feel intimidated by the process, code inspections have not always been readily accepted. Additionally, there has not always been enough evidence (metrics) to provide that for the time and effort invested, the process has any value in reducing defects and improving overall software quality. Since the early days, the process has become better understood and documented, and recent articles have provided concrete metrics and other evidence to justify the value of the process.

This paper describes our experiences in bringing the code inspection process to HP's Application Support Division (ASD). We describe both the positive and negative findings related to using code inspections. Although we only have metrics for one project, out main goal here is to present how we implemented the inspection process and to illustrate the type of data to collect and what might be done with the data.

[Bollinger 1992]
Bollinger, Donald E., Frank P. Lemmon, and Dawn L. Yamine. "Providing HP-UX kernel Functionality on a New PA-RISC Architecture." Hewlett-Packard Journal, Vol. 43, No. 3, Jun. 1992, pp. 11–15.

Abstract: Hewlett-Packard Co's HP 9000 Series 700 workstation development goals required that the HP-UX kernel laboratory change the normal software development process, the number of product features and the management structure. The laboratory wanted to change or add the minimum number of HP-UX kernel functions that meet customer needs and its own performance goals while also adapting to a new I/O system. The resulting HP-UX kernel code is called minimum core functionality (MCF). The management structure was changed to allow small teams of individual developers and first-level managers to make important program decisions quickly and directly. The performance team included members from hardware, kernel, languages, graphics and performance measurement groups; the team's goal was to maximize system performance in computation, graphics and I/O. The quality control plan, certification process, design and code reviews, branch and source management and test setup process are described.

[Britcher 1988]
Britcher, Robert N. "Using Inspections to Investigate Program Correctness," IEEE Computer, Vol. 21, No. 11, Nov. 1988, pp. 38–44.

Conclusion: As we develop better tools for recording and compiling software designs and code, those who think about and practice programming will take greater interest in the more obscure aspects of a program: its intent, meaning, resilience, and developmental history. Although the problem of writing correct programs, especially those embedded within large systems or products, remains largely unsolved in practice, the situation is improving. We can use inspections to further the investigation into how correct programs are constructed. Several such inspections will be carried out to determine their usefulness and refine their practice. The purpose of incorporating correctness arguments into inspections is not to improve inspections, but to improve programming. This is not a modest objective. Steps will necessarily be small.

[Brothers 1990]
Brothers, L., V. Sembugamoorthy, and M. Muller. "ICICLE: Groupware for Code Inspection," CSCW 90: Proceedings of the ACM Conference on Computer Supported Cooperative Work, Oct. 1990, pp. 169–181.

[Brykczynski 1993]
Brykczynski, Bill, and David A. Wheeler. "An Annotated Bibliography on Software Inspections," ACM Software Engineering Notes, Jan. 1993, Vol. 18, No. 1, pp 81–88.

[Buck 1981]
Buck, F. O. "Indicators of Quality Inspections," IBM Corp., Technical Report TR21.802, Sep. 1981.

Abstract: Management of a software development effort using the formal inspection process requires constant monitoring of the quality of those inspections. The number of errors found during an inspection is not an adequate indicator of a quality inspection. The number of errors found is just as much a function of the quality of the materials being inspected as it is a function of the quality of the inspection itself. This report presents an analysis of the results of many code inspections on the same materials. With constant quality materials, the alternative inspection indicators could be more accurately evaluated.

[Buck 1984]
Buck, Robert D. and James H. Dobbins. 1984. "Application of Software Inspection Methodology in Design and Code," Software Validation, H. L. Hausen, ed., Elsevier, Amsterdam, pp. 41–56.

[Bush 1990]
Bush, Marilyn. "Improving Software Quality: The Use of Formal Inspections at the Jet Propulsion Laboratory," 12th International Conference on Software Engineering, 1990, pp. 196–199, IEEE Computer Society Press.

Abstract: Finding and fixing defects early in the software development life cycle is much cheaper than finding and fixing the same defects later on. After surveying detection practices in the best of industry, JPL Software Product Assurance decided that the most cost-effective early defect detection technique was the "Fagan inspection" procedure. This paper will describe this technique, how it was introduced to JPL, some of the difficulties involved in "transferring technology" and the first provisional set of results.

[Chaar 1992]
Chaar, J. K., M. J. Halliday, I. S. Bhandari, and R. Chillarege. "In-process Metrics for Software Inspection and Test Evaluations," IBM Corp., Technical Report 80725, 1992.

[Christenson 1987]
Christenson, Dennis A. and Steel T. Huang. "Code Inspection Management Using Statistical Control Limits," National Communications Forum, Vol. 41, No. 2, Chicago, IL, 1987, pp. 1095–1100.

[Christenson 1988]
Christenson, Dennis A. and Steel T. Huang. "A Code Inspection Model for Software Quality Management and Prediction," GLOBECOM '88. IEEE Global Telecommunications Conference and Exhibition, Hollywood, FL, 1988, pp. 468–472.

[Christenson 1990]
Christenson, Dennis A., Steel. T. Huang, and Alfred J. Lamperez. "Statistical Quality Control Applied to Code Inspections," IEEE Journal on Selected Areas in Communications, Vol. 8, No. 2, Feb. 1990, pp. 196–200.

Abstract: Code inspections have been used on the 5ESS Switch project since 1983. Beginning with a training program for all the developers involved in the project, code inspections have improved with each new 5ESS Switch generic. The improvement in code inspections has been the result of hard work and innovation on the part of the 5ESS Switch software developers, and the use of some "Statistical Quality Control" (SQC) techniques.

Variations on a standard SQC technique, the control chart, have been used to track the metrics indicative of the effectiveness of code inspections. Parameters used in the computation of these metrics include the preparation effort, inspection time, number of inspectors, the size of the inspected unit of code, and the number of errors found at the inspection. The exact form that these "control charts" have taken has evolved and improved with experience.

[Collofello 1987]
Collofello, James S. "Teaching Technical Reviews in a One-Semester Software Engineering Course," ACM SIGCSE Bulletin, Vol. 19, No. 1, Feb. 1987, pp. 222–227.

Abstract: Software technical reviews are essential to the development and maintenance of high quality software. These review processes are complex group activities for which there exist an abundance of basic concepts evolved over years of practical experience. In a typical one-semester software engineering course very little of this information is adequately conveyed to students. Texts supporting this course are also very weak in this area. This paper provides a practical approach for teaching about software technical reviews in a one-semester software engineering course. The contents for two to three lectures on this topic are described as well as suggested exercises and an approach for integrating technical reviews with the usual team project. An extensive annotated bibliography is also provided to assist instructors and students.

[Collofello 1988]
Collofello, James S. "The Software Technical Review Process," Curriculum Module SEI-CM-3-1.5, The Software Engineering Institute, Carnegie-Mellon University, Pittsburgh, PA, Jun. 1988.

Capsule Description: This module consists of a comprehensive examination of the technical review process in the software development and maintenance life cycle. Formal review methodologies are analyzed in detail from the perspective of the review participants, project management and software quality assurance. Sample review agendas are also presented for common types of reviews. The objective of the module is to provide the student with the information necessary to plan and execute highly efficient and cost effective technical reviews.

[Cross 1988]
Cross, John A., ed. "Support Materials for the Software Technical Review Process," Support Materials SEI-SM-3-1.0, Software Engineering Institute, Pittsburgh, PA, Apr. 1988.

[Crossman 1977]
Crossman, Trevor D. "Some Experiences in the Use of Inspection Teams," 15th Annual ACM Computer Personnel Research Conference, Aug. 1977, p. 143.

[Crossman 1979]
Crossman, Trevor D. "Some Experiences in the Use of Inspection Teams in Application Development," Applications Development Symposium, Monterey, CA, Oct. 1979, pp. 163–168.

[Crossman 1982]
Crossman, Trevor D. "Inspection Teams, Are They Worth It?" Proceedings 2nd National Symposium on EDP Quality Assurance, Chicago, IL, Mar. 24–26, 1982.

[Deimel 1991]
Deimel, L. E. "Scenes of Software Inspections. Video Dramatizations for the Classroom," Software Engineering Institute, Carnegie-Mellon University, Pittsburgh, PA, CMU/SEI-91-EM-5, May 1991.

Abstract: This report describes the videotape "Scenes of Software Inspections," which contains brief dramatizations that demonstrate appropriate and inappropriate conduct of software inspections. The tape also includes scenes that show other kinds of group interactions. Any of these scenes can be incorporated into lectures, self-study materials, or other educational delivery mechanisms, to illustrate how to perform inspections, an important software engineering technique.

[Dichter 1992]
Dichter, C. R. "Two Sets of Eyes: How Code Inspections Improve Software Quality and Save Money," Unix Review, Vol. 10, No. 2, Jan. 1992, pp. 18–23.

Abstract: Programmers can detect a large percentage of software bugs by inspecting code to supplement testing. Testing alone will not determine if code will work on different platforms, if it is written efficiently and whether it adheres to particular coding guidelines or standards. Inspections and walkthroughs are two kinds of software reviews. Programmers perform inspections by sequential reading of code to search for bugs by using an inspection checklist. In walkthroughs, inspectors play the role of the computer by searching the code for logical errors. Programmers can start improving code by using advanced linter tools and then inspecting code for errors the linter will not catch. Code-counting tools are also helpful. Programmers may find that inspections on code of more than 1,000 lines will help find bugs that testing would not turn up and which would be more expensive to correct later.

[Dobbins 1987]
Dobbins, J. H. 1987. "Inspections as an Up-Front Quality Technique," Handbook of Software Quality Assurance, G. G. Schulmeyer and J. I. McManus, eds., pp. 137–177, NY: Van Nostrand Reinhold.

[Doolan 1992]
Doolan, E. P. "Experience with Fagan's Inspection Method," Software-Practice and Experience, Vol. 22, No. 2, Feb. 1992, pp. 173–182.

Abstract: Fagan's inspection method was used by a software development group to validate requirements specifications for software functions. The experiences of that group are described in this paper. In general, they have proved to be favourable. Because the costs of fixing errors in software were known, the payback for every hour invested in inspection was shown to be a factor 30. There are also other benefits that are much more difficult to quantify directly but whose effect is significant in terms of the overall quality of the software.

Some pointers are given at the end of this paper for those who want to introduce Fagan's inspection method into their own development environment.

[Ebenau 1981]
Ebenau, R. G. "Inspecting for Software Quality," Second National Symposium in EDP Quality Assurance, 1981. DPMA Educational Foundation, U.S. Professional Development Institute, Inc., 12611 Davon Drive, Silver Spring, MD 20904.

[Fagan 1976a]
Fagan, Michael E. "Design and Code Inspections to Reduce Errors in Program Development," IBM Systems Journal, Vol. 15, No. 3, 1976, pp. 182–211.

Abstract: Substantial net improvements in programming productivity have been obtained through the use of formal inspections of design and of code. Improvements are made possible by a systematic and efficient design and code verification process, with well-defined roles for inspection participants. The manner in which inspection data is categorized and made suitable for process analysis is an important factor in attaining the improvements. It is shown that by using inspection results, a mechanism for initial error reduction followed by ever-improving error rates can be achieved.

[Fagan 1976b]
Fagan, M. E. "Design and Code Inspections and Process Control in the Development of Programs," IBM Corp., Poughkeepsie, NY, Technical Report TR 00.2763, Jun. 10, 1976. This report is a revision of "Design and Code Inspections and Process Control in the Development of Programs," IBM Corp., Kingston, NY, Technical Report TR 21.572, Dec. 17, 1974.

Abstract: Substantial net improvements in programming quality and productivity have been obtained through the use of formal inspections of design and code. Improvements are made possible by a systematic and efficient design and code verification process, with well defined roles for inspection participants. The manner in which inspection data is categorized and made suitable for process analysis is an important factor in attaining the improvements. Using inspection results, a mechanism for initial error reduction followed by ever improving error rates (down to minimum process average levels) can be achieved.

[Fagan 1977]
Fagan, Michael E. "Inspecting Software Design and Code," Datamation, Oct. 1977, pp. 133–144.

[Fagan 1986]
Fagan, Michael E. "Advances In Software Inspections," IEEE Transactions on Software Engineering, Vol. 12, No. 7, Jul. 1986, pp. 744–751.

Abstract: This paper presents new studies and experiences that enhance the use of the inspection process and improve its contribution to development of defect-free software on time and at lower costs. Examples of benefits are cited followed by descriptions of the process and some methods of obtaining the enhanced results.
    Software inspection is a method of static testing to verify that software meets its requirements. It engages the developers and others in a formal process of investigation that usually detects more defects in the product— and at lower cost—than does machine testing. Users of the method report very significant improvements in quality that are accompanied by lower development costs and greatly reduced maintenance efforts. Excellent results have been obtained by small and large organizations in all aspects of new development as well as in maintenance. There is some evidence that developers who participate in the inspection of their own product actually create fewer defects in future work. Because inspections formalize the development process, productivity and quality enhancing tools can be adopted more easily and rapidly.

[Fowler 1986]
Fowler, Priscilla J. "In-Process Inspections of Workproducts at AT&T," AT&T Technical Journal, Vol. 65, No. 2, Mar./Apr. 1986, pp. 102–112.

Abstract: In-process inspections are examination meetings held to find defects in design and development work products, including intermediate versions of the product or system in requirements and design documents. Because these inspections delimit the phases of design and development processes, they can prevent the passage of defects from one phase to the next and significantly reduce the number of defects released to customers. Software development projects within AT&T's research and development community have been using in-process inspections effectively for several years to reduce defects, and hardware projects began using them one and a half years ago. In addition, the experience of installing in-process inspections in project organizations has yielded a wealth of information on technology transfer. This article defines inspections, describes the installation process, and discusses some uses for inspection data.

[Freedman 1982]
Freedman, Daniel P. and Gerald M. Weinberg. 1982. Handbook of Walkthroughs, Inspections, and Technical Reviews: Evaluating Programs, Projects, and Products. 3rd ed. Boston, MA: Little, Brown and Company.

[Gilb 1991]
Gilb, Tom. "Advanced Defect Prevention Using Inspection, Testing, and Field Data as a Base, " American Programmer, May 1991, pp. 38–45.

[Graden 1986]
Graden, Mark E. and Palma S. Horsley. "The Effects of Software Inspections on a Major Telecommunications Project," AT&T Technical Journal, Vol. 65, No. 3, May/Jun. 1986, pp. 32–40.

Introduction: Software inspections are a highly formalized and rigorous technique used for the identification and removal of errors in software products. Faithfully applied, they have beneficial impact on the productivity and quality of a project. As a result, software inspections were selected as a critical ingredient in the overall Software Quality Assurance Plan to guide the development and evolution of a major, real time telecommunications software project.

This paper describes how the results of software inspections have been used to explain differences in end-product quality and identifies useful techniques for applying the results of software inspections to manage the software development process.

[Hale 1978]
Hale, R. M. "Inspections in Application Development—Introduction and Implementation Guidelines," IBM Corp., Form GC20–2000-0 (Jul. 1977) updated by TNL GN20-3814 (Aug. 1978).

[Hollocker 1990]
Hollocker, Charles P. 1990. Software Reviews and Audits Handbook, NY: John Wiley & Sons.

[IBM 1976]
IBM. "Code Reading, Structured Walkthroughs, and Inspections," IBM Corp., Report GE–19-5200, Zoetermeer, Netherlands, 1976.

[Kelly 1992]
Kelly, John C., Joseph S. Sherif, and Jonathan Hops. "An Analysis of Defect Densities Found During Software Inspections," Journal of Systems and Software, Vol. 17, No. 2, Feb. 1992, pp. 111–117.

Abstract: Software inspection is a technical evaluation process for finding and removing defects in requirements, design, code, and tests. The Jet Propulsion Laboratory (JPL), California Institute of Technology, tailored Fagan's original process of software inspections to conform to its software development environment in 1987. Detailed data collected from 203 inspections during the first three years of experience at JPL included averages of staff time expended, pages covered, major and minor defects found, and inspection team size. The data were tested for homogeneity. Randomized samples belonging to the various phases or treatments were analyzed using the completely randomized block design analysis of variance (a = 0.05). The results showed a significantly higher density of defects during requirements inspections. The number of defect densities decreased exponentially as the work products approached the coding phase because defects were fixed when detected and did not migrate to subsequent phases. This resulted in a relatively flat profile for cost to fix. Increasing the pace of the inspection meeting decreased the density of defects found. This relationship held for major and minor defect densities, although it was more pronounced for minor defects.

[Kindl 1992]
Kindl, Mark R. "Software Quality and Testing: What DoD Can Learn from Commercial Practices," US Army Institute for Research in Management Information, Communications, and Computer Sciences, ASQG-GI-92-012, 31 August 1992.

Abstract: With regard to software testing in DoD, we can summarize our conclusions in two fundamental ideas. First, DoD knows how to produce quality software at low cost. This is because organizations such as DoD STEP, Army STEP, and Software Engineering Institute have already researched and documented policies for DoD. A few commercial software developers practice many of the DoD policies and directives now, and produce quality software (for example, IBM FSC Houston). Second, quality cannot be tested into software. Only a well-defined, well-disciplined process with a continuous improvement cycle can ensure software quality. However, testing cannot be underestimated. Systematic testing activities that detect error earliest in the life cycle are necessary to drive process improvement and optimize the development of quality software. Such testing methods as formal inspection find defects early. This enables cost-effective error resolution, identification and removal of defect causes, and thus, prevention of future defect insertion. If practiced with discipline, such methods can evolve a self-correcting software development process that is stable, modeled, measured, and therefore, predictable. This development process engineers quality software faster at reduced cost.

[Kitchenham 1986]
Kitchenham, B. A., Kitchenham, A. P., and J. P. Fellows. "Effects of Inspections on Software Quality and Productivity," ICL Technical Journal, Vol. 5, No. 1, May 1986, pp. 112–122.

[Knight 1991]
Knight, John C. and Ethella Ann Myers. "Phased Inspections and their Implementation," University of Virginia, Computer Science Report No. TR-91-10. May 12, 1991. Also published in ACM Software Engineering Notes, Vol. 16, No. 3, Jul. 1991, pp. 29–35.

Abstract: Since the 1970s, non-mechanical review methods have become very popular as verification tools for software products. Examples of existing review methods are formal reviews, walkthroughs, and inspections. Another example is Fagan Inspections, developed in 1976 by Michael Fagan in an effort to improve software quality and increase programmer productivity. Fagan Inspections and other existing methods have been empirically shown to benefit the software development process, mainly by lowering the number of defects in software early in the development process. Despite this success, existing methods are limited. They are not rigorous, therefore, they are not dependable. A product that has been reviewed with an existing method has no quantitative qualities that are ensured by the method used.

This thesis presents a new review method, Phased Inspection, that was developed to be rigorous, reliable, tailorable, heavily computer supported, and cost effective. Phased Inspection consists of a series of partial inspections termed phases. Each phase is intended to ensure a single or small set of related properties. Phases are designed to be as rigorous as possible so that compliance with associated properties is ensured, at least informally, with a high degree of confidence.

A detailed description of Phased Inspection, an evaluation framework and preliminary evaluation, and a prototype toolset for support of Phased Inspection is presented.

[Kohli 1975]
Kohli, O. Robert. "High-Level Design Inspection Specification," IBM Corp., Kingston, NY, Technical Report TR 21.601, Jul. 21, 1975.

Abstract: This report is written to be used as a specification for the inspection of high level design materials. This inspection (called I0) together with the inspections of low level (detailed) design (I1) and code (I2) constitute an efficient process for detecting and removing programming errors prior to any machine testing. The report describes in detail the process of inspecting high level design materials against specific exit criteria. Satisfaction of the exit criteria constitutes meeting the high level design complete checkpoint. Thus, I0 provides a checkpoint for management to enable better control of the programming process. Inspections are applicable in both systems and application programming environments.

[Kohli 1976]
Kohli, O. Robert and Ronald A. Radice. "Low-Level Design Inspection Specification," IBM Corp., Kingston, NY, Technical Report TR 21.629, Apr. 1976.

Abstract: Examination of program design by people other than the designer is recognized as a tangible method for improving duality in programing. This report is intended for use as a specification for conducting an inspection of detailed (low level) design. This inspection (called I1), together with the inspection of high level design (I0) which precedes it and code (I2) which follows it, constitute an efficient process for detecting and removing programming errors prior to any machine testing. Inspections are applicable in both systems and application programming environments.

[Koontz 1986]
Koontz, W. L. G. "Experience with Software Inspections in the Development of Firmware for a Digital Loop Carrier System," IEEE International Conference on Communications, 1986 Conference Record, pp. 1188–1189.

[Larson 1975]
Larson, Rodney R. "Test Plan and Test Case Inspection Specification," IBM Corp., Kingston, NY, Technical Report TR21.585, Apr. 4, 1975.

Abstract: Inspections of design and code have proven to be a valuable part of the development cycle of a software component. Similar benefits can be derived by applying inspection techniques to the functional verification test plan and test cases. This report addresses how to apply an inspection process to the functional verification test plan and test cases.

[Martin 1990]
Martin, Johnny and W. T. Tsai. "N-fold Inspection: A Requirements Analysis Technique," Communications of the ACM, Vol. 33, No. 2, Feb. 1990, pp. 225–232.

Abstract: N-fold inspection uses traditional inspections of the user requirements document (URD) but replicates the inspection activities using N independent teams. A pilot study was conducted to explore the usefulness of N-fold inspection during requirements analysis. A comparison of N-fold inspection with other development techniques reveals that N-fold inspection is a cost-effective method for finding faults in the URD and may be a valid technique in the development of mission-critical software systems.

[McCormick 1981]
McCormick, K. K. "The Results of Using a Structured Methodology, Software Inspections, and a New Hardware/Software Configuration on Application Sys-

tems," Second National Symposium in EDP Quality Assurance, 1981. DPMA Educational Foundation, U.S. Professional Development Institute, Inc., 12611 Davon Drive, Silver Spring, MD 20904.

[McKissick 1984]
MoKissick, John Jr., Mark J. Somers, and Wilhelmina Marsh. "Software Design Inspection for Preliminary Design," COMPSAC '84: 1984 Computer Software and Applications Conference, Las Vegas, NV, Jul. 1984, pp. 273–281.

Abstract: The continuing need for improved computer software demands improved software development techniques. A technique for the inspection of preliminary software designs is described in this paper. Experience and results from the application of this technique are presented.

[Myers 1978]
Myers, Glenford J. "A Controlled Experiment in Program Testing and Code Walkthroughs-Inspections," Communications of the ACM, Vol. 21, No. 9, Sep. 1978, pp. 760–768.

Abstract: This paper describes an experiment in program testing, employing 59 highly experienced data processing professionals using seven methods to test a small PL/1 program. The results show that the popular code walkthrough/inspection method was as effective as other computer-based methods in finding errors and that the most effective methods (in terms of errors found and cost) employed pairs of subjects who tested the program independently and then pooled their findings. The study also shows that there is a tremendous amount of variability among subjects and that the ability to detect certain types of errors varies from method to method.

[O'Neill 1991]
O'Neill, Don. "What is the Standard of Excellence?" IEEE Software, May 1991, pp. 109–111.

[Peele 1982a]
Peele, R. "Code Inspections at First Union Corporation," COMPSAC '82: 1982 Computer Software and Applications Conference, Chicago, IL, Nov. 8–12, 1982, pp. 445 –446, IEEE Computer Society Press.

Abbreviated Introduction: During 1980, a task force was formed within the Systems Development Division of First Computer Services to examine the coding and testing functions and to recommend ways to increase productivity and improve the duality of these functions while maintaining high staff morale. The task force evaluated the Design and Code Inspection process developed by Mike Fagan of IBM and concluded that this approach offered [several] potential quality assurance benefits.

[Peele 1982b]
Peele, R. "Code Inspection Pilot Project Evaluation," Second National Symposium in EDP Quality Assurance, DPMA Educational Foundation, U.S. Professional Development Institute, Inc., 12611 Davon Dr., Silver Spring, MD 20904.

Abstract: At First Computer, a code inspection is conducted after the coding of a program or module is complete as indicated by a clean compilation of the program and prior to unit testing of the program. The completed program specifications and a clean compilation are the entry criteria for the inspection process. An inspection team at First Computer consists of four members: one moderator and three inspectors. The moderator is the key person in the process with the responsibility to ensure the best possible review of the program. The moderator approves the team members for the inspection and makes the necessary decisions related to scheduling and conducting the sessions. The moderator is the facilitator of the inspection meetings but is also an active participant charged with finding defects. The moderator must log all defects found during the sessions, ensure that all defects found are corrected by the author, and decide whether or not to reinspect the code.

[Reeve 1991]
Reeve, J. T. "Applying the Fagan Inspection Technique," Quality Forum, Vol. 17, No. 1, Mar. 1991, pp. 40–47.

Abstract: This paper asks and briefly explains what Fagan inspection is, and how it differs from more established techniques. It proposes how the technique may be used as an integral part of the product appraisal process from initial proposal to release to customer. A proven plan of action for establishment of the technique is also proposed, together with evidence of its success.

[Remus 1984]
Remus, Horst. 1984. "Integrated Software Validation in the View of Inspections/Reviews," Software Validation, H. L. Hausen, ed., pp. 57–64, Elsevier, Amsterdam.

Abstract: The Software Development Process is being looked at as to the specific contribution of inspections/reviews to the discovery of wrong design directions or implementations. The benefits are evaluated under the aspects of quality/productivity improvement and/or cost savings.

[Runge 1982]
Runge, B. "The Inspection Method Applied to Small Projects," 6th International Conference on Software Engineering, 1982, pp. 416–417.

Abstract: The Inspection Method is a quality-control for written material. It is used on large projects and takes 3 to 8 persons for correct use. This excludes small projects with less than three persons from proper inspection. This paper shows how the personnel restriction may be circumvented in small projects. An example of inspection in a small project (writing a report) is given.

[Russell 1991]
Russell, Glen W. "Experience with Inspection in Ultralarge-Scale Developments," IEEE Software, Vol. 8, No. 1, Jan. 1991, pp. 25–31.

Abbreviated Introduction: Inspections can be very cost-effective and highly beneficial, even when scaled up for ultralarge projects. Here I present quantitative results based on a 1988 study of inspection of 2.5 million lines of high-level code at Bell-Northern Research.

The data represent one of the largest published studies in the industry and confirm that code inspection is still one of the most efficient ways to remove software defects. In the box on pp. 28–29, I describe how to successfully introduce inspections in large-scale production environments.

[Schneider 1992]

Schneider, G. Michael, Johnny Martin, and W. T. Tsai. "An Experimental Study of Fault Detection in User Requirements Documents," ACM Transactions on Software Engineering and Methodology, Vol. 1, No. 2, Apr. 1992, pp. 188–204.

Abstract: This paper describes a software engineering experiment designed to confirm results from an earlier project which measured fault detection rates in user requirements documents (URD). The experiment described in this paper involves the creation of a standardized URD with a known number of injected faults of specific type. Nine independent inspection teams were given this URD with instructions to locate as many faults as possible using the N-fold requirements inspection technique developed by the authors. Results obtained from this experiment confirm earlier conclusions about the low rate of fault detection in requirements documents using formal inspections and the advantages to be gained using the N-fold inspection method. The experiment also provides new results concerning variability in inspection team performance and the relative difficulty of locating different classes of URD faults.

[Sherif 1992]

Sherif, Joseph S. and John C. Kelly. "Improving Software Quality Through Formal Inspections," Microelectronics and Reliability, Vol. 32, No. 3, Mar. 1992, pp. 423–431.

Abstract: The software inspection process was created for the dual purpose of improving software quality and increasing programmers' productivity. This paper puts forward formal inspections as an alternative to and a better method than technical walkthroughs in the software lifecycle reviewing process. Examples of benefits gained in the development of defect-free software by utilizing formal inspections are cited.

[Shirey 1992]

Shirey, Glen C. "How Inspections Fail," 9th International Conference on Testing Computer Software, Jun 15–18, 1992, Washington, D.C., pp. 151–159.

Abstract: This paper discusses an experience in the application of inspections in software development and how a concentration on the mechanics of the technology rather than acting on the information it provides failed to improve product quality. In this paper practitioners will find a comprehensive inspection model used to audit the inspection practices of the group studied. Managers will find examples of how to integrate the information provided by inspections into their Software Development Process.

[Weinberg 1984]
Weinberg, Gerald M. and Daniel P. Freedman. "Reviews, Walkthroughs, and Inspections," IEEE Transactions on Software Engineering, Vol. 12, No. 1, Jan. 1984, pp. 68–72.

Abstract: Formal technical reviews supply the quality measurement to the "cost effectiveness" equation in a project management system. There are several unique formal technical review procedures, each applicable to particular types of technical material and to the particular mix of the Review Committee. All formal technical reviews produce reports on the overall quality for project management, and specific technical information for the producers. These reports also serve as an historic account of the systems development process. Historic origins and future trends of formal and informal technical reviews are discussed.

[Weller 1992a]
Weller, Edward F. "Experiences with Inspections at Bull HN Information Systems," 4th Annual Software Quality Workshop, Aug. 2–6, 1992, Alexandria Bay, NY.

Abstract: Bull's experiences with the inspection process over the last two years will be discussed by using four case studies. Several successes as well as one "failure" are included. Data for requirements, design, and code inspections, and how it has been used outside the inspection process, are also presented.

[Weller 1992b]
Weller, Edward F. "Lessons Learned from Two Years of Inspection Data," 3rd International Conference on Applications of Software Measurement, Nov. 15–19, 1992, La Jolla, CA, pp. 2.57–2.69. Also published in Crosstalk: The Journal of Defense Software Engineering, No. 39, Dec. 1992, pp. 23–28.

Abstract: Bull HN Information System's Major Systems Division in Phoenix initiated an inspection program in April 1990. Data collection was crucial to early buy-in to the inspection process. During the last 2 years, this data has been used to highlight potential direction for continuing process improvement. The data is also the basis for continuing development staff and management commitment to the program. Various metrics and the conclusions we have drawn from them will be discussed. A "case study" approach will highlight both the "good" and "bad" uses of inspection data for software process management.

[Wenneson 1985]
Wenneson, G. "Quality Assurance Software Inspections at NASA Ames: Metrics for Feedback and Modification," Tenth Annual Software Engineering Workshop, Dec.10, 1985, Goddard Space Flight Center.

Part II—Review/Walkthrough-related References

[Bias 1991]
Bias, Randolph. "Walkthroughs: Efficient Collaborative Testing," IEEE Software, Vol. 8, No. 5, Sep. 1991, pp. 94–95.

[Hart 1982]
Hart, J. "The Effectiveness of Design and Code Walkthroughs," COMPSAC '82: 1982 Computer Software and Applications Conference, Chicago, IL, Nov. 8–12, 1982, pp. 515–522, IEEE Computer Society Press.

[IEEE 1988]
"IEEE Standard for Software Reviews and Audits," ANSI/IEEE STD 1028–1988, IEEE Computer Society, Jun. 30, 1989.

[Lehman 1976]
Lehman, John H. "Software Engineering Techniques in Computer Systems Development," Department of the Air Force, Report No.: SM-ALC/ACD-76-04. 15 Dec. 1976.

[Lemos 1979]
Lemos, Ronald S. "An Implementation of Structured Walkthroughs in Teaching COBOL Programming," CACA, Vol. 22, No. 6, Jun. 1979, pp. 335–340.

[MILS 1985]
Military Standard for Technical Reviews and Audits for Systems, Equipments, and Computer Software. United States Department of Defense. 1985 MIL-STD–1521B.

[Myers 1988]
Myers, Ware. "Shuttle Code Achieves Very Low Error Rate," IEEE Software, Vol. 5, No. 5, Sep. 1988, pp. 93–95.

[Parnas 1987]
Parnas, David L. and David M. Weiss. "Active Design Reviews: Principles and Practices," Journal of Systems and Software, No. 7, 1987, pp. 259–265.

[Remus 1979]
Remus, Horst and S. Zilles. "Prediction and Management of Program Quality," 4th International Conference on Software Engineering, Sep. 1979, pp. 341–350, IEEE Computer Society Press.

Abstract: Techniques such as design reviews, code inspections, and system testing are commonly being used to remove defects from programs as early as possible in the development process. The objective of the authors is to demonstrate that predictors can be devised which tell us how well defects are being removed during the defect removal process.

[Shelly 1982]
Shelly, Gary B. and Thomas J. Cashman. 1982. "Implementation of Structured Walkthroughs in the Classroom," Section 12 of Handbook of Walkthroughs, In-

spections, and Technical Reviews: Evaluating Programs, Projects, and Products, 3rd ed., pp. 425–434. Boston, MA: Little, Brown and Company.

[Waldstein 1976]
Waldstein, N. S. "The Walk-Thru—A Method of Specification, Design, and Review," IBM Corp., Poughkeepsie, NY, Technical Report TR 00.2436, 1976.

[Weinberg 1971]
Weinberg, Gerald M. 1971. The Psychology of Computer Programming. NY: Van Nostrand Reinhold.

Part III—Software Engineering Textbooks Discussing Reviews, Walkthroughs and Inspections

[Dunn 1984]
Dunn, Robert H. 1984. Software Defect Removal. NY: McGraw-Hill Book Co. pp. 102–125.

[Dyer 1992]
Dyer, Michael. 1992. The Cleanroom Approach to Quality Software Development. NY: John Wiley & Sons. pp. 96–99.

[Gilb 1987]
Gilb, Tom. 1987. Principles of Software Engineering Management. Reading, MA: Addison-Wesley Publishing Co. pp. 205–226, pp. 403–422.

[Grady 1992]
Grady, Robert B. 1992. Practical Software Metrics for Project Management and Process Improvement. Prentice Hall, Englewood Cliffs, NJ.

[Humphrey 1989]
Humphrey, Watts. 1989. Managing the Software Process. Reading, MA: Addison-Wesley Publishing Co. pp. 463–486.

[Jones 1986]
Jones, Capers. 1986. Programming Productivity. NY: McGraw-Hill Book Co.

[Jones 1991]
Jones, Capers. 1991. Applied Software Measurement. NY: McGraw-Hill Book Co.

[Myers 1976]
Myers, Glenford J. 1976. Software Reliability: Principles and Practices. NY: John Wiley & Sons. pp. 17–25.

[Pressman 1992]
Pressman, Roger S. 1992. Software Engineering: A Practitioner's Approach. 3rd Edition. NY: McGraw-Hill Book Co. pp. 558–570.

[Yourdon 1989]
Yourdon, Edward. 1989. Structured Walkthroughs, 4th Edition. Englewood Cliffs, NJ: Yourdon Press.

Index

ABOUT THE AUTHORS

ROBERT G. EBENAU is president of RGE Software Methodologies, Inc. a consulting firm that specializes in the software inspection process. He has assisted Bell Laboratories, among other corporations, to implement software inspections and he was their resident inspections expert for a number of years. Mr. Ebenau was formerly a member of the staff and senior instructor at the IBM Systems Science Institute and has a Master of Engineering degree from Columbia University.

SUSAN H. STRAUSS has spent more than 20 years at Bell Labs working on computer systems engineering. She has been actively involved in applying the inspection process in R&D and training employees in its use.